CLINICAL SUPERVISION:
Special Methods for the Supervision of Teachers
Second Edition

Robert Goldhammer

Robert H. Anderson
Texas Tech University

Robert J. Krajewski
Auburn University

HOLT, RINEHART AND WINSTON
New York   Chicago   San Francisco   Dallas
Montreal   Toronto   London   Sydney

LB
2805
.G54
1980

Library of Congress Cataloging in Publication Data

Goldhammer, Robert
  Clinical supervision.

  Includes index.
  1. School supervision.   I. Anderson, Robert Henry, 1918–
joint author.   II. Krajewski, Robert J., joint author.   III. Title.
LB2805.G54   1980   371.2′013   79-25334
ISBN 0-03-046571-0

FOREWORD

In any conceptualization of instructional leadership, the task of teacher supervision must be included. This revised edition on clinical supervision affords an up-to-date account of the state of the art with a detailed analysis of the carefully conceived stages of this process. It promises to be an important book as the supervisory relationship with teachers matures.

Robert Anderson and Robert Krajewski both have labored in the supervision vineyard for many years. As teachers and scholars in the field, they bring a rich experience to this book which probes deeply into the delicate interpersonal relationship which must be cultivated if a climate of mutual trust and respect is to prevail between the teacher and supervisor.

That this relationship is delicate has always been known. As schools and systems grew larger in size over the last several decades, many abuses developed in the supervisory relationship. Often these occurred simply out of ignorance of the impact on teachers of the threatening elements in this process which has often been equated with evaluation for tenure purposes.

This book makes an enormous contribution to the entire field of instructional leadership. As we witness the press for higher quality in the schools (as opposed to the problems of quantity we faced for so many years), the demand for *instructional* leadership from both line and staff personnel is increasing. What are the tasks involved in such leadership?

I believe that building principals who would be called *instructional* leaders would spend at least half their time engaged in the following activities: 1) curriculum planning; 2) clinical supervision; 3) staff development; and 4) teacher evaluation.

Current evidence suggests that many principals spend scarcely 15 percent of their time in all four areas *combined*. They are compelled to spend considerable time in discipline, operations, parental communication, and general supervision (for example, in hallways and lunchrooms). With continuing reduction in staff supervisory personnel, principals will need training in this important supervision component if a productive relationship with teachers is to be developed. The supervision task is frequently avoided simply because the principal is not comfortable with it.

Staff-level supervisors also need to understand the concept of clinical supervision if they are to overcome skepticism. This book lays out the deep feelings many teachers have about supervision. Knowledge of these feelings must be understood and dealt with if a mature and helping relationship is to prevail.

The clinical supervision movement will be assisted by this work. It has come a long way from the early conceptualization of Morris Cogan and the subsequent refinement of Robert Goldhammer. Both Anderson and Krajewski have contributed greatly in assuring that the complexities of the supervisory relationship are better understood and incorporated into practice.

Gordon Cawelti, Executive Director
Association for Supervision and Curriculum Development
Washington, D.C.

CONTENTS

Chapter 1

CLINICAL SUPERVISION: Concept or Method?

When Robert Goldhammer died in 1968, with his book nearly ready for publication, the term *clinical supervision* was not yet in wide use and its literature was only beginning to take shape. In fact, another five years passed before the milestone volume of the same title by Morris Cogan (Goldhammer's principal mentor) appeared. Even in 1978–1979, as this second edition of the Goldhammer volume is being prepared, it can be said that the ideas and practices associated with clinical supervision are insufficiently known and appreciated. All the same, much has happened over the past decade within the parent field of general supervision and also in that more specific discipline concerned with hands-on, in-classroom, face-to-face supervisor/teacher interactions.

For those who have been close to the ongoing research, development, and publications over the decade, it has seemed a fruitful and exciting time. Our assumption is that if Goldhammer had lived to be a part of that excitement, he would have undergone both some changes of heart and some bolstering of previously held convictions, as did we. Having taken on the task of updating the original Goldhammer volume, we found ourselves wondering how Goldhammer himself would have chosen to do so; and, in our speculations and fantasies, we eventually invented the idea of a three-way interview through which could be revealed at least one set of predictions or estimates of Goldhammer's viewpoint were he still alive.

What follows, then, is a partially hypothetical discussion. The questions and statements profferred by us are authentic enough, and we hope that most of the views ascribed to a revivified Goldhammer are also authentic, or at least highly likely given what is known about his history and his beliefs.

In this setting, we three authors are assembled around a conference table, which is covered with copies of the 1969 volume and several tentative outlines of the projected revision. Anderson (RHA) is reading a portion of the 1969 Foreword, to refresh his memory. Krajewski (RJK) turns to Goldhammer (RG):

RJK: Bob, a lot of water's passed over the dam in the past ten years. Many exciting arguments and discussions, both profound and superficial, have been addressed to the topic of clinical supervision, a number of which can be attributed to your fine book. Bob Anderson and I have been inspired to follow up that work, concentrating in part on how teachers' and supervisors' needs, attitudes, and perspectives toward this important subject have changed. Recently, ideas seem to be falling into a pattern. We hear supervisors and teachers saying that emphasis no longer can be placed primarily on the process aspect of clinical supervision. Rather, they say, a sharper focus on the concept of clinical supervision must be provided both to establish clearer objectives and goals for supervisors and teachers and to enable them to work together more productively. This then allows them to formulate their own processes for clinical supervision which may better fit their climate or environment.

RG: Yes. I too believe the concept of clinical supervision is the most fundamental aspect of the whole of clinical supervision. But you must remember that when I initially wrote my book, schools were in great need of immediate instructional improvement. Thus, I thought it more useful to present a basic method to which teachers and supervisors could turn, thereby speeding up the growth of clinical supervision within the school systems. You may recall that I stated:

> In its present stage of development, the clinical supervision that our minds can formulate and which we practice does not completely fulfill the ideology that occupies our imaginations. Day by day we know better, what it is, in life and in professional life, that we're after. And by small increments, we are getting to know better, how to get what we're after.

I did indeed have in mind how essential the concept of clinical supervision was, but felt at that time it was more relevant to begin with the method, therefore giving the supervisor and teacher something solid to grasp and use.

RHA: Bob, if you remember the old days at Harvard when we talked about clinical supervision with Cogan[1] and several others, it was during the time of the Harvard–Newton Summer Program[2] and the Harvard–Lexington Summer Program (1962 and 1963). We who were involved in those programs talked at length about the concept of clinical supervision, but in those days

---

[1] Morris Cogan is given credit for coining the term "clinical supervision" during his work at Harvard.

[2] The Harvard–Newton Summer Program, first offered in 1955, brought recent college graduates without Education training into an intensive student-teaching experience, usually four or five under direction of the same master teacher. Cogan and Anderson were faculty members in this program, within which Cogan developed various clinical, peer-supervision technologies. The Harvard–Lexington Summer Program (HLSP), by contrast, was offered in the Summers of 1961 through 1965 to experienced teachers and administrators seeking training in team teaching. The five-stage model of clinical supervision described in this book was developed in HLSP.

we thought it better to put a version of clinical supervision into practice. Since we were working with training programs, our minds were centered around practical aspects of the concept, and not necessarily around the concept itself.

RG: And there was yet another problem. Right from the start, clinical supervision received slow acceptance, probably due in part to the name itself. Perhaps if it had been called by a different name, teachers would have been less reluctant to accept it, and the growth of clinical supervision could have been more rapid and more extensive than it was then or is presently. I was somewhat disappointed with all aspects of supervision in school systems when I wrote my book, and was more interested in trying to get clinical supervision integrated into school systems than I was in anything else. But today, I see that before this process will work efficiently (and there has been some improvement in instructional supervision), the concept must first be accepted by teachers and supervisors so that they are not only aware of it, but understand why clinical supervision exists, and so that they are motivated to continue using, improving, and evaluating the method.

RHA: In the 1969 edition, you insisted on the inclusion of an opening chapter that dealt only slightly with supervision per se, but expressed your own very strong feelings about things that are wrong in the schools and that therefore cry out for correction. You realized when you wrote it that it was an emotional, somewhat exaggerated statement of the troublesome and ironic experiences that confront many teachers and children. I guess that you were trying to cause the readers to become so concerned about the anomalies that they would be all the more eager to promote the widespread adoption of excellent supervisory practices.

RG: You're right, I wanted the reader's adrenalin to flow.

RHA: The adrenalin of *some* of the readers almost spilled over, in fact! At any rate, we hope you agree that in the second edition it would probably be redundant to include that same chapter.

RG: I'll agree to that — but reluctantly. Nearly all of the problems I cited are still very much with us, and the urgency of correcting them is at least as great now as it was a decade ago.

RJK: That's true, and any readers who are curious about that chapter could still consult it in the 1969 edition. Now, then, let's get back to our discussion of the word *clinical*. As you were implying, for some persons a word like *clinical* may at first be troublesome. It carries different meanings for different people, most of them having to do with the medical field. In effect, people generally tend to think of the word negatively. It suggests cold, formal, uniform, cut-and-dried procedures that leave out the personal elements of human contact.

RG: When you think of a clinic, you usually think of a place with formica surfaces, an unfriendly receptionist, and maybe even someone with a needle ready to draw blood from you.

RJK: Maybe not always — but in the world of education teachers and supervisors find themselves almost afraid of words like *clinical* and draw back. Few of them understand the concept behind the method, and thus clinical supervision becomes meaningless to them and nonfunctional in the school system.

RHA: Clinics are usually nonprivate places, also, and the clinicians get down to discovering some pretty basic truths about you.

RJK: Yes, clinical *supervision* can actually intimidate teachers because weaknesses in the classroom are exposed many times, especially during the analysis stage. If teachers knew (and accepted the fact) that the purpose behind this exposure is to improve instruction and learning for the students, rather than to embarrass teachers or to find potential reasons for their dismissal, they might actually welcome the analysis and cooperate with the supervisor in efforts to implement clinical supervision.

RHA: We've talked about what the term *clinical* might mean to various people, but let's discuss what it actually means and how we can best get this meaning across accurately to teachers and supervisors.

RG: Clinical supervision means that there is a face-to-face relationship between supervisor and teacher. Clinical supervision is sometimes confused with ordinary supervision, which has in the past been thought of as supervision conducted at a distance, with little or no direct teacher contact, by someone such as a supervisor of curriculum development. Clinical supervision methods can include group supervision between several supervisors and a teacher or a supervisor and several teachers. When discussing what clinical supervision actually means, we envision a relationship developing between a supervisor and a teacher which is built on mutual trust, through the setting of mutual goals and objectives; through professionalism, harmonious interaction; and through a certain human autonomy which enhances freedom for both the teacher and the supervisor to express ideas and opinions about how the method of supervision should be implemented to best improve teaching.

RHA: When clinical supervision is mentioned, I think mostly about those things that involve the direct intervention — the deliberate and direct intervention — by a skillful observer into the professional performances or episodes of teaching behavior in which the person being helped engages. Usually that happens in a class; if it's for a counselor, it happens in a guidance office. There are other settings, but, for the most part, we are talking about a teacher who is in a school building working with students. The clinical part refers to the hands-on or eyes-on aspect of the supervisor who is attempting to intervene in a helpful way.

RG: That's congruent with my idea of clinical supervision.

RJK: Similarly, I think of clinical supervision as a subset of instructional supervision. The supervisor must establish and maintain rapport between self and teacher; that rapport must extend throughout the entire supervision program or method. My idea differs somewhat from Goldhammer's, as expressed in the first volume, in that I believe rapport is important throughout the entire process rather than just at the beginning of it.

RG: No, we don't differ on this point — I too now see the need for continuous rapport.

RJK: Of course, all three of us (and Cogan as well) propose somewhat different approaches, which indicates how many methods one can derive to achieve the objectives or goals one is trying to reach after first establishing the concept of clinical supervision.

RHA: Yes, there are many possible variations or approaches to use (after determining one's concept of clinical supervision). But going back to what we talked about before, it is difficult for supervisors and teachers to grasp this concept, given the present name of clinical supervision. Perhaps we should seek to find a better name — maybe something related to counseling and guidance. Whatever the wording used, it should include the idea that this kind of supervision is observational, meaning that the supervisor actually observes the teacher's classroom behavior and then discusses the behavior afterward with the teacher in a counseling–guidance setting. The whole goal of clinical supervision, in my mind, is to help teachers perform a job better according to their capabilities, so that they can continually improve and become more efficient in communicating with students and thereby give them the proper motivation for wanting to learn. I like to think of the supervisor as a teacher of teachers.

RJK: In a way, the inherent responsibilities of supervisors and teachers are closely related to those of teachers and students. The supervisor must motivate teachers to want to learn how to better teach and motivate their students. It is a continuous cycle, and when one part of it breaks down, the whole thing can quickly collapse. Teachers may become confused, afraid of losing their jobs, jealous of certain peers who understand the concept, and afraid of evaluation and competition. They will then try to avoid the supervisor.

RG: That situation infuriated me from the beginning. I saw the school system working against itself. No one seemed to know what the objectives or goals for his or her work were; all seemed to concentrate more on their individual careers, forgetting who was having to pay for the inability of school personnel to work together effectively — the children. It was so clear to me what needed to be done that it appeared that the teachers must know, too. Instructional improvement wasn't being accomplished, but then I was on the outside looking in.

RHA: To accomplish it requires that all school personnel work together and that they know where they want to go and how they want to get there. Where they want to go should be similar for schools throughout the country; how they do it, on the other hand, can differ in accord with the structural makeup of their environment and other factors.

RJK: Yes, our way of thinking in the past has been to regard only one or two methods as effective. This might restrict clinical supervision — both in concept and method. I'd like to reemphasize the importance of understanding concept.

RHA: The method is important, too. Even when the concept is well understood by school personnel, it may be difficult to implement. The implementation ought to follow some plan that is owned psychologically by both the supervisor and the teacher. Also, we must use method as an instrument for measuring how well the teachers and the supervisor are accomplishing the objectives and goals of clinical supervision.

RG: Yes, that's exactly why I put the most emphasis on method in my book. Krajewski is right when he says it all comes back to understanding concept. That is essential, and must be accomplished first. However, we must not concentrate on it alone and lose sight of how important the method is as a tool for accomplishing improvement in instruction. I can see the two working hand in hand for the best results.

RHA: With respect to method, do you still feel that teachers need some fairly structured, step-by-step procedures to follow, of the sort emphasized in the book?

RG: Yes, I feel that on the whole, clinical supervision should be systematic. But there are times when the teacher and supervisor must be flexible and not stick to a systematic pattern day-in and day-out. A patterned routine such as that can lose its effectiveness. I guess that the method is probably always changing, or should be, to allow for changes occurring in the outside factors that teachers must deal with. I'm talking about changing technological and social conditions affecting both teachers and students, which are beyond the school system's control but which do affect students' learning and interests. Clinical supervision, then, must change with the times in order to be effective. Only in this way can we be sure that instructional improvement will remain positively oriented.

RHA: Although we've said that the method should be jointly determined by the teachers and the supervisor, I think that the supervisor should be the one to start the ball rolling. The supervisor must have more expertise in the analysis of teaching and in applying principles of learning than do the teachers. It is difficult to gain respect for the designated role of supervisor without that knowledge and understanding. The teachers shouldn't fear the supervisor or regard him or her to be egotistical, but at the same time, they shouldn't consider the supervisor to be just another teacher. There should be a notable difference between the supervisor and the teachers, in skills and in the ability to analyze and understand the overall view of the school system's needs. The supervisor must be able to observe skillfully and therefore detect more in a teaching sequence than a teacher is able to. The supervisor has a certain amount of responsibility for ensuring that there is a positive school climate and for keeping the teachers working on improving their teaching — in an informal operational manner. He or she has to create and maintain an atmosphere conducive to change. If the teacher is convinced that he or she will benefit from the observations and recommendations, then a close working relationship between the supervisor and teacher can develop.

RG: One comment along the same lines, Bob. I imagine the supervisor as having the principal effect of expanding the sense of gratification experienced by the teachers and thus by the students. Teachers should feel gratification at being involved in the process and gratification in knowing that their work is helping to reach the common goal of improved instruction. After all, what is it that makes people want to be part of a team or want to work harder at their jobs? It is knowing that they are helping to bring about something important — and this makes each individual feel important. Thus, it is the responsibility of the supervisor to help the teachers see themselves in this light.

RJK: In order to do this, though, a supervisor must be a particularly knowledgeable person with sufficient training in this area and must possess a distinct capacity for motivating others. The supervisor should also possess humanistic skills, but at the same time must maintain sight of objectives. With his or her advanced knowledge of the concept and method of clinical supervision, he or she must be able to communicate this knowledge to teachers and illustrate its importance and relationship to individual situations.

RHA: I'll agree. Although the supervisor to a certain degree must have strong feelings about his or her work and care about the teachers — personally as well as professionally — I still believe that the intelligence of the supervisor makes the most difference. Feelings are important and so are the technical skills, but what you really need is the ability to fit things together skillfully and to understand things more quickly than the average human being understands. You can't be much of a leader unless you are more alert than those you're leading, because if they think first, they'll do the leading. The supervisor must have excellent cognitive attributes.

RG: To get all of the things accomplished that must be done if instructional improvement is to occur, it appears that the supervisor may have to be almost superhuman. I think the trouble in the past was that most supervisors or potential supervisors didn't know what was expected of them and neither did the teachers. In fact, there were few training programs, if any, that outlined supervisors' responsibilities and needed skills; nor were there any types of programs designed exclusively for the instructional or clinical supervisor. Before, we usually just hired an experienced teacher as the supervisor without any required further training. Today, it appears that better training programs at the university level are being considered and being implemented, at least for general supervision. It's a step in the right direction, and eventually instructional supervision skills — then clinical supervision skills — will be a standard feature of the training programs.

RHA: As was implied when we agreed earlier, Bob, rapport is one of the factors on which we must focus a lot more in the new volume than you did back in 1969.

RG: Yes, at that time, I opined that rapport was already so much treated in literature that it could be assumed by the reader without much explanation on my part. In fact, I devoted only several sentences to it. It now seems as though the readers will be better served by our including its rationale.

RJK: The changing educational/social scene and personnel almost necessitate its inclusion. It's desirable that teachers have healthy self concepts and feel secure in their teaching and in their relationships with (clinical) supervisors. It is imperative for the supervisor to effect those feelings within teachers. Rapport is the key. I'm pleased that we've decided to emphasize rapport nurturance as a skill requisite for the supervisor, and one which all supervisor training programs should include.

RG: It's clear that training and in-service programs in the 1980s will have to be even more elaborate and intense than those I called for in the late 1960s. We need a much larger vision of what the supervisor's role should be.

RJK: I believe that change is forthcoming. A 1977–1978 ASCD working group on roles and responsibilities of supervisors gathered current information on the role of the instructional supervisor through both review of literature and empirical research. As a member of that group, one of my tasks was to conduct a telephone survey of executive directors of various national education associations and selected practitioner representatives from those groups (AACTE, AASA, AFT, ASCD, COPIS, NAESP, NASSP, NEA,[3] and Professors of Curriculum). One question asked was, what should be the activities of instructional supervision? Forty-nine of the 63 suggestions offered involved the techniques and practices of clinical supervision. Another question asked what the preparation program for instructional supervisors should include. Those interviewed suggested that the majority of formal classwork should be in the area of clinical supervision. Overall, they believed that clinical supervision is the process whereby the instructional supervisor gains insight into the quality of interaction among instructional personnel. So, growth of programs in clinical supervision appears to be likely. The future should hold not only clinical supervision classes for supervisors, but

[3]American Association of Colleges for Teacher Education, American Association of School Administrators, American Federation of Teachers, Association for Supervision and Curriculum Development, Council of Professors of Instructional Supervision, National Association of Elementary School Principals, National Association of Secondary School Principals, and National Education Association.

also classes for teachers (both preservice and in-service) containing the concepts and various alternative methods utilized by clinical supervisors.

RHA: Yes, but we need a way to inform and involve all present teachers and supervisors, as well as future teachers and supervisors!

RJK: Definitely! Teachers should learn various teaching patterns and methods of clinical supervision through well planned preservice programs. They should also be made aware of the concept of clinical supervision so that they in turn can help the supervisor to understand *why* observation, analysis, and conferencing are important as vital components of instructional improvement. With courses of this nature for teachers and supervisors, clinical supervision can be introduced into the schools. School systems share responsibility for training supervisors, not only by making universities aware of the type of training desired — as borne out in the ASCD project telephone interviews — but also by providing funds, time, and personnel for training.

RHA: We have to be more tough-minded in insisting that the universities respond to this need *and* that personnel *avail* themselves of training opportunities. In fact, supervisors should not be hired unless they have had both basic supervision courses and successful teaching experience. It should be the school systems' duty to employ only well qualified and trained supervisors, and to require that all teachers have some basic courses that prepare them to participate in supervision.

RG: I agree. There is no reason why today's schools should have to put up with unqualified personnel. If they would only make their demands and expectations more exacting, the universities and colleges would have to follow suit. The only way instructional improvement will come about is through upgrading the standards of those whom we select to put in the classroom and whom we hire to supervise our teachers. With improved quality of training and knowledge of skills, there should be (little reason not to expect) rapid advances in clinical supervision and in its impact on instructional improvement in the schools.

RJK: I feel this present textbook can become a catalyst in bringing about better quality in clinical supervision training. Because we stress the inclusion of both concept and method, not only will the book aid universities in initiating courses, but it will also provide guidelines for covering the ideas of clinical supervision as many see it now — and as it may be in the future.

RG: One of the main thrusts of this text (whether for neophytes or experienced teachers and supervisors) should be that supervisors need to be supportive of and empathic toward teachers, and that teachers in turn need to respond and give feedback to their supervisors. The teachers and supervisors must treat one another decently, responsibly, and affectionately. Colleges and universities need to emphasize these behaviors, and the concepts from which they are generated, so that teachers and supervisors whom they prepare will be highly qualified individuals. The objectives and goals of clinical supervision should be made clear in this text, with the understanding that school personnel must be productive and striving toward instructional improvement, while at the same time moving forward in their own personal careers. By honestly cooperating in understanding the clinical supervision *concept* and *methods* in their school systems, both teachers and supervisors will have rewarding encounters as they provide better learning for students.

RHA: In the first edition, Bob, you felt that many school personnel already had these high ideals and thoughts but just could not reach the point of accomplishing such goals. Do you think conditions have improved since you made that statement?

RG: Yes, because today we're beginning to put more of our ideas into action. There are many examples of this, although not as many as there should be. Perhaps this is because of what Bob Krajewski said before, that many people were trying to implement the clinical supervision method but all had varying ideas of why they were doing it. What this second edition should make perfectly clear to everyone is that clinical supervision is based on concept and that the concept should be clear in one's mind prior to implementing a method, thereby eliminating any possible underlying conflicts which slow down the methods and render them unusable.

RJK: I believe that clinical supervision will have more power if it is thought of as concept and not just a method which may or may not fit into the school system's operational philosophy. That should also be emphasized in this second edition, and I feel that emphasis will be well received. Supervisors and teachers have reached the point where they no longer are satisfied with doing something (method) just because it's always been done that way or because they were taught in a class to follow a certain pattern. They can see whether or not it is working in their own particular school system, and they should not feel tied down to a given method. By studying the concept, as explained in this text, teachers and supervisors can understand what it is supposed to accomplish. If the teachers know that it is the goals and not the methods that are *most* important, they will be more willing to offer suggestions and new ideas as to what method might better accomplish the desired objectives for both teachers' and children's needs. When you've got an interaction such as this and all are motivated toward a similar idea and/or goals, then clinical supervision will become a healthy reality in our school systems.

RHA: Teachers might understand the concept of clinical supervision, but it's putting the concept into practice that is the hardest part. A particular problem for *some* teachers is being observed and evaluated by other professionals. But as we mentioned before, observation will not look so scary once teachers know the concept behind it and realize that it is to their benefit to be observed in the classroom. In fact, I don't think you can have too much of it (observation); but the supervisor usually has so many other responsibilities (especially if he or she is the principal) that an opportunity to observe a classroom occurs only once every couple of months — if even that often. So the teacher who is not used to a supervisor's visit may become disturbed, and thus think something is wrong, because the supervisor is observing his or her classroom.

RJK: Putting clinical supervision into practice may appear to be the hardest part only because of this lack of understanding of what is to be accomplished. That is why most of the methods fall apart, especially in the analysis area. What we are aiming for, then, is total knowledge, for both teachers and supervisors, of the concept of clinical supervision in order to make the methods work in school systems today.

RG: I put it another way in the first edition of *Clinical Supervision:*

> The aims of clinical supervision will be realized when largely by virtue of its own existence, everyone inside the school will know better why he is there, will want to be there, and, inside that place, will feel a strong and beautiful awareness of his own, individual identity and a community of spirit and of enterprise with those beside him. These are the values that motivate our work and give rise to our ambitions. While we cannot, obviously, make promises that are as large as our dreams, we can proclaim those dreams and let ourselves be guided by them.

I took forward to this second edition in which our ideas on concept will be better delineated, while at the same time we continue to recognize the importance of explaining method to be utilized in implementing that concept with teachers in school systems.

And so the hypothetical interview ends. Krajewski and Anderson take leave of the conference table and head towards their respective desks. Both express the hope, in their hearts, that the revision will be a fitting tribute to their departed friend.

Chapter 2

SUPERVISOR ROLE RESPONSIBILITIES

* **Supervision as a Field**
* **Role**
* **Instructional Supervision**
* **Clinical Supervision**
* **Implications**

When one uses the term *supervision* in education, what does the term imply? What are the kinds of activities in which supervisors engage? In one statement, issued in 1931 by the Department of Supervisors and Directors of Instruction of the National Education Association, these questions were answered by including:

> . . . all activities by which educational officers may express leadership in the improvement of learning and teaching. Such activities as observation of classroom instruction, conduct of teachers' meetings and of group and individual conferences are clearly within the meaning of this term. The development and execution of plans looking toward increased effectiveness in reading, arithmetic, and some other area of the school program, and the organization or reorganization of curriculum and method are still further examples of what is meant by supervisory activities.[1]

While it is commendable that the Department's list began with reference to classroom observation, the general ambiguity of the statement is immediately evident. Regrettably, a half century later the activities which comprise the supervisor's role remain somewhat less than exacting in the minds of those who

---

[1]*Evaluation of Supervision*, The Fourth Yearbook of the Department of Supervisors and Directors of Instruction of the National Education Association (New York: Teachers College, Press, 1931), p. 3.

propose definitions or who are seeking to learn about them. Furthermore, in the absence of clarity it is possible for the perceptions of educators, whether those who supervise or those who are supervised, to be colored by the personal values, political orientations, and educational philosophies that operate in the background. In turn, the varied perceptions cause the individual to elect certain activities and to accept certain responsibilities while at the same time rejecting other possibilities.

In such a loosely organized situation, it is possible that some individuals in each group perceive the supervisor's role as emphasizing quality control, or the production of new courses of study and curricula. Others may conceive of the role as being largely concerned with evaluating curriculum and/or instruction. Still others see it as working with professional personnel to seek new answers, or releasing the potential energies of teachers who wish to find answers for themselves. Many other possibilities come to mind. And so it may be useful to provide, at this early stage in the volume, a brief overview of supervision as a field, and then to examine at least briefly the role that instructional and clinical supervision play or could play within it.

SUPERVISION AS A FIELD

Often linked with educational administration and invariably connected with the concept of educational leadership, supervision is today seen as that dimension of the teaching profession which is concerned with improving instructional effectiveness. Nearly all definitions state or imply that supervision is the task assigned to certain school employees, whether in a line or staff relationship to classroom teachers (or counselors), to stimulate staff growth and development, to influence teacher behaviors in the classroom (or counseling center), and to foster the selection, development, use, and evaluation of good instructional approaches and materials. Some definitions place particular stress upon the role of communication skills in supervision, and in recent years there has emerged a strong emphasis upon helping teachers with problem-solving, with interpersonal relationships within the school, and with the creation of a more humane atmosphere to surround children and the adults who teach them. Nearly all discussions of supervision, in textbooks and periodicals over a half century, have wrestled with the difficult problem of separating *helping* behaviors from *evaluating* behaviors on the part of supervisors, since the helping functions have most often been assigned to the same persons (principals, department heads, directors) who are at times responsible for employment, promotions, and/or salary decisions. Most of the time, too, textual discussions have suggested that nearly everything that leadership people do in the course of their professional lives is in some way a part of supervision. For these and other related reasons, the fairly extensive (although generally mediocre) literature of supervision rarely gets beyond truisms and platitudes, to the effect that all sorts of activities make some potential contribution to teacher growth. Given such a history, it is little wonder that supervision has had a rather low standing among the education disciplines; and even the major professional organization to which supervisors belong, the Association for Supervision and Curriculum Development, devotes only a relatively small fraction of its activities (for example, in annual convention programs) and publications to supervision per se.

Teachers generally dislike being the object of supervision. They tend to perceive supervision as inherent in the administrative hierarchy and to see the supervisor as being somewhat of a threat. Supervisors, on the other hand, perceive supervision as teacher-oriented, leading to an improvement in teaching, curriculum, and the total educational program. They envisage their role as helping teachers to improve instruction, a basic goal of supervision. That still other perceptions are held by administrators, with diverging viewpoints of supervision as either a staff or line role, further becloud the supervisor's role.

What is the role of the supervisor? Is it one of instructional leader, manager, administrator, or a combination of many positions? What has been the supervisor's role in the past? Has it remained the same or do we find the role changing today? Where does the supervisor presently fit in the total educational program? These are but a few of many questions asked by educators and others concerning supervisory roles. Describing the role of the supervisor, however, is not a task that is easily accomplished.

During the last 50 years, supervision has progressed, at the theoretical level at least, through overlapping stages. Changing emphases as presented in three current analyses appear in Table 1.

The review of supervision during the 1900s indicates that writers in the field have generally agreed as to the developing phases and characteristics of supervision. However, they have differed in terminology relating to the predominant features of each period and in the limits of any periods, indicating the difficulty of setting beginning and ending dates for phases which continually overlap.

Admittedly, supervision in the 1970s and in the 1980s cannot be neatly categorized; inspection practices of the early 1900s still linger in more than isolated situations, and classroom demonstrations continue to serve exclusively in too many situations. For the most part, however, supervision today — and actually for the past 25 years and longer — embraces a wide variety of activities and personnel directed toward a major goal: the improvement of instruction. The current concept of supervision has its natural roots in the emphasis on "cooperative group work" and "democratic human relations" of the thirties, forties, and fifties. During the last ten years, a staggering variety and plethora of input factors have intended to overwhelm and confuse supervisory personnel. Questions were and are being raised, such as:

Table 1

Comparison of Periods of Supervision:
Early 1900s to Present

Eye, Netzer and Krey[2]	Alfonso, Firth and Neville[3]	Gwynn[4]
1876–1936 — Efficiency orientation	1900–1920 — Scientific supervision	1920–1960 — Scientific supervision
1937–1959 — Cooperative group effort in the improvement of teaching and learning	1930–1950 — Sporadic application of cooperative — democratic approach	1930–1960 — Supervision as democratic educational leadership
1960–present — Research orientation	1950–present — Mutual concern and cooperative interaction toward organizational improvement goals	1930–1960 — Creative supervision, with allied concepts of supervision as guidance, curriculum improvement, group processes, and indigenous to instructional teams

"Should I use micro-teaching?"

"Are student ratings valid?"

"Can I video tape a classroom lesson and obtain a true representation?"

"Are minicourses too expensive?" "Do they do any good?"

"Are objective analysis systems what they're 'cracked up' to be?" "Can I learn to use them effectively?"

"Will I be able to accept myself as a resource person?"

"How will they hold me accountable?"

"Will the federal government ever stop confusing us?"

"Can I (still) 'cut it' as a supervisor?"

The very fact that supervisor personnel have been asking and continue to ask such questions is in itself a positive indication of progress. Answers to these questions have ranged from a very definite "yes" to a lukewarm "maybe" and at times a "no". Fortunately, many supervisors have eagerly capitalized on experimental ideas and productive innovations and have put them to work in their own situations. Fortunately, too, many supervisors who at first had been

[2]Glen G. Eye, Lanore A. Netzer, and Robert D. Krey, *Supervision of Instruction* 2d ed. (New York: Harper & Row, 1971), pp. 23–28.

[3]Robert J. Alfonso, Gerald R. Firth, and Richard F. Neville, *Instructional Supervision: A Behavior System* (Boston: Allyn and Bacon, 1975), pp. 16–27.

[4]J. Minor Gwynn, *Theory and Practice of Supervision* (New York: Dodd, Mead, 1969), pp. 3–17.

reluctant to do little more than add a few new terms to their professional vocabularies have conquered their defense mechanisms and gone to work. A hesitant supervisor, for instance, may attend a meeting where one of the several objective analysis systems is presented and demonstrated. He or she asks, "Can I ever learn all these categories? Do I really want to? If I do decide to try this out, will I ever be able to get our teachers to try it?" Dissipating those fears, the supervisor tries the system, becomes competent with it, begins to use it frequently, and learns to appreciate its effectiveness in improving instruction.

ROLE

Role may be defined as "a socially expected behavior pattern usually determined by an individual's status in a particular society,"[5] — behavior expected of an individual by those for whom and with whom the person works. Alfonso[6] relates that there is great confusion concerning the superivisor's role. Many role studies have been made but little emphasis has been placed on the relationship of the supervisor's role to the organization of the school, let alone to the administrative structure. The perennial question asked by teachers and administrators, "Should the supervisor be in a staff or line position?" seems to be, as Alfonso indicates, a factor in the role confusion. But there are other factors as well — and it is difficult to consider each factor in any one given study of the supervisor's role. Yet most practitioners and researchers admit to the fact that we must continue the efforts of defining the supervisor's role. The supervisor's role is very often too generally defined, and it varies from school system to school system. In addition, the supervisor can be referred to by any of such various titles as helping teacher, resource teacher, instructional specialist, master teacher, coordinator, curriculum specialist, educational assistant, consultant, advisor, instructional assistant, assistant superintendent (for curriculum or instruction), department head, director, and the like.

Many of the recognized problems concerning varying role perceptions in supervision are due to the fact that specific supervisory role assignments still remain in developmental stages, and many newly appointed and experienced supervisors accept responsibilities having had little, if any, preparation. The evolving supervisory role is being shaped by a myriad of forces, both social and educational. Yet, the bottom line for the supervisory role is, as Muriel Crosby says, "to make it possible to help teachers help themselves become more skilled in the processes of fostering childrens' learning."[7] The demand for students' learning is becoming greater, through we still do see, in some situa-

[5]*Webster's New Collegiate Dictionary* (Springfield, Mass.: Merriam, 1973), p. 1003.
[6]Alfonso et al., *Instructional Supervision*, p. 123.
[7]C. Taylor Whittier, "The Setting and New Challenges," in William H. Lucio (ed.), *The Supervisor: New Demands New Dimensions* (Washington, D.C.: Association for Supervision and Curriculum Development, NEA, 1969), p. 8.

tions, promotions to a supervisory position of those personnel who possess neither the requisite skills nor the preparation.

INSTRUCTIONAL SUPERVISION

One need only make a cursory examination of the literature to substantiate the fact that the supervisor, through historical development, has been many things to many people. Perhaps therein lies part of the reason for the present confusion toward supervision per se. The changing societal expectations for schools also contribute to the confusion. Definitions of supervision vary in both content and specificity. The *Dictionary of Education* defines supervision as:

> All efforts of designated school officials directed toward providing leadership
> to teachers and other educational workers in the improvement of instruction;
> involves the stimulation of professional growth and development of teachers,
> the selection and revision of education objectives, materials of instruction,
> and methods of teaching, and the evaluation of instruction.[8]

Instructional supervision is a subset of supervision. Even as supervision has varied interpretations so that the role of the supervisor is not consistent between and sometimes within school systems, so have instructional supervision and the role of the instructional supervisor. Study of instructional supervision in public schools is constrained by the very nature of the subject. Though seemingly a plausible term, instructional supervision has not, in the past, been adequately defined; thus it may be appropriate to seek more current views. Harris defines supervision of instruction as:

> What school personnel do with adults and things to maintain or change the
> school operation in ways that directly influence the teaching processes em-
> ployed to promote pupil learning.[9]

Eye, Netzer, and Krey define supervision of instruction as:

> That phase of school administration which focuses primarily upon the
> achievement of the appropriate instructional expectations of educational sys-
> tems.[10]

Intrinsic to these definitions is that instructional supervision is both a concept and a process to improve the instruction afforded the pupil.

---

[8]Carter V. Good (ed.), *Dictionary of Education*, 2d ed. (New York: McGraw-Hill, 1959), p. 539.

[9]Ben M. Harris, *Supervisory Behavior in Education*, 2d ed. (Englewood Cliffs, N.J.: Prentice-Hall, 1975), pp. 10–11.

[10]Eye et al., *Supervision of Instruction*, p. 30.

Given that the definition of instructional supervision is agreed upon by most present supervision authorities and significant others as those activities engaged in by school personnel for the improving of instruction through changing of teacher behavior, the role of the instructional supervisor ostensibly would seem not too difficult to comprehend. But such is not the case. There remains yet today an imprecise structure to instructional supervision and perhaps somewhat of a lack of consensus as to the nature of instructional supervision, its goals, and processes to attain these goals. Even more perplexing is the lack of agreement as to who should perform the instructional supervision functions — and why.

Disagreements on instructional supervision philosophy, worth, and practice abound. At present there is no progress toward resolution; neither is there sufficient structure and/or desire to foster the initiative toward resolution, or sufficient leadership necessary to achieve it. Instructional supervision development in public schools has not been proactive. As such, the developmental pattern is unstable (reflecting a reactive pattern). Also, the dispersed nature and conduct of instructional supervisory activities creates confusion, inhibits effective interaction among the parties involved, and thereby delays or impedes the instructional supervisory process.

This confusion arises because seldom is there a person or agency within the school system solely responsible for providing instructional supervision; neither ther is there a single client constituency — a group or activity which is the beneficiary of such supervision. Rather, instructional supervision responsibilities are assigned to whichever person/agency is best able to absorb them without much disturbance of the on-going operation. This piecemeal arrangement is hardly satisfactory and certainly not of much benefit to anyone.

In today's school systems, therefore, the role of instructional supervisor remains ambiguous and *varied*. Some instructional supervisors profide *staff* consultation of curriculum, program, and materials, some provide *staff* evaluation of teacher competence and performance, some provide *staff* assistance of a clinical nature for dealing with specific exceptional problem situations, and some provide only administrative assistance.

The approach never seems quite adequate to accomplish the instructional supervision goals. In it, neither human nor material resources are utilized properly, creating conflicting internal objectives and contradictory strategies. There is no constituent body of personnel who are classified as "instructional supervisors." If a school system has instructional supervisors, they keep quite busy but not often in the roles in which they should be utilized. Far too many voices in varying positions demand, discuss, and decide what jobs the instructional supervisor's role will include. They then seek the person (often from within the system) who will fulfill the job "required" but not, characteristically one who will fulfill the real role of an instructional supervisor.

There is little doubt that each school system area personnel, administrators, guidance personnel, curriculum heads, principals, teachers, and the public need the services of an instructional supervisor. However, each needs the skills provided on different levels and to different degrees. To date, few school systems have taken the initiative or even attempted the logical task of deciding how to blend their interests and needs enough to establish a more appropriate/definitive role expectation for the instructional supervisor. This is most unfortunate, for not only is each area not receiving expected services from the instructional supervisor (mainly because the supervisor is spread too thin and has too many expectations for services), but few are happy with the results. None finds its needs completely served, and in the long run the students are the ones who suffer.

CLINICAL SUPERVISION

Morris Cogan defines clinical supervision as:

> the rationale and practice designed to improve the teacher's classroom performance. It takes its principal data from the events of the classroom. The analysis of these data and the relationship between teacher and supervisor form the basis of the program, procedures, and strategies designed to improve the students' learning by improving the teacher's classroom behavior.[11]

Sergiovanni and Starratt say that clinical supervision:

> refers to face-to-face encounters with teachers about teaching, usually in classrooms, with the double-barreled intent of professional development and improvement of instruction.[12]

Flanders sees clinical supervision as:

> a special case of teaching in which at least two persons are concerned with the improvement of teaching and at least one of the individuals is a teacher whose performance is to be studied. . . .[I]t seeks to stimulate some change in teaching, to show that a change did, in fact, take place, and to compare the old and new patterns of instruction in ways that will give a teacher useful insights into the instructional process.[13]

These and other definitions have several elements in common. Our own definition is consistent with the others and enhances those common elements. Clinical supervision as we see it, then is: that phase of instructional supervision which draws its data from first-hand observation of actual teaching events, and involves face-to-face (and other associated) interaction between the supervisor

---

[11]Morris Cogan, *Clinical Supervision* (Boston: Houghton Mifflin, 1973), p. 9.

[12]Thomas J. Sergiovanni and Robert J. Starratt, *Supervision: Human Perspectives*, 2d ed. (New York: McGraw-Hill, 1979), p. 305.

[13]Ned A. Flanders, "Interaction Analysis and Clinical Supervision," *Journal of Research and Development in Education*, 9 (Winter 1976), pp. 47–48.

and teacher in the analysis of teaching behaviors and activities for instructional improvement.

The clinical dimension of supervision, it seems to us, is more clearly defined and causes less role confusion than do the more general dimensions of instructional supervision, or general supervision. Because it is more specific, and because of the greater amount of interaction and participation on the part of the teacher and the supervisor, it is probably easier for the parties to understand and accept their respective roles. Because in each case of clinical supervision a specific teacher is the direct client of the supervisor and has a direct stake in the outcomes of the supervisory process, it is more likely that the teacher will connect with the supervisor's services than when a supervisor engages in instructional supervision activities that are aimed at groups of teachers.

IMPLICATIONS

From the discussion on role responsibilities, one can infer that describing the role of the supervisor and instructional supervisor is a task which is not easily realized. Yet, from this debate, one question remains unanswered and demands immediate attention. That question centers around the present non-existence, for the most part, of a role description for the instructional supervisor. Instructional supervisors must be defined. Ideally, this role description should be derived by instructional supervisors and their client constituency, be understood and accepted by all parties concerned, and be utilized as agreed upon. The role delineation should be available for reading by all professional personnel in the school system. Once a role description is derived and circulated — and the instructional supervisor's role is understood and accepted by the client constituency — the instructional supervisor must carry out those tasks outlined in the job description and be held accountable for their effectiveness.

The supervisor's role encompasses these basic components: administrative, curricular, and instructional. It is difficult, if not virtually impossible, to view these as mutually exclusive entities of the supervisor's role, or for that matter, of the instructional supervisor's role. In fact, it may not be desirable to completely separate them. Let us for the moment accept that supervision includes everything mentioned, and represent all of the ingredients or entities in a Venn diagram by the universal set U. Let us further seek to represent all of the activities that are not curricular or administrative, but are instead related to *instructional* supervision. This will be a subset A of the universal set U. Then we can further subdivide the space represented in the A portion of U, by referring to all of the activities of clinical supervision in the subset B. Figure 1 therefore helps us to see that of all the things a supervisor does, only the things reflected in space B involve direct, in-class, instruction-related contacts.

Figure 1.

The proportions that are shown may or may not be realistic or typical, and hopefully many readers will protest that in their own experience, both A and B are a larger part of U than Figure 1 suggests. That is well and good. We would like to suggest that Figure 2 comes closer to an ideal toward which American education ought to aim:

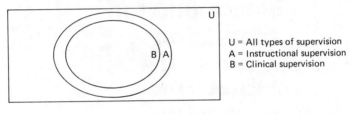

Figure 2.

Figure 1 suggests that, first of all, instructional supervision probably does not comprise even a third of all of supervision; rather, its total is relegated to a smaller amount or proportion of the whole. As we have previously noted, instructional supervision's role is still ambiguous, and often the persons who serve in that role are not really free to actuate the kinds of activities they feel are necessary to fulfill the role. We also opine that with better preparation programs for supervisors and more emphasis on instructional improvement procedures within these preparation programs, instructional supervision will assume a greater role within supervision. Should this happen, and many indicators point to the fact that it will and is already beginning to happen, clinical supervision will assume a greater role as well. In fact, we envision that in the near future clinical supervision's role in the public school will be closer to the ideal as shown in Figure 2.

Chapter 3

A MODEL OF CLINICAL SUPERVISION

---

* The Concepts of
  Clinical Supervision
* A Conceptual
  Background for
  Supervision
* A Framework
  of Values for
  Supervision
* The Structural Model-
  Its Rationales
  and Purposes
* The Model

THE CONCEPTS OF CLINICAL SUPERVISION

Before we go much further into clinical supervision, it may be helpful to examine some of the concepts that underlie or are associated with the term. Already evident is that clinical supervision is a subcategory of the general term *supervision* as it is commonly used in education to indicate all of the activities, functions, maneuvers, and nurturing conditions that are intended to help teachers (and various other educational workers) to upgrade their performance. The adjective *clinical*, which was appropriated from other sciences for education in about 1958 by Morris Cogan[1] conveys the idea that such efforts are based upon data collected in actual classroom (or other instructional) situations where the teacher is working directly with the learners and the supervisor is present as a witness if not a participant. Sometimes the term *hands-on* is used as a metaphor, although for some persons this may be confusing. Suffice it to say that in the "clinic" (which is itself a potentially troublesome metaphor) of the classroom, the supervisor is a part of the ongoing activity, and as a result the supervisor carries away a more accurate and complete understanding of what actually occurred. In the succeeding events, to pursue the clinical analogy, the supervisor and teacher meet face-to-face for purposes of reviewing the occurrences and their import.

This differentiates clinical supervision from such legitimate helping activities as: (1) conducting faculty discussions on classroom management; (2) sending teachers to visit other classrooms; (3) bringing in speakers and lecturers; (4) encouraging and enabling teachers to read professional books and magazines; (5) demonstrating good teaching practices in the presence of teachers (although this activity admittedly has a clinical dimension); (6) organizing staff study groups and/or curriculum committees; (7) setting up teacher centers; (8) providing opportunities for graduate study; and (9) stimulating other kinds of staff development activities (for example, by establishing a team teaching organization for the school). These and dozens of other approaches that are subsumed under the term *general supervision* are important concomitants of hands-on activities, but this book does not address them. Furthermore, the authors strongly believe that of all the things that educational leaders do to promote the professional growth of teachers, those involving direct contact with, and response to, each teacher's work with children have by far the greatest value. In fact, even though supervisors cannot or do not ordinarily devote more than one-fourth or so of their time to clinical supervision, our conviction is that such work is at least equal in value to all the rest of what the supervisor does.

Supervision has had a dubious reputation at least in part because its clinical dimension has been neglected. If supervisors were to spend more of their energy in in-clasroom visits followed by helpful conferences, we believe that teachers would probably have more friendly attitudes toward supervision.

We believe that the concept of clinical supervision, the emergence and the literature of which are discussed in this volume, has enriched and expanded the overall field of supervision and helped to expose the naiveté and the general inadequacy of prior definitions and role reconmendations. We think that supervisors have too long been misled into believing that they could keep profitably busy without spending much time in classrooms. If this seems a harsh

---

[1]Cogan's role as prime developer of clinical supervision and some of his struggles getting the adjective accepted in view of its negative medical connotations are described in his important book, *Clinical Supervision* (Boston: Houghton Mifflin, 1973).

criticism, let the reader consult the usual textbook to see how many pages deal with direct classroom-based involvement. Our role in this volume is to tilt the supervisor's interests in the direction of such involvement, and to redefine the role of supervisor accordingly.

Reference was made above to the establishment of team teaching. This organizational arrangement, which was advocated and tested by John Dewey around the turn of the century, was one of the most powerful and promising of the so-called innovations that emerged in the late 1950s and developed in the next decade or so. At first controversial because of ill-founded faith in the self-contained classroom as a presumably ideal environment for children, the arrangement soon gained almost unchallenged theoretical and conceptual support. However, habits established over centuries proved difficult to displace, and neither teacher education nor supervision made the necessary adjustments to orient and equip teachers for teaming. Therefore, at the end of the 1970s, team teaching remained an essentially neglected option. All the same, the idea remains alive, and over the next several decades it could gradually gain more universal acceptance.

Team Teaching. Most of the descriptive literature of team teaching is now on dusty shelves, and since the mid-1960s little if anything has been added by way of definition. This is not surprising, since the concept is not very complicated; but the early literature[2] was aimed at an audience almost blindly loyal to self-containment, and the pioneer authors sought to furnish not only definitions but examples and philosophic justifications for abandoning the familiar arrangement. The alleged advantages of self-containment came to seem less sacred, however, and by 1966, Anderson's point-by-point disavowal of those advantages[3] did not stir up much, if any, controversy. In fact, one finds virtually no negative references to team teaching or positive support for the self-contained classroom in current educational literature. Fairly common, especially in books dealing with staff development, are statements such as the following:

> Informal staff-development approaches should be encouraged and supported. Indeed, the benefits derived from such approaches are a good reason for supervisors and administrators to advocate patterns of instruction which encourage teachers to plan and work together. Team teaching, schools within the school, and family grouping are examples of arrangements which naturally stimulate informal staff-development activities.[4]

There are many possible versions of the recommended pattern. The most desirable, and certainly the most effective, of these provide for collaboration in

[2]Notably, Judson, T. Shaplin and Henry F. Olds, Jr, (eds.), *Team Teaching* (New York: Harper & Row, 1964).

[3]Robert H. Anderson, *Teaching in a World of Change* (New York: Harcourt, 1966), pp. 71–108.

[4]Thomas J. Sergiovanni and Robert J. Starrett, *Supervision: Human Perspectives*, 2 ed. (New York: McGraw-Hill, 1979), p. 296.

all phases of the educational program and enable (we do not say "require") the teachers to be heavily involved in the sharing of ideas, information, techniques, and criticism. The latter, a word that invariably raises eyebrows, is probably the most crucial of all the interchanges that are possible; and in our definition of team teaching at its best, the most important element is that of critical exchange within a framework of peer supervision.

Our ideal conception of team teaching includes at least 12 features, as outlined below:

1. The teaching is conducted within flexible space that is open at least to some extent; all of the space, equipment, and instructional materials within that space is communal property.
2. The program is nongraded (some authors might prefer the word "open"), focusing upon promoting each individual child's maximum development.
3. The children served by the teaching team are multiaged, preferably within a three-year age span but in any case not less than a two-year span. This applies to both elementary and secondary situations.
4. All team members (including children, wherever possible) participate in formulating broad overall objectives for the total program.
5. All team members participate at least weekly in formulating the more immediate objectives of the program.
6. All team members have an opportunity from time to time to contribute to the specific daily planning of their colleagues, and vice versa. That is to say, Miss Jones's lesson plan for Thursday afternoon is presented, discussed, and (it is hoped) modified for the better in Tuesday's team planning session, and, in turn, Miss Jones has equivalent opportunities to examine and improve the plans of her teammates.
7. Therefore, all team members are at all times at least conversant with the specific daily plans and professional repertoires of the other team members. As a result, it would be relatively easy for any team member to step into a colleague's teaching shoes in an emergency.
8. All team members at least occasionally (that is, several times a week) carry on teaching functions in the actual presence of colleagues who are either taking some part in the same lesson or simply sitting in as interested observers. Here is where processes of clinical supervision can come into play. See Item 10.
9. All team members participate periodically (weekly, if possible) in evaluation sessions of the overall as well as the current program.
10. Each team member is the beneficiary of at least one weekly conference in which episodes of his own teaching (preferably those to which one or more colleagues were witnesses) are carefully and objectively analyzed and out of which emanate specific suggestions and ideas for professional management.
11. Periodically, for example, at least once within every six-week progress-reporting cycle, all members of the team engage in a full-scale discussion and review of each child's school progress.
12. Role specialization exists at least to some extent, including both professional and paraprofessional functions.

We recognize that few schools have thus far developed team teaching programs that satisfy all the foregoing requirements. Probably those that come closest to doing so are the more mature programs associated with the Individually Guided Education (IGE), as developed by the Institute for Development of Educational Activities (I/D/E/A), an affiliate of the Kettering Foundation. Of importance to this volume is that clinical workshops and other training activities sponsored by /I/D/E/A/ for the benefit of individuals and school systems involved in IGE, are built around peer-observation processes and have, for at least a decade, followed the five-stage observation cycle as recommended in these chapters.

Teachers who have had IGE-type training or some other exposure to clinical supervision and who work together in teams, can build observation cycles into their daily or weekly schedules and thus enjoy many benefits associated with the process. Such teachers tend very quickly to shed some of the anxiety (and even fear) that most teachers have about being supervised and criticized; and the levels of professional conversation and technical sharing in such situations tend to be very high. Experience and research strongly suggest, however, that in order for such sharing practices to emerge, the building principal and others in supervisory roles must (1) have great understanding not only of team teaching but also of the observation cycle; (2) possess and manifest a strong personal commitment to teaching and to the use of the observation cycles as a professional tool; and (3) provide resources, time, and other necessary assistance so that such activities can actually be worked into the busy schedule of the school. The aforementioned understanding and commitment are likelier to exist if the supervisors have a good conceptual grasp of clinical supervision and its elements.

A CONCEPTUAL BACKGROUND FOR SUPERVISION

We hope that you as our reader enjoyed the imaginary conversation that was presented in Chapter 1, in our attempt to link this volume to its predecessor and to acquaint you with some of its major ideas and concepts. Sifting through some of the interview material, you may have discerned that we associate at least nine characteristics or notions with clinical supervision; it:

1. is a technology for improving instruction.
2. is a deliberate intervention into the instructional process.
3. is goal-oriented, combining school and personal growth needs.
4. assumes a working relationship between teacher(s) and supervisor.
5. requires mutual trust, as reflected in understanding, support, and commitment for growth.
6. is systematic, yet requires a flexible and continuously changing methodology.
7 creates productive tension for bridging the real–ideal gap.

8. assumes the supervisor knows more about instruction and learning than the teacher(s).
9. requires training for the supervisor.

The last two items in the above list may merit discussion since at first glance Item 8 may seem somewhat arrogant or at least condescending with respect to the knowledge base from which teachers work, and Item 9 requires clarification with respect to the elements of training.

In the 1966 publication by Anderson, cited earlier, there was presented a definition of teaching as a career, symbolized by a right triangle at the extremities of which were shown the Curriculum (things that are to be learned by the child), the Teacher, and the Learner. The vertical leg of the triangle connected the Teacher to the Curriculum and represented in effect the substantive knowledge base undergirding the Teacher's work. The horizontal leg of the triangle connected the Teacher to the Learner and represented both the Teacher's efforts to know about the Learner and his needs (diagnosis) and the rapport that exists (or should exist) between the Teacher and the Learner and, ideally, results in *trust* (see Item 5 in the above list). The hypotenuse of the triangle represented the pedagogical dimension, connecting the Learner to the Curriculum. Anderson's reason for choosing a right triangle was that he wanted to imply, through a slight distortion of the well-known Pythagorean theorem (hypotenuse squared equals leg squared plus leg squared), that command by the teacher of pedagogy is equal in importance to command of knowledge plus ability to relate to learners. In the mid-1960s, that argument seemed to make sense because most teachers seemed in need of strengthening their pedagogical repertoires.

Supervision as Teaching. In 1967, in a pamphlet published by the Commission on Supervision Theory of the Association for Supervision and Curriculum Development[5] Anderson proposed that supervision is in fact a teaching role and developed an analogy that was reflected in the following figure.

Note from the illustration that there are three kinds of knowledge and skill that supervisors must command if they are to succeed in helping teachers to increase their own command of the three-dimensional teaching role. On the horizontal dimension is reflected the need for supervisors to know how to examine each teacher's role-improvement needs, and also how to build rapport (see Chapter 5 of this volume) of the sort that is based on trust. The hypotenusal dimension illustrates what the supervisor does, in the form of supervision, to help the teacher to experience growth-in-service. We might describe this as the technical knowledge (or skill) base of the supervisor. On the vertical dimension is reflected the *substantive* knowledge base (in this instance, about the teacher's role) that undergirds the supervisor's work.

---

[5] William H. Lucio, (ed.) *Supervision: Perspectives and Propositions* (Washington, D.C.: Association for Supervision and Curriculum Development, 1967), pp. 29–41.

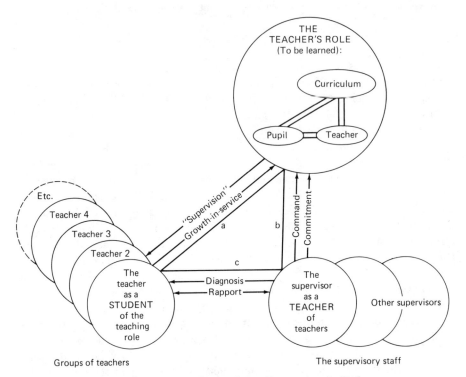

Figure 3.   **Dimensions of the Supervisor's Role**

Anderson in 1980 would prefer to draw both of the above-mentioned triangles as equilateral, which therefore would show each dimension as equal in importance to the others. With reference to teaching, this reflects his awareness of the greater need of teachers to increase their command of *what* is taught, and also his realization that over the past decade or so, teachers have likely become more expert pedagogically than they were before. With reference to teaching, similarly, it seems possible to argue that teachers' skills in learning more about their role have become greater, whereas supervisors may need more command of teacher-role knowledge than was implied in Figure 3. A 1980 artistic version of the supervisor's role might therefore be the one shown in Figure 4.

If the reader is by now comfortable with the teaching analogy that has been drawn, and accepts the argument that a supervisor in order to be helpful must have a larger and deeper understanding of teaching than the persons he or she seeks to help, then perhaps we can safely proceed to the further development of the model on which this volume is built.

For those reluctant to ascribe greater knowledge or skill to the supervisory role, at least as a theoretical ideal, perhaps some comfort can be found in the somewhat softer position that even persons of lesser skill can, under favorable circumstances, provide useful assistance or insight to colleagues. In the case

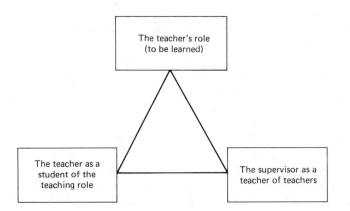

Figure 4. **The Supervisor's Role (Revised Illustration)**

of peer supervision (for example, within a teaching team) we are confident that teachers at whatever respective levels of skill can be extremely helpful to each other. Further, we have no doubt that almost any supervisor, unless downright inept, can under favorable circumstances be of significant assistance to the World's Greatest Teacher (if any such person does in fact exist in this century). However, we see little real hope for the development of a true profession in teaching unless and until we can claim with reasonable confidence that those entrusted with the important work of supervision will themselves be the best exemplars and analysts of the work teachers try to do.

A FRAMEWORK OF VALUES FOR SUPERVISION

Our ideas and practice of clinical supervision arise from a framework of values in connection to which the discipline acquires its purposes and its rationales. We value certain educational priorities that are reflected in most of the literature of innovative practice since the mid-1950s and that concentrate, in particular, upon the notion of individual human autonomy for people generally and, in our specific frame of reference, particularly for teachers and their supervisors. We are driven by images of teaching that enhance the learners' self-sufficiency and freedom to act; of supervision that facilitates such teaching and aims for a parallel condition in the teacher's own existence; and, finally, of a supervision in which the supervisor's own capacities for autonomous functioning are heightened by the very practice in which he himself (or she herself) engages.

We value learning that focuses upon its own processes and structures as well as upon external objects. We value inquiry, analysis, examination, and evaluation, especially when such activities of the mind are self-initiated and self-regulated. We believe that any supervision intended to facilitate such outcomes must be inherently humane, conceptually tough, grounded in intellectual humility, and based upon a determination to discover more about reality and to construct behaviors that are rationally related to such discoveries.

The supervision we envisage is intended to increase teachers' incentives and skills for self-supervision and for supervising their professional colleagues. It is additionally intended to become progressively more useful as teachers become increasingly capable of employing it creatively. We imagine, in other words, a supervision that becomes more and more productive as the teacher achieves higher and higher levels of technical and professional sophistication, most notably the ability to reach out for the special provisions that clinical supervision incorporates potentially. Our minds struggle for images of a supervision whose principal effect is to expand the sense of gratification experienced by students, teachers, and supervisors, gratification in being and gratification in the work they do.

In its present stage of development, the clinical supervision that our minds can formulate and that we seek to practice does not completely fulfill the ideology that occupies our imaginations. Day by day we know better what it is, in life and in professional life, that we are after. And, by small increments, we are getting to know better how to get what we are after. The following model of clinical supervision and the writing that surrounds it are mainly an expression of our trials. They show more of what we are trying for than of what we can assuredly do, although, to the degree that we can do anything at all, our existing proficiencies are also described.

In the way we teach children and supervise teachers and prepare clinical supervisors, we want, in each case, to be supportive and empathic; to perfect technical behaviors and the concepts from which they are generated; to increase the efficiencies and pleasures of learning and of becoming; to treat one another decently and responsibly and with affection; to engage with one another in productive and rewarding encounters; and to move toward our own destinies and toward one another's honestly.

In practice we cannot always behave as we would like to behave or accomplish the ideals we cherish. Ironically, at moments when we feel that the stakes are highest and, consequently, when we want most to achieve our desired effects, we trip upon our individual frailties and wind up with other, less desirable outcomes. We are, nonetheless, committed to success and plea for our efforts to be tolerated.

If technical improvement stands as an important objective for clinical supervision, and if the results of improved teaching and supervisory technique should constitute a betterment of everyone's condition, then the means we employ toward that end must incorporate a profound measure of human compassion and patience and a great sense of one's own behavior and of its impact upon others. The outcomes we prize are very difficult to achieve and shall be permanently elusive if our feeling of urgency impels us toward immoderate behavior that, by its failure to be compasssionate, becomes self-defeating.

We also value intellectuality for its own sake, and we dream of helping people, especially teachers, to think more clearly and more creatively about the world and the pieces of it that they seek to know. Related to this value is a respect for knowledge in its own right, and a concern for the accuracy, the salience, and the significance of what is taught. We long for the day when teachers will in all of their behavior reflect a scholarly, well-integrated, and value-oriented perspective upon the world, and when children in classrooms will find in their teachers exemplars not only of humane and honorable citizenship but also of intelligent truth-seeking.

The aims of clinical supervision will be realized when, largely by virtue of its own existence, everyone inside the school will know better why he is there, will want to be there, will be concerned with important curriculum questions, and, inside that place, will feel a strong and beautiful awareness of his own, individual identity and a community of spirit and enterprise with those beside him. These are the values that motivate our work and give rise to our ambitions. Although we cannot, obviously, make promises that are as large as our deams, we can proclaim those dreams and let ourselves be guided by them.

THE STRUCTURAL MODEL — ITS RATIONALES AND PURPOSES

As we turn to discussion of our basic five-stage model, it may be helpful to acknowledge that ours is only one of several models designed to accomplish essentially the same purposes. As participants in, or at least as intrigued observers of, the early stages of model development at Harvard University, Anderson and Goldhammer engaged in events that at first involved work with graduate students preparing for teaching careers and soon involved working with experienced teachers, principals, and others being trained to work in teaching-team projects. Known as the Harvard-Lexington Summer Program (HLSP), the ultimate setting within which the five-stage "cycle of supervision" evolved in their experience was one over which Anderson had a major directing responsibility and in which Goldhammer served as a junior faculty member. In those days Cogan's ideas provided the basic foundations, and in fact Cogan was a part of HLSP (which was operated in the summers of 1961, 1962, 1963, 1964, and in Boston in 1965) in the first year or two. Goldhammer, on whose doctoral committee Anderson served and who worked with Cogan at the University of Pittsburgh following Cogan's departure from the Harvard scene, did his dissertation on the topic of clinical supervision; and the appearance of his 1969 volume (of which this book is the second edition) represented a major event in the literature.

In HLSP, teams of trainees spent alternate weeks under faculty supervision in team curriculum planning, in team teaching (carrying out the plan), and in team observations of the teaching being done by fellow trainees. The observation activities, as it turned out, were remarkably more exciting, more dramatic, and more educative for the trainees than were the other two phases of the training cycle; and, in fact, offshoot training programs still in existence in the late 1970s (for example, IGE clinical workshops) have telescoped the planning and teaching phases so that more trainee energy can go into the "ob cycle."

The 1969 Goldhammer description of the ob cycle followed the eventual HLSP pattern, which embraced five stages. By 1973, when Cogan's long-awaited volume appeared, the cycle was presented by Cogan in eight phases, the first three of which (establishing the teacher–supervisor relationship, planning with the teacher) correspond with Goldhammer's Stage 1, and two others of which (analyzing the teaching-learning process, and planning the strategy of the conference) correspond with Goldhammer's Stage 3. Cogan's final phase (Number 8, renewed planning) treats the postobservation activity in a way somewhat different from Goldhammer's; but it seems reasonable to claim that there are no major differences in the structure of the cycle of supervision as described by the two authors. This is not to deny that the two authors make unique and somewhat different contributions, however.

In this second edition of Goldhammer's work we have elected to stay with the five-stage description and largely to update and reinforce, rather than drastically to alter, Goldhammer's views. Because of our admiration for Cogan's treatment of the topic, however, we suggest that many readers will want to consult his presentation as well as our own.

THE MODEL

The basic model, as already indicated, consists of five stages to which we will refer collectively as the "sequence of supervision." A collection of such sequences will be called the "cycle of supervision." Our plan for the remainder of this volume is first, to describe the general purposes and rationales of each of the five stages; second, to present methodological techniques employed at each stage; third, to examine certain problems that often arise at each stage in practice; and finally, to examine some aspects of our past and of our future. Taking the model's structure as the organizing principle of this writing, we will identify its major underlying premises and the system of values from which it has grown, step by step as the presentation progresses.

THE FIVE STAGES

The prototype of a sequence of clinical supervision consists of the following five stages: (1) preobservation conference; (2) observation; (3) analysis and strategy; (4) supervision conference; and (5) postconference analysis. Let us imagine a hypothetical sequence of supervision occurring sometime after the supervisory relationship has been inaugurated. Initial sequences pose special problems and incorporate certain unique goals that we will consider later on as a special case and in relation to a spread of issues concerning "beginnings" in supervision.

Stage 1: Rationales and Purposes of the Preobservation Conference

This stage is mainly intended to provide a mental and procedural framework for the supervisory sequence to follow. Although its functions can be viewed somewhat differently by the teacher and the supervisor, in general, in our practice, it has served the following purposes:

Confirming and Nurturing the Teacher-Supervisor Relationship If the sequence about to occur is a first, at least for these particular persons, various prior events serve to initiate a relationship within which, it is hoped, both parties will begin to feel comfortable with each other. If the sequence represents continuation of an ongoing relationship, the trust already earned and the history already recorded provide a basis for reestablishing, and perhaps raising to higher levels, the bases for productive supervision.

Fluency Both Teacher and Supervisor require fluency in Teacher's plans for the teaching that will, presumably, be observed. The teacher's fluency is demanded for seemingly obvious reasons: The better the teacher knows his or her own intentions, both means and ends, the better they can be implemented. The supervisor must know the teacher's intentions in order to share a framework of meaning and to understand the teacher's reasons, premises, doubts, explicit professional motives, and the specific payoff envisioned.

Understanding the teacher's frame of reference is necessary for either of two purposes: for helping the teacher to function successfully in his or her own terms or for modifying plans according to concepts existing in the supervisor's frame of reference. In the latter case, for Supervisor to introduce constructs into Teacher's thinking, particularly if such constructs lead logically to changes in Teacher's plans and subsequent teaching behavior, the reasons and justifications for such changes should make sense in the teacher's existing conceptual framework. Although the technical modifications that the supervisor proposes may be novel in the teacher's experience, the reasons for them must be communicable in language with which the teacher is already familiar.

Another assumption about requirements for fluency is that there is generally a positive relationship between one's explicit knowledge of one's intentions and operational strategies and one's subsequent control over instrumental behavior. Although intuitiveness and spontaneity often appear as elements of "successful" teaching, it seems nonetheless true that beyond certain limits, predominantly intuitive approaches are more likely to wind up on the rocks than explicitly planned approaches. Retroactive analyses of teaching often reveal that loss of control or focus or efficiency was due to absence of explicit understanding of certain prior assumptions or of other elements of the teaching in question.

The principal means, in this stage, for enhancing both members' fluency, is for the teacher to present his or her most polished and updated version of plans whose formulation was begun during the prior sequence of supervision in this cycle. That presentation serves dual purposes: Supervisor learns just what Teacher has in mind, and Teacher is able to test and increase self-fluency by verbalizing ideas to Supervisor.

Rehearsal In a rudimentary sense, we can imagine that the simple enunciation of plans provides Teacher with a degree of rehearsal for the teaching lesson, at least a conceptual rehearsal. Additional opportunities exist in Stage 1 for more thorough rehearsal of instructional behavior. For example, should either member anticipate that at certain points in the lesson problems might be created by the pupils' failure to produce some specific verbal response or by some pupil's verbalization of an unanticipated response, Teacher and Supervisor might role-play those episodes of the lesson in order for Teacher to sharpen resiliency and to heighten readiness to refocus the inquiry or to prosecute some new line of inquiry, should the proper indications arise.

Although one might argue that under such circumstances rehearsal would be overly specific, Supervisor cannot role-play every unanticipated response. Nonetheless, experience has shown that Teacher's general capacity to cope with unexpected outcomes can be heightened by this practice and that in many instances their combined imagination, which is rooted in Teacher's and Supervisor's backgrounds of classroom experience, often enables the members to predict "unanticipated" responses and to be consequently forearmed to deal with them. We suspect that this general capacity consists partly of developing an emotional tolerance for surprises and partly in knowing the general categories of distortion or misunderstanding in which pupils' spontaneous responses are likely to occur.

Analogously, a student of flying learns very specific techniques for dealing with unexpected stalls, spins, turbulence, icing, instrument failure, and the like. It is true, however, that in every emergency, every storm, and every cross-wind landing, the aircraft's behavior is unique in some respect, as are environmental variables and elements of the student's psychological functioning. The student cannot rehearse every conceivable condition of flying; still, rehearsal of various aeronautical crises can provide students with both emotional fortitude and sufficient experience with general problems to enable them to make specific behavioral adaptations to cope with unexpected terrors when they must.

Another possibility for rehearsal arises from circumstances in which, although the teacher knows generally what key questions and directions to use, he or she has not formulated them verbatim. If Teacher or Supervisor suspects that because of improper or ambiguous phraseology, Teacher's questions or directions may fail to achieve their intended outcomes, such key items can be rehearsed by role-play or other means and committed to more precise forms. For example, if one of Teacher's goals is to start things off by posing a question that demands a highly developed response from the pupils (because, let us suppose, Teacher has attached a high priority to pupils' verbal participation in this instance), and if he or she should then commence teaching by stating a complex question that is answerable by a single word or by an otherwise meager response, the strategy would thereby be undone. Anticipating this eventuality, Supervisor can exercise Teacher by helping him or her through successive approximations of a maximally efficient question until both are satisfied that the risks involved have been substantially reduced. Such problems for rehearsal may arise from either Teacher's or Supervisor's concerns and may be initiated by either member in the preobservation conference.

Revisions Besides providing Teacher with a chance to rehearse planned episodes of his instruction, Stage 1 creates an opportunity for last-minute revisions in the lesson plan. As you might suspect, certain spine-tingling problems are often associated with this practice and will be examined below when we talk about problems in the supervisory sequence.

Contract However you might choose to think about it — for example, as role definition, as defining shared goals, or as agreeing to ground rules — imagining, metaphorically, a supervisory "contract" is an easy way to get a handle on this concept. We mean to suggest that the preobservation conference is a time for Teacher and Supervisor to reach explicit agreements about reasons for supervision to occur in the immediate situation and about how supervision should operate.

Among other things, after the teacher's goals have been established, the question ought to be raised of whether observation and the rest of the sequence should take place at all. If it makes sense and can be useful to the teacher (in Teacher's own terms) for supervision to continue, then surely it is worthwhile to take the trouble to say how and why and to make deliberate decisions about what is to be done. If, on the other hand, convincing reasons do not seem to exist for continuing the sequence, then it is best to ascertain that fact in time to quit.

The best way we can think of to avoid ritual commitment to the supervisory sequence, or supervision that is motivated by conflicting purposes, is to talk the matter over beforehand and to arrive at some contractual understanding before anything else happens. Once having reached agreements, both members must be ready at later stages to modify the contract if necessary and they must understand that any such modifications must be made explicitly. In other words, after certain rules have been decided upon, — "This is what you will do, this is what I will do, and here's why" (the contract) — those rules should not be changed in the middle of the game except by mutual agreement and with mutual understanding.

The need for setting a priori contracts is indicated by two common conditions: (1) that supervision is often enacted ritualistically — "My job is to supervise, your job is to be supervised, today's the day, let's get it over with"; and (2) that without explicit prior agreements (sometimes even with them), supervision is likely to operate according to social conventions, to become basically a social process, rather than to aim for specific technical and process outcomes which require behavior governed by specialized professionl conventions. When it is a tea party or a wrestling match, it is not supervision.

While Stage 1 contracts are generally short-term affairs, applying principally to a specific supervisory sequence, long-range contracts affecting cycles of supervision and long-term supervisory relationships can also exist and may provide contexts for Stage 1 dialogue. What we do today should be focused on specific problems with which Teacher is attempting to cope today. Those problems, however, rather than coming from nowhere, may derive from a sequence of problems that constitute the basis and orientation of Teacher's professional development and for the supervision intended to facilitate it.

Stage 2: Rationales and Purposes of Observation

The supervisor observes the lesson so that he or she may analyze it with the teacher afterward. Toward this end, data are recorded in appropriate ways. Whether analysis will be centered on problems identified beforehand (in Stage 1) or will emerge freshly from the new data, it is crucially important that the data constitute as true, as accurate, and as complete a representation of what took place as possible. If the data are seriously distorted, then the analysis will be worthless because, never existing for its own sake in clinical supervision, its chief purpose is to provide a sound basis for planning future teaching. "Futurity" is one hallmark of a successful conference and the more explicitly it exists, the better.

Today's data are employed as a source of tomorrow's agenda for supervision. To be isolated for supervisory treatment, problems should have some consequence for Teacher. But if, in effect, tomorrow's problems and plans are structured upon false representations of reality, then the whole business will have been a terrible waste and will not be likely to result in anything better than disenchantment. Even worse, if things keep up that way, Teacher's demoralization and withdrawal from the supervisory relationship can easily follow.

One reason for Supervisor to observe is that Teacher, being engaged in the business of teaching, cannot usually see the same things happening that a disengaged observer can. By adding eyes, the data are increased. Another reason — this also backfires occasionally — is to demonstrate commitment to Teacher, a serious enough commitment to justify paying such close attention to his behavior as the observer must. And, in this condition, Supervisor's work at observation gives weight to the technical balance in supervision and should serve as evidence that the relationship is not merely a social one: that social incentives are not sufficient in the supervisory framework.

Another rationale for Stage 2 is that by being in close proximity to the teacher and the pupils at the very moments when salient problems of professional practice are being enacted, the supervisor occupies a position from which to render real assistance to Teacher, in Teacher's terms, and according to specific observational foci (tasks) and instrumentation that Teacher may have defined in Stage 1. If observational data can be used for developing solutions to problems of practice, then such data can also be employed to authenticate the existence of certain problems, to make sure they are real, and as bases for articulating previously undefined problems.

Perhaps we should make clear that by *problems* we mean complex or problematical issues in teaching. Problems are not necessarily bad; they do not necessarily imply weaknesses. A problem, for example, might be how to secure some element of practice that seemed to be particularly productive; how to understand better under what circumstances it should be used; how to elevate it to a more general level of teaching. "Why do objects fall?" and "How do you blow glass?" are problems in this sense.

An ancillary benefit may result from observation, namely, that using given observational techniques as a model, Supervisor can teach them to Teacher who, in turn, may employ them for self-learning when opportunities to observe other teachers arise. In a more direct manner, Teacher can learn methods of systematic observation for use in the classroom and, in this fashion, can become more independently able to obtain broader data for self-analysis.

In the most general sense, observation should create opportunities for supervisors to help teachers test reality, the reality of their own perceptions and judgments about their teaching. We have argued that supervision should result in heightened autonomy for Teacher and, particularly, in strengthened capacities for independent, objective self-analysis; and that supervision which increases Teacher's dependency upon Supervisor to know whether the teaching is good or bad (that is, supervision in which Supervisor's unexamined value judgments predominate) is bad supervision. But the supervisor's perceptions and evaluations, rather than counting for nothing, represent a potentially excellent source of data from which consensual validation can be obtained: given the supervisor's own perceptions of what has taken place, Teacher can test "reality" by ascertaining whether Supervisor's observations (and later, value judgments) tend to confirm or to oppose his or her own.

Stage 3: Rationales and Purposes of Analysis and Strategy

Stage 3 is intended for two general purposes: first, in Analysis, to make sense out of the observational data, to make them intelligible and manageable; and second, in Strategy, to plan the management of the supervision conference to follow — that is, to determine what issues to treat, which data to cite, what goals to aim for, how to begin, where to end, and who should do what.

If, as we have suggested, observation is a fundamental element in clinical supervision, then analysis is its heart. Rationales for analysis can be formulated either historically or methodologically. Historically, supervision has been deeply entrenched in evaluation (rating), and supervisory evaluations have generally had only the most tenuous relationships to objective evidence. One common pattern has been for Supervisor to observe some teaching and then, through feedback, to render judgments to Teacher either on the way out, later in the office, later in a written memo, or much later in a summary evaluation of Teacher's work during the year.

Supervisor's comments have often concerned superficial aspects of teaching — bulletin boards, window shades, physical posture, and the like — and have dealt with arbitrarily selected issues, often in an arbitrary and capricious manner. This is to say that if, conventionally, supervisors' value judgments have been reasoned at all, they have not been reasoned out explicitly for the teacher in common practice. It is, and has been, even more rare for supervision to provide systematically for teachers to participate in developing evaluations of their own teaching.

One problem has been that because educational values and principles of educational practice are so ambiguous and uncertain, professional evaluators have almost been forced to choose issues and evaluation criteria arbitrarily. Another problem is that, by and large, supervisors have not known very much about educational theory or practice — being untrained or poorly trained in poor ideas — and, not having been schooled in any special discipline, have had to function idiosyncratically, according to home remedies, that is, as eclectics in the worst sense. The supervision they have performed has generally mirrored the poor supervision they received as teachers. They have focused upon elements of teaching that their own supervisors treated and that, in the absence of a professional discipline or a scientific method, are authentic only in the sense that they exist, enduringly, in the folklore and mores of teaching.

A third problem is that since supervision has never really been defined as a professional practice, no special conventions have been invented to govern supervisory behavior. Being untechnical, supervisory practice has failed to generate a body of specialized technique. It is little wonder that, not having been confronted with problems of supervision in their own training, supervisors evaluate arbitrarily or glibly: there are few reasons for them to do otherwise, and no useful models of how else to operate have been available. Unlike the psychiatrist, for example, the supervisor has no special theory to learn, no special competencies to master, no body of case material to study, and no regular supervision of his or her own practice.

From a historical perspective, a rationale for extensive analysis of empirical data in supervision is that teachers' anxieties and mistrust of supervision can be alleviated only if teachers of the future learn that supervision is (or can be) an essentially rational practice, that it methods are those of logical reasoning and forthright analysis, and that it incorporates neither the sanctions nor the mysteries nor the vagaries that have made them so helpless, so disquieted, and so independent in the past.

The analytical component of clinical supervision is intended to make it safer — less whimsical, less arbitrary, less superficial — than supervision of the past. And particularly when Teacher is trained to participate in the teaching analysis, based on the truest and most comprehensive representations of that teaching that can be created, his or her chances of benefitting from the enterprise are most favorable. Perhaps the best way that supervision can outlive its unfortunate history is by becoming something useful in the teacher's existence. Except for teachers who feel endangered by realism — we will examine this problem later — analysis of their teaching should be the most useful thing that anyone else can do in relation to it.

Methodologically, analysis exists for the sake of understanding true events in order to exercise greater control over future events. In other words, analysis of today's teaching is primarily for the sake of greater power, for a higher probability of success in tomorrow's teaching. Besides eliminating inequities from supervision — for example, hierarchical inequities and injustices arising from the imposition, by an outsider, of unexamined value judgments — analysis provides possibilities for Teacher to be vigorously engaged in examination of his or her work and to function autonomously, rather than dependently, in framing decisions that affect the work. The problem of having to accept someone else's word on faith is largely avoided. If, as your supervisor, I have shown you the (recognizable) evidence that has led me to certain questions or judgments about what you have done, and if I have enunciated the sequence of reasoning by which I traveled from perceptions of your teaching to inferences about it, then I have made myself sufficiently vulnerable for you to discover logical inconsistencies in my reasoning, to be able to read the data differently, to offer alternative interpretations, to provide missing data, to isolate other issues, to frame questions that may be truer or, in some way, more productive to treat — or, if it works out that way, to be persuaded by my evidence and by my reasoning and to commit yourself to work through the problems I have identified.

At the very least, my involvement in analysis of your teaching should demonstrate my degree of commitment to you — I have not simply verbalized it; I have done actual work to show it — and should at least reassure you that I am not carefree in my attention to your professional behavior. To have matched your energy and sobriety in connection to issues that are very important to you should make the work I do seem at least tentatively trustworthy. In any event, analysis as a supervisory method is used in clinical supervision as a mode of learning and as a medium through which to modify teaching behavior. In a later chapter, we will illustrate some of the specific analytical techniques that clinical supervision employs.

Supervisor's next step, after having performed an analysis of the observational data, is to make decisions about how the supervision conference should be conducted. The principal rationale for Strategy, like that for instructional planning, is that a planned approach toward specified goals by deliberate processes is more likely to work out than a random one. Obviously, this simple formula fails if, for one reason or another, the plan is poor. In any case, it is theoretically acceptable to think of planned conferences and to suppose that if the plan is a good one it should enhance Supervisor's responsiveness to Teacher instead of retarding it and should culminate in behavior that Teacher finds useful.

If Strategy exists for the sake of efficiency, it is also intended for protection. It is generally safe to assume that the teacher feels that teaching is important and that even if the teacher's conscious motives for teaching are superficial or extrinsic (for example, teaching represents a stable source of income and provides attractive fringe benefits), observation and analysis will, nonetheless, be important — if only because of its evaluative character and of the emotional implications evaluation carries for most people.

Given the assumption, therefore, that the business to be transacted in the supervision conference will be emotionally important for the teacher (and, presumably, important in other terms as well), it follows that the conduct of such business ought to be considered carefully in advance. If the emotional stakes may be high, then possibilities for feeling hurt or being hurt may be high. Where possibilities for pain exist (that is, for someone else's pain to arise more or less directly from our behavior toward the teacher), at the very least we are responsible for exercising some deliberate control over our behavior. In this context it would seem that one's self-interest — our investment in supervision — functions to protect the supervisee's interests as well as our own.

Strategy is also intended to provide continuity in supervision. If it becomes important to stick to certain specific lines of inquiry throughout a cycle or over longer periods of time, if supervision has become a vehicle for "longitudinal" development of one kind or another, or if, for any other purposes, it seems important for supervision to have a fabric, a cohesiveness, a unity, then Strategy provides a natural time to pick and choose issues from the analysis for continuity's sake.

In a more general sense, if supervision is intended to result in process outcomes as well as in purely technical ones, that is, if it is intended to affect patterns of behavior and underlying psychological predispositions as well as simply to transmit substantive information, then it is more difficult to prepare for supervision than it would be otherwise. Rather than simply having to prepare one's material, as for a lecture, one must additionally prepare oneself for collaboration intended to benefit one's supervisee. Both technical and process outcomes depend very much upon one another. We must prepare in several integrated dimensions; and Strategy is the time for doing so, if we conceptualize supervision in these terms.

Another rationale for Strategy, which is perhaps more a hope than a reason, is, again, that Teacher's confidence in supervision is more likely to be inspired if he or she perceives that Supervisor has put a great deal of work into it than if Supervisor appears to be working off the cuff. Another rationale, when it is possible for Teacher to be freed from other responsibilities in order to have time to develop self-strategies for supervision before the conference — this possibility should always exist, although, in actual practice, it generally does not — is to enable the teacher to compose ideas beforehand. If Teacher is functioning well in supervision, is relaxed, intelligent, committed, professionally creative, and functioning autonomously, then Strategy will allow time for ordering priorities and screening issues for the conference accordingly. Viewing supervision as a battleground, however, the teacher has an equal chance with the opponent to mobilize forces (although nevertheless handicapped inasmuch as it is his or her teaching that is at stake). In more realistic terms, Teacher can be protected from the disadvantages of having to deal all at once, without forethought, with problems that are already well rehearsed for Supervisor.

Stage 4: Rationales and Purposes of the Supervision Conference

All roads lead to the conference. Whereas it is sometimes appropriate to omit earlier stages of the clinical sequence for special reasons, and whereas even on certain occasions shortages of time may preclude any supervisory contact except a conference, once a sequence has been begun it is almost never acceptable to quit that sequence before the conference. If a lesson does not happen, or if things go very poorly, it would generally be indicated that a conference of some kind, even a very abridged one, should be held. Such a conference might be used, first of all, to help Supervisor test impressions of Teacher's condition. Additionally, it might focus upon a teacher's seeming anxiety rather than on the teaching. Or, it might serve simply as a time to offer reassurances and to make decisions about what should happen next. Or, it might be used for planning future teaching without including systematic analysis of the observed teaching, and the like.

But in one way or another, some kind of conference is almost always preferable to no conference at all — for example, if only to signify that Teacher is important to Supervisor (whether plans are executed or not) and that Supervisor is not going to abandon the relationship at moments of failure or crisis when Teacher is more likely to require support than at any other moment. One of the principles underlying this reasoning is that supervision is most likely to succeed if Supervisor can accept the existence of problems without attaching any stigma to Teacher for having them.

Another thought, in this connection, is central in clinical supervision. Understanding that even under the most favorable conditions observation is likely to be accompanied by some feeling of stress, we propose that a minimum responsibility incumbent upon the observer is to discuss what was observed in Teacher's lesson. In many cases supervision is less punishing, even when it must address very inadequate teaching, than it is when Teacher is left only with fantasies about how Supervisor feels because, having observed the teaching, Supervisor did not follow through with conversation about it. The probability of such an outcome is especially vivid when, as it commonly happens, Teacher does depend very much upon Supervisor's evaluation and has not yet learned to value self-initiated analysis or, indeed, any form of analysis in favor of prompt and positive feedback from Supervisor. In our work with supervision students in professional practicums, rule number one is, generally, "Stay out of the classroom unless you are committed to a full sequence of supervision. Your participation in a conference is what earns you your right to observe."

This idea can be expressed in yet another variation: Before they have met in conference, Teacher has been highly vulnerable while Supervisor has been practically invulnerable. Again, it seems true that in any supervisory type of relationship, the supervisee experiences an inevitable handicap inasmuch as it is his or her work (rather than anyone else's, including Supervisor's) that is being examined. Whatever handicaps Teacher must endure in supervision ought not to be avoidable artifacts that result from what Supervisor does, particularly when Supervisor could have elected other alternatives.

Our sense of the teacher's vulnerability can be imagined best in connection to observation. Whereas Teacher's mistakes may be apparent, Supervisor's perceptual errors and errors of interpretation are invisible. It is additionally true that in Preobservation, while Supervisor has nothing to lose, Teacher's sense of intention and plans for instruction can be thoroughly undermined. And, as it most often happens, by conference time Supervisor enjoys a relatively organized intellectual preparation, whereas Teacher is still panting from other responsibilities during the intervening period.

In the conference, as he or she becomes an active agent and must enunciate ideas, Supervisor begins to generate behavior and products that are as vulnerable in analysis as Teacher's. Especially when committing to judgments concerning elements of the teaching, Supervisor's constructs, patterns of reasoning, and professional assumptions — the logical and substantive integrity of what is said — have become public and exposed and open to examination.

In succinct terms, the supervision conference is additionally intended to:

1. Provide a time to plan future teaching in collaboration with another professional educator. Perhaps the best measure of whether a conference has been useful, in Teacher's framework, is whether it has left him or her with something concrete in hand, namely, a design for the next sequence of instruction.
2. Provide a time to redefine the supervisory contract in order to decide what directions supervision should take and by what methods it should operate (or whether supervision should be temporarily terminated).
3. Provide a source of adult rewards. In common practice, teachers have few opportunities for their value to be acknowledged by other adults who have professional sophistication and who know their work (that is, Teacher's work) intimately.
4. Review the history of supervision — that is, of the problems that Supervisor and Teacher have addressed formerly and to assess progress in mastering technical (or other) competencies upon which Teacher has been working.

5. Define treatable issues in the teaching and to authenticate the existence of issues that have been sensed intuitively.
6. Offer didactic assistance to Teacher, either directly or by referral, in relation to information or theory that Teacher requires and of which Supervisor may have relatively advanced knowledge.
7. Train Teacher in techniques for self-supervision and develop incentives for professional self-analysis.
8. Deal with an array of factors that may affect Teacher's vocational satisfaction and technical competency. The queston of what issues of this kind are appropriate to treat in supervision depends largely upon the participants' inclinations, Supervisor's specials skills for such work, pertinent situational variables, and the overriding question of how supervision can be therapeutic (small "t") without becoming Therapy (large "T").

Whether a conference begins to fulfill any of these potentialities depends partly on what has come before, partly on psychological variables that operate for or against successful work, and largely upon the manner in which Supervisor operates. As with other stages of the sequence, there are never any guarantees. Simply because clinical supervision offers a conference and even though Supervisor may conceptualize *conference* in all the right terms, conferences may nevertheless fail terribly by any reasonable criteria that one might choose. Strategies to minimize risks and to alleviate problems that commonly occur should therefore have been devised duing Stage 3.

Stage 5: Rationales and Purposes of the Postconference Analysis

Because Stage 5 was invented in the Harvard training program in a context of group supervision in which some member(s) could analyze the supervisory behavior of some other member(s) after the supervision conference was over, it is difficult to describe Postconference Analysis as a solo activity. Nevertheless, we can examine the concept and talk about its rationales, leaving methodological questions for later on.

In retrospect, it seems that although each of the stages reviewed so far has plural purposes and multiple rationales, each nevertheless seems also to have some essential commitment. Preobservation serves largely to set the contract; Observation takes place to capture realities of the lesson; Analysis is intended to make the data intelligible by unearthing logical relationships among them; Strategy produces an operational plan for supervision. In essence, the Conference Analysis serves as clinical supervision's superego — its conscience.

It is the time when Supervisor's practice is examined with all of the rigor and for basically the same purposes that Teacher's professional behavior was analyzed theretofore. In both instances our principal rationale is that examined professional behavior is more likely to be useful — for everyone — than unexamined behavior; that, perhaps, the only truly worthwhile existence is an examined existence. In one sense, this can be construed as an ethical rationale:

As supervisors — the same holds for teachers — we are responsible for protecting the interests of the people we serve and, given the profession's clinical character, our first line of defense for them is represented by deliberate consciousness of, and purposeful control over, what we do. According to this view, decisions affecting the conduct of our future behavior must arise, in large part, from objective analysis of our past behavior and from as fine an understanding as we can develop of what consequences it has had.

Again, the Conference Analysis arises from pragmatic, methodological, and historical considerations. First, it represents a basis for assessing whether supervision is working productively, for ascertaining its strengths and weaknesses, and for planning to modify supervisory practices accordingly. In this context, any and all variables are appropriate to review: supervisory technique, implict and explicit assumptions, predominating values, emotional variables, technical and process goals, and the like. Second, Supervisor can demonstrate skills of self-analysis by familiarizing Teacher with the work to be done in the Postconference Analysis, perhaps by videotaping it for analysis by Teacher afterwards. Third, Teacher's awareness of Supervisor's regular practice of Postconference Analysis shoud help to offset misgivings that may exist concerning Supervisor's commitment and the historical disparity between his or her professional vulnerability and Teacher's.

When Supervisor operates alone (that is, in one-to-one supervision rather than in group supervision), Postconference Analysis is a solitaire. By and large, Supervisor directs attention to behavior in the conference, reaching back to material from observation notes, and so on, when analysis of the conference requires it. Supervisor's methods are essentially the same as those employed in analysis of the teaching. One of the obvious advantages of group supervision — that is, of supervision undertaken collaboratively by two or more supervisors — is that in such practice certain members may be assigned responsibility for conducting the Postconference Analysis and, from the beginning, can collect data at each stage of the supervisory sequence for that purpose. Particularly when Supervisor is not yet able to perform an objective, full-bodied self-analysis, the utilization of other analysts to examine Supervisor's behavior may be crucial for both Supervisor's and Teacher's professional growth and for the protection of Teacher's interests.

Even at the most advanced stages of his or her technical development, we propose that Supervisor's practice should, itself, be supervised from time to time. Also needed, therefore, is a model that incorporates supervision of supervision as well as supervision of teaching.

Chapter 4

SETTING
THE STAGE
FOR CLINICAL
SUPERVISION

---

* Rapport
* Self-acceptance
* Rapport Nurturance

[T]he supervisory program is the nervous system of the school. It is, above all else, the mechanism for adaptation; it represents that ability to adapt to new conditions which an organism — or school — must have or die.[1]

The supervisory aspect of any school system is vital to the success that system has in producing a top-quality educational network in which teachers and students interact and grow. One may liken curriculum to a sport, and the skill and technique utilized in that sport to instructional effectiveness. Within any sport, the proper equipment occupies an important role — yet equipment alone is hardly sufficient for success. A knowledge base of the sport and its rules is necessary, as well as skill in application of that knowledge base. Consider briefly, the sport of golf. One may own an excellent set of clubs, use the finest golf balls, and wear a top-notch pair of golf shoes. But the finest equipment cannot guarantee a quality golfer. The acquisition and maintenance of skills is necessary. Even the best professional tour golfers must, from time to time (and some on a regular basis) seek the help of a master analyst/teacher to sharpen their game and regain self confidence, working out the problems in their swings, thus allowing them to be able to maintain skills necessary to retain their status on the tour.

[1]Fred T. Wilhelms, *Supervision in a New Key* (Washington, D.C.: Association for Supervision and Curriculum Development, 1973), p. 1.

Now consider an individual school. It may be a well designed building, having an excellent curriculum, and contain the latest equipment in its various labs. However, without teachers who care for professional development to improve their teaching techniques and skills in working with students, the school may not excel, in either achievement of pupils or reputation for professionalism.

Just as the professional golfer, or any other sports person, must have both the knowledge base and the skills to implement that knowledge, so too must the teacher. In order to be effective in the teaching profession, the teacher must have a knowledge base and the skills to implement that knowledge base. Just as professional golfers must periodically sharpen their skills, so must teachers refresh their instructional and interactional skills — through obtaining the assistance of a master analyst who can also help them regain the self-confidence needed for successful performance. As the golfer turns to an advisor he trusts, so does the teacher turn to a supervisor he trusts.

The analogy between professional athletics and teaching is an apt one. The assumption is that we are dealing with competent people, and at the same time it is taken for granted that skills maintenance and skills improvement are regularly required. The *most* skillful persons, in fact, may well be the ones most eager for further improvement and therefore for further counsel. We are reminded of the legendary Ted Williams, of the Boston Red Sox, who never ceased to be an ardent student of batsmanship and who, even at the peak of his career, constantly discussed the science of hitting with top players, coaches, and retired baseball stars.

So it should be with teachers. There is probably no more desirable attribute in professional teachers than an eagerness to improve (through change) their teaching methods and content for the students. Clinical supervision makes this possible because, in it, instructional improvement is an ongoing procedure that does not require the typical in-service and university involvement that traditional professionl growth implies. Morris Cogan succeeds in capturing the nature of clinical supervision when he says, "Clinical supervision does not mean that the teacher is in training. It means that he is continually engaged in improving his practice, as is required of all professionals."[2]

Clinical supervision makes available to the teacher who is so motivated the teaching professional who can be of direct assistance and who draws upon a fund of knowledge about the best way to "hit the ball." That advisor, furthermore, bases his responses and suggestions upon data gathered directly in the classroom, and utilizes techniques for data analysis and of providing feedback that contribute not only to methodological/instructional improvements but also to the teacher's well-being.

The well-qualified and well-motivated clinical supervisor uses techniques that have nearly universal applicability. No supervisor can possibly have a strong

[2]Morris L. Cogan, *Clinical Supervision* (Boston: Houghton Mifflin, 1973), p. 21.

background in all curriculum subjects, nor is it likely that most supervisors have an extensive background of training and experience at all levels (preschool, elementary, middle school, secondary, and postsecondary) of schooling. This obviously means that certain kinds of questions may be more challenging to some supervisors than others. We recognize that certain questions, especially relating to the content, probably cannot be addressed at all by some supervisors. However, we believe that most of the techniques that are associated with clinical supervision are relevant to the whole gamut of educational situations, and that a skillful supervisor can work successfully with any teacher of any subject at any level. One need not understand physics at all, for example, yet one could be capable, through analysis of classroom dynamics or use of space and materials, of literally transforming a mediocre physics teacher into a good one. Similarly, a former physics teacher, childless and largely ignorant about five-year-olds, could be enormously helpful to a kindergarten teacher in such domains as interaction, curriculum content, communications, and lesson pacing.

We hope this argument will make sense, and reduce the resistance that teachers sometime offer when they perceive that the supervisor comes out of a different background from their own. Perhaps especially at the secondary level this is often a problem. Secondary teachers tend, more than elementary teachers, to be heavily committed to the content of their field(s) of specialization, and they are likelier to be concerned about content questions than about methodological matters or about nuances of teacher-pupil and pupil-pupil relationships. Their initial expectations of supervisors are therefore likely to relate to *what* they are teaching. In such cases, supervisors must earn the confidence of teachers not by their demonstrated command of subject-matter knowledge, but by their ability to raise questions about the content, about the apparent responses of pupils to the content as presented, and about the larger setting within which the teacher, the pupils, and the content ideas are interacting.

In all instances, but perhaps especially in cases where the supervisor has to build a supervisory relationship from scratch, it is essential for the supervisor to be conscious of *rapport* as a facilitating condition. To this topic we will turn in a moment. Another important and related concept to guide supervisor behavior is that supervision has as one of its main goals the nurturance of healthy and confident self-concepts in teachers, and through teachers' behaviors toward pupils, in the pupils as well. Our enthusiasm for clinical, as opposed to other, more distant types of supervision, is fueled by our awareness that clinical approaches are particularly conducive to influencing and increasing teachers' self-respect and healthy, positive regard for learners.

By its very nature, in-classroom observation connects supervisors to the learners, to the teacher in action, and to the various forces that impinge upon the morale and the productivity of the various participants. By being one of the participants, at least to some extent, the supervisor enters into the morale picture; and every response or suggestion flowing out of that participation is a potential contribution to the ways that teachers and students feel about the content, about their relationships to it, and about themselves and each other.

Some general principles should therefore guide the supervisor toward making *positive* rather than negative contributions to such feelings. One is that every effort must be made to reduce the teacher's natural tendency to be apprehensive about supervision. Especially when the supervision involves a great deal of direct, face-to-face contact, many teachers are actually frightened about possible negative consequences. Such is the nature of clinical supervision. Instructional supervision sometimes instills an apprehensive feeling within teachers. In comparison, "clinical" supervision, due in part to the name and in part to its inherent activities, downright scares them.[3] Such fears can be reduced by tactful, sympathetic, nonjudgmental, helpful, and ego-supportive responses to the teacher's work.

A second guiding principle is that supervisors should seek to enhance the teacher's sense of professional autonomy. For teachers to grow professionally, they must feel important, in a personal sense, to the cause of the organization. They need to know who they are, and learn to respect and appreciate themselves. Teachers should be free to think for themselves, to form and express their own opinions, make decisions, and act on those decisions. Their skill and freedom to do those things will help to contribute to self-confidence and in turn allow for improved instruction. Supervisors can promote such skills and freedom. They must respect teachers for what they are and how well they do. Clinical supervisors must also know and respect themselves so they can respect others' ideas.

A third principle is that supervisors should seek to encourage initiative in teachers and respond to creative efforts. Change in the school program centers around the teachers, since it is they who have most contact with the students and have, therefore, the most influence on them. An environment should be established in which teachers can be creative, and willing to improve their teaching. To encourage teachers to be creative is to have them strive for excellence, plan, test, and then revise new approaches — always keeping the student in mind. Clinical supervisors should encourage teachers to try new ideas frequently, and assist them in evaluation of the results.

Two other principles come to mind, both having to do with the teacher's feelings. First, teachers need to feel good about working with young people, and therefore to be eager to establish good relationships with their pupils and among their pupils. As both self-respect and regard for others is increased, teachers are better able to relate to students in healthy ways and to encourage interaction from the students because of their increased confidence in their

[3]Robert J. Krajewski, "Some Thoughts on Clinical Supervision: Theory and Practice," *Professional Educator*, *1*(2) (Fall 1978), p. 20.

ability to cope with any situation. If teachers feel good about themselves, they will be more apt to transmit this feeling to the students.

Clinical supervision improves not only instruction, but curriculum as well. Thus, how the teacher *feels* about the content of the subject, for example, will influence the character it assumes as it is mediated to the students. Therefore, the supervisor should make every effort to help the teacher feel comfortable about what he is teaching, to deal with perceived gaps in his knowledge, and especially to make certain that his enthusiasm for the content is not concealed from the children. An enthusiastic interest in the subject matter as expressed by the supervisor sometimes heartens the teacher and rekindles enthusiasm that repetitious presentations, over the years, may have cooled.

A final principle, implicit in most of the others, is that supervisors must be eternally conscious of the importance of maintaining rapport with teachers. This admonition is so important to us, in fact, that we want to stop for a moment and examine rapport as an integral aspect of supervisory effectiveness.

RAPPORT

To be effective in a given position, especially in a position as a clinical supervisor, the person in that position needs a knowledge base built upon a foundation of theory in administration and supervision. Among the most relevant theories in these fields are those relating to the importance of motivation and of having a positive view of self. These we consider to be the foundation of rapport. By definition, rapport is a harmonious relationship with and between people. Rapport suggests positive feelings between people, and it reflects the fact that people get along well together. To cultivate a harmonious relationship with and between people, a clinical supervisor needs to utilize a knowledge base of supervision, to include elements of learning theory, motivational theory, and administration theory. To be effective, clinical supervisors must command a knowledge of both instructional theory and of skill in its practical application with teachers. Throughout the process, rapport is vital. A clinical supervisor needs to know how to deal with the various anxiety feelings that are revealed by teachers — whether conscious or subconscious. The supervisor also needs to know how to assess, and then to contribute toward the improvement of, the self-view (both personal and professional) that the teacher appears to have. In order to do so effectively, the supervisor must himself or herself possess a healthy, positive self-concept. If you as a supervisor feel good about yourself and what you do, both as a person and as a professional (in other words, if your self-concept is healthy), you will be much better equipped to work effectively with teachers and students than if you do not. Without self-acceptance, no one can really work very well with other people.

The corollary of such reasoning is that the teacher cannot expect to work well with children, or expect to be able to help them to work well with each other, if the teacher's self-acceptance and self-definition are negative. It also seems probable that relationships between people depend in part upon acceptance, even admiration, of the self-definitions that the relators perceive in each other. If Joan feels good about herself with respect to a certain set of skills or characteristics, if Fred feels good about himself in similar ways, if Joan is pleased about the way Fred appears to feel and Fred feels pleased about the way Joan appears to feel — then it would seem that Joan and Fred are going to feel good about their relationship.

Now, if Joan (the supervisor, who feels good about herself) and Fred (a teacher who feels good about himself) do not know very much about each other's self-definitions, it is not as likely that a productive relationship will exist, at least for now, and an immediate need is to set various get-acquainted activities in motion. Since our postulation is that both persons are in good psychological shape (at least with respect to the roles in question) it seems likely that rapport can be developed in fairly short order. More effort will be involved if Fred has a low self-concept; and we hesitate even to deal with the effort needed if Joan, the supervisor, also has low self-esteem or, worse, is the one of the two with such a problem. We believe strongly that the profession cannot tolerate this weakness in supervisors; and in this volume the overriding assumption is that the supervisor possesses a healthy, positive self-concept. Unless this is in fact the case, teachers will almost surely be poorly served.

We examine rapport, then, largely under the assumption that the supervisor has the necessary personal strength both to merit the confidence and respect of teachers and also to be able to cope with some of the problems and stresses that can arise when dealing with low-self-concept personnel.

Rapport is much more than just a single aspect of clinical supervision. It cannot be so limited. It is, rather, a total encapsulation, a constant throughout the process of working with people toward a given end. It is a necessary ingredient without which we cannot begin to effect improvement in the school. In essence, we envison rapport as a continual and overriding aspect of the clinical supervisory process, an ingredient required in all phases. Its apparent lack in many of the supervisory situations in schools today is probably a major cause of the sad state of affairs in supervision generally. Too many teachers expect supervision to be punitive, to be anchored in an odious system of administrative sanctions. One might guess that what many teachers have learned best from their experiences with supervision is how to second-guess supervisors, how to anticipate what will please them, how to stage appropriate classroom performances for them to observe, and how to jolly them up for their (the teachers') own protection. Given the mystique that inevitably surrounds unexplicit systems of evaluation, an anachronistic result is that teachers' dependencies upon supervisory evaluation have grown very strong, despite its fearful and threatening aspect.

How can we make a transfer from the prevailing poor image of supervision in the schools to one in which rapport will characterize all interactions between supervisor and teacher?

SELF-ACCEPTANCE

Already established is that the supervisor must know, and feel good about, himself or herself as a person, and also as a professional. Another need is for the supervisor to understand and be committed to the promotion of certain conditions in the climate of the school that are believed to foster growth. Finally, the supervisor needs skills that enable him or her to connect in a productive way to the teachers served.

The Association for Supervision and Curriculum Development has issued many excellent publications over the years, but none has been more influential or received more acclaim than the 1962 yearbook, *Perceiving, Behaving, Becoming*. Still a strong and relevant statement after nearly two decades, the yearbook deserves attention by all persons who seek guidance about the kind of classoom climate and working relationships that must be present in order for teachers to effect a proper learning climate with students. One chapter calls for classroom climates that:

1. Encourage self-revelation rather than self-defense.
2. Give each person a feeling of belonging.
3. Create the impression that difference is good and desirable.
4. Encourage children to trust their own organisms.
5. Emphasize the existential, ongoing character of learning.
6. Finally, acceptance requires the establishment of an atmosphere which is generally hopeful.[4]

Although the above climate descriptions were intended to be used by teachers working with students, they can just as easily be applicable for supervisors working with teachers. In fact, such a climate must be present for supervisors to be able to affect changes with teachers. As the yearbook describes it:

> Teachers in service should be treated in the same way that teachers are expected to treat students. Becoming teachers are more likely to see evidence

[4]"Acceptance and The Accurate View of Self," in Arthur W. Combs (ed.), *Perceiving, Behaving, Becoming: A New Focus for Education*, 1962 Yearbook (Washington, D.C.: Association for Supervision and Curriculum Development, 1962), pp. 125 and 126.

of becoming in students. Teachers should be helped to grow through accepting, understanding and assisting them in identifying problems which they feel need solution. The supervisor who is aware that teachers are in the process of becoming works in ways which help them develop a positive view of self.[5]

Some cues for supervisors seeking to establish this sort of climate may be found in the following suggestions for self-awareness and self-acceptance:

1. *Know yourself.* Once in a while it is a good idea to sit down and ask yourself "Who am I? What am I?" You might also occasionally ask others those same questions about yourself. By asking others, you may discover things about yourself that you were not previously aware of; things you probably ought to know about yourself. Asking others is, in a sense, inviting constructive criticism. Each of us is unique, a composite of values, attitudes, and experiences. If we accept this fact, we will also accept the fact that we view others both directly through our experiences and reflectively through theirs. The clinical supervisor who knows himself and is cognizant of experiences that have contributed to his present status can interact with others more openly and more professionally.

2. *Accept yourself.* Accept yourself for what you are; if you do not, you will find it most difficult to accept others for what they are. As a clinical supervisor working with teachers this acceptance is paramount for establishing a trust base. Self-confidence enhances confidence in others, and the self-confident clinical supervisor can pass confidence on to teachers, who in turn can accept and encourage students.

3. *Respect yourself.* Self-respect is also a must for the clinical supervisor. If you do not respect yourself, how can you get others to respect you? Believe in yourself; evaluate your innate abilities; strengthen your weaknesses by building from your strengths; gain sufficient knowledge in all aspects of the supervisorship; keep current and active professionally; listen to ideas of others.

4. *Respect others.* Success in such efforts will better equip supervisors with a readiness to respect others. For teachers to gain respect from students, they must first show respect for them. Similarly, for clinical supervisors to garner the respect of the teachers with whom they work, they must first show respect. By listening to others and accepting their ideas and mannerisms we build respect, both for ourselves and for others.

RAPPORT NURTURANCE

As previously stated, clinical supervisors must command both a knowledge of instructional theory and skill in its practical applications with teachers.

---

[5]"The Process of Becoming," in Arthur W. Combs (ed.), *Perceiving, Behaving, Becoming: A New Focus for Education,* 1962 Yearbook (Washington, D.C.: Association for Supervision and Curriculum Development, 1962), pp. 246 and 247.

Throughout that implementation, rapport is vital. The term *nurturance* means to nourish or to promote development or growth. Thus rapport nurturance is the nourishing and developing of a harmonious relationship between the clinical supervisor and teachers. The responsibility for nourishing this type of relationship belongs to the clinical supervisor. The nurturance must be a continual, conscious process. It necessitates use of human relations skills, in appropriate degrees and with appropriate timing.

How can the clinical supervisor get better rapport with teachers — and how may it be nurtured? Rapport nurturance should be the subject of a specific self-inservice program, in connection with which we have a brief list of suggestions:

1. Examine thoroughly the present types of contacts the clinical supervisor has with teachers which could either promote or injure rapport. Then, from that list, choose ten types of contacts you believe will promote rapport and for each of them, discuss ways to cultivate advantages of those pleasant contacts. From the original lists, choose ten types of contacts you believe injure rapport nurturance and for each of these discuss ways in which these contacts could be made more nurturant.
2. Examine the types of praise clinical supervision affords teachers. Then analyze the types of praise you, as a clinical supervisor, use with teachers, and how you may praise more effectively.
3. Have supervisors participate in simulation exercises designed to show the importance of both verbal and nonverbal communication.
   a. Pair two supervisors. Have them, in turn, read a selection of names (or advertisements) from the telephone directory to each other, reading as if they were bored; exasperated; thinking this is the greatest; unhappy; in a hurry; confiding in someone.
   b. Pair two supervisors and have them shake hands showing the same feelings as listed in (a) above.
   c. Pair two supervisors and have them, in turn, use body gestures or movements and facial expressions to demonstrate the feelings as presented in (a) above.

Chapter 5

THE PREOBSERVATION CONFERENCE

---

* Methods
* Problems

METHODS

How the supervisor prepares for the preobservation conference depends to a great degree upon what he or she already knows about the teacher from previous interaction. In the same vein, how successful the supervisor is depends on the existing teacher–supervisor rapport. Above all, it is important in the preobservation conference to continue nurturing the rapport previously established. If there is nothing that the supervisor can do to enhance the teacher's probabilities of success — perhaps nothing needs to be done — at the very least the supervisor should not reduce the teacher's chances.

In any given supervisory relationship one must learn, largely by trial and error, what the individual teacher is likely to find useful, before the supervisory observation. In some instances it seems sufficient to pay a courtesy call: to ask, simply, whether the plans discussed yesterday are still set for today's teaching: to signify, by one's appearance, "I am here, just as we planned; all systems are go."

There are many times when you, as a supervisor, are unable to have a formal conference in advance with the teacher you will observe. This means that you are left on your own to make inferences or assumptions about what the teacher intends to do during the lesson to be observed. Sometimes you are facing an ad lib or extemporaneous situation where perhaps the teacher did not have an intention ahead of time but creates one along the way. But whether a teacher has a plan in mind or not, it makes good sense to confer with the teacher about the lesson to be observed, find out exactly what kind of help he or she would like to have from you, and then plan the observation accordingly. Thus the rationale for the preobservation conference in which the supervisor and teacher discuss the lesson to be observed, how it is to be observed, under what conditions, and so forth. A sample outline format of the preobservation conference is shown in Table 2.

Table 2

Sample Format Preobservation Conference

1. Establish a "contract" or "agreement" between the supervisor and the teacher to be observed, including:
   a. Objectives of the lesson.
   b. Relationship of the lesson objectives to the overall learning program being implemented.
   c. Activities to be observed.
   d. Possible changing of activity format, delivery system, and other elements based on interactive agreement between supervisor and teacher.
   e. Specific description of items or problems on which the teacher wants feedback.
   f. Assessment procedures of activities and problems.
2. Establish the mechanics or ground rules of the observation including:
   a. Time of observation.
   b. Length of observation.
   c. Place of observation.
3. Establish specific plans for carrying out the observation.
   a. Where shall the supervisor sit?
   b. Should the supervisor talk to students about the lesson? If so, when? Before or after the lesson?
   c. Will the supervisor look for a specific action?
   d. Should the supervisor interact with students?
   e. Will any special materials or preparations be necessary?
   f. How shall the supervisor leave the observation?

Planning for the preobservation conference by both supervisor and teacher is essential; the items to be considered in the planning are those listed in Table 2 — as a minimum. Then, in the preobservation conference, how the supervisor proceeds depends on what tasks must be performed. It is very important for the supervisor to be sure he or she understands exactly what it is that the teacher wants to do and what the teacher wants the supervisor to do and, with such understanding, to function responsively. Or, if it is the other way around, the supervisor should take pains to ensure that the teacher understands the supervisor's intent and is presently capable of moving within the supervisor's directions, before diving into the work. Our reasoning, with regard to this statement, is that if the teacher sees fit to raise questions, it follows that such questions are likely to have a large measure of importance for him or her. And if that is the case, then it becomes all the more urgent for the supervisor to respond as adequately as possible to the teacher's questions rather than to his or her own misinterpretations or misunderstandings of the teacher's questions.

When time is short and the stakes are high, it can represent a major economy to make sure that communications are straight. The same reasoning applies if the supervisor wants to broach questions of his or her own in those precious moments, knowing full well that to do so may undermine the teacher's equilibrium in the lesson to follow.

A good rule of thumb is to deal in the teacher's terms — that is, in the teacher's frame of reference during the preobservation conference (if not all of the time) and to reserve issues arising from the supervisor's imagination for treatment later during the supervision conference. If there is any chance that should the supervisor introduce his or her own constructs the teacher's equanimity would become unsettled or confusion would set in, it is best that the supervisor not do so immediately before the teaching.

One way for the supervisor to keep preobservation in the teacher's frame of reference is to be indirect and ask questions of the teacher — for example: What, exactly, is the sequence of instruction that you intend to follow? What key questions do you intend to ask? Will you give the directions before you distribute the materials or afterwards? About which sequences of the lesson, if any, are you uncertain? What are your thoughts about how this technique will operate to achieve the goals you're after? What decisions have you made concerning the unresolved issues we talked about in yesterday's planning? In some instances, when supervision has ripened and communication has become very efficient, it is possible to begin almost anything by some simple opening, such as "Ready?" — depending on the teacher's current frame of mind. "How should we approach this observation?" If the teacher's response is that there are no specific needs to which the supervisor can attend, then the supervisor should present the sample format list to the teacher and they can review it together.

If supervision is operating properly, complex decisions relating to teaching will be formulated early enough beforehand (either before or during the preobservation conference) for a sufficient margin of time to exist in which the teacher can assimilate a definite and specific plan, rehearse it conceptually, and produce last-minute refinements. Goal setting, developing rationales for instruction, and laying out instructional methods are appropriate to the preobservation stage. What tasks then are appropriate to tackle, and what supervisory methods are likely to succeed?

The supervisor's choice of methods should depend upon the specific tasks, and upon whatever identifiable psychological variables may be operating. For example, if the teacher's expressed problem is to be certain that the intended wording to be used in a specific set of directions during the lesson is precise enough, the supervisor might appropriately run through the wording of the directions in question to see how they sound to new ears. But this solution is not so simple because of the question of whether it matters or in what ways it can matter — that is, by what specific technique the supervisor performs that function. This is, in effect, a problem of supervisory priorities, a question of relationships among technical and process goals.

If, for example, supervision (in this hypothetical case) is also intended to increase the teacher's professional autonomy through encouraging of initiation of self-issues in supervision, by reinforcing spontaneous self-initiated inquiry when it occurs, and by creating conditions conducive to self-evaluation, then it would seem inconsistent with such goals (at least, at face value) for the supervisor to begin:

SUPERVISOR: How can I help you; what can I do for you this morning?
TEACHER: I'm not sure that I've got these directions buttoned down the way you want them.
SUPERVISOR: All right. Supposing you run through the directions right now. I'll tell you whether they seem adequate. Go ahead.

The supervisor's emphasis upon giving help (implicitly, "My job is to help; your job is to be helped"), on doing something for the teacher; the teacher's emphasis on doing things the way the supervisor wants them done; and the supervisor's evaluative posture (implicitly, "It is for me to decide whether your peformance is adequate") and directiveness (implicitly, "In this relationship, I decide what is to be done") all seem more likely to increase the teacher's dependency and to cast the teacher as a passive agent than to achieve opposite effects.

The qualification "at face value" is included to allow for the possibility that in a supervisory relationship in which the teacher does take major initiative and does function autonomously, it might not matter so much if, on isolated occasions, the supervisor moves in quite aggressively. Supervisors are unlikely to injure teachers who are basically self-sufficient by rendering judgments about their work or offering advice or directions from time to time. On the contrary, if teachers are neither excessively dependent upon supervisors nor afraid of them and if the supervisors should say something like "that lesson was not good," it would not matter very much to the teachers — which is as it should be — especially if the teachers perceived evidence to the contrary. If you (the teacher) trust in your own perceptions and judgmental adequacy, supervisor evaluations may represent useful data to you, but you are not, in any event, at the mercy of these evaluations.

In the example above, the teacher seems to betray an opposite condition in stressing "the way you (supervisor) want them." Although we should not be excessive in "diagnosis" based on such a limited excerpt, a guess that the teacher has learned to depend upon the supervisor for evaluation and looks to the supervisor for direction would seem better founded than the contrasting hypothesis. Consider a very different example:

SUPERVISOR: How do things stand?
TEACHER: It's pretty well set, but I'm still not sure that the directions will be clear to everybody.
SUPERVISOR: Would it help to run through them?

TEACHER: Yeah — I think I'm just too close to them right now to see them clearly. Let's give it a try.

(Teacher recites the directions).

SUPERVISOR: Well?

TEACHER: Actually, that sounded OK to me.

SUPERVISOR: Yeah. You know, I was a little worried as I read these directions in your plans — they're sort of complicated — but as you said them, the pauses you made and the way you used your voice to emphasize certain things — "Be sure to turn off the oxygen first; first the oxygen and then the acetylene" — really made things very clear.

TEACHER: Ah, yes. I was thinking so much about what words to use that I didn't really think about my voice. I think that's the solution. If I take it slow and listen to what I'm doing, that ought to take care of it.

SUPERVISOR: I think so.

This excerpt communicates a substantially different flavor. Rather than implicitly defining a role as "helper" (which, incidentally, tends to put a supervisor one up on the teacher), the supervisor's opening question expresses considerably more confidence in the teacher. It does not suggest that the teacher is helpless; rather, it asks for appraisal, perceptions, and judgments — in short, for the teacher to take things in any direction that seems useful. The teacher expresses an uncertainty, but one that is considerably more specific than that expressed in the first case. Instead of saying, in effect, "I'm not sure whether my plans will meet your approval," the teacher asserts that the plans satisfy self-criteria, by and large, but identifies one technical problem that remains. The supervisor's response, framed as a question, leaves room for the teacher to elect many alternatives, for example, "No, I think it would be best not to fuss with it any more," or "I think it might help me if you read these directions out loud so that I could get a better perspective on them."

The supervisor might, indeed, have simply waited for the teacher to prescribe an exercise of some sort instead of suggesting a rehearsal. However, the supervisor apparently decided, perhaps for efficiency's sake, to introduce the idea, tentatively, as one possible course of action. Prior experiences with the teacher may have suggested that directiveness of this magnitude would be appropriate. The teacher, in turn, provided a rationale for following the supervisor's suggestion and affirmed the suggestion. After directions were recited, the supervisor passed the initiative for evaluation back to the teacher. Once the teacher was committed, the supervisor offered consensus and, moreover, provided a reasoned rather than an arbitrary consensus. The teacher expanded the supervisor's concept by translating it into an operational strategy for the lesson. Once again, the supervisor offered consensus.

Although it is clear, in this case, that the teacher did depend upon the supervisor for assistance, the quality of that dependency does not seem inconsistent with essentially autonomous behavior. Having used the supervisor as a source of reactions, the teacher made productive use of the supervisor's responses through self-initiative. Again, such sparse data do not justify very elaborate interpretations, but somehow one does not feel that the supervisor's evaluations were prized for their own sake, as reflections of approval. Whereas this teacher may value approval by others, as most people do, at least the teacher does not seem to be gasping for it. The conscious focus is upon mastering problems in his or her own technical behavior.

The brief examples raise some interesting questions about promoting either autonomy or dependency in supervision. Other examples having no direct relationship to problems of autonomy could have been used here equally well. In any case the examples should serve to demonstrate the point that how the supervisor behaves may be as consequential as, or more so than, the substantive content and the technical focus of the remarks. The teacher learns things from both dimensions of the supervisor's behavior. At the very same moment that the two of us are talking about sociometric variables in your classroom, you may be learning about who knows more and who decides what is best — any number of self-definitions and definitions of our relationship, the goals of the relationship, roles in the relationship, and all kinds of other things about what is appropriate in supervision and what is proscribed — simply from the supervisor's conduct. For this reason the supervisor's decisions about how to operate in the preobservation conference are monumentally more difficult than they would be if the only decision to be made was what to talk about. During the preobservation conference the supervisor must be conscious of and must exercise deliberate control over interactional behavior, in addition to thinking about the issues being discussed.

In the event that reasons do not seem to exist for rehearsal or review of the teaching plan during the preobservation conference, it is useful to reaffirm or to redefine the goals for that sequence of supervision — that is, to address the supervisory aspects as well as the teaching to be performed. Should definitions of what the supervisor and the teacher will do in supervision have been especially complex, a statement of the agreement could ensure that both parties understand the course to be followed. If a variety of plausible agreements were previously identified and discussed, and if it was decided to hold selection in abeyance until the teacher could sleep on the possibilities for awhile, then the preobservation conference would be the natural time for final agreements to be made.

Again, the supervisor's technical conduct is important in relation to incidental learnings likely to arise from it:

1. *SUPERVISOR:* Now remember what we decided: your objective for the lesson will be to avoid asking multiple questions. My task will be to keep track of your questioning and to note every multiple question you ask.
2. *SUPERVISOR:* OK, I'll try to be especially careful to get your questions down verbatim and the children's responses to them so that we can examine the questioning patterns afterward.
3. *SUPERVISOR:* Yes, it makes good sense to me to work on questioning

patterns if you'd like to. I remember that the last time we focused on questioning (some months ago) you brought that pattern of rhetorical questions under control very quickly. Do you think it would be useful for me to limit my data (gathering) to those episodes of the lesson containing questioning sequences, or should I get the whole business down?

4. *SUPERVISOR:* Well, since we've got the problem pretty well defined at this point (having treated it through several sequences of supervision), suppose I stop observing for a while so that you have a chance to work on it by yourself? I think your idea about tape-recording your teaching and then analyzing the tapes for questioning patterns afterward is a very good one, particularly because you seem so comfortable with the recorder going and the kids have apparently gotten used to it. You know where to reach me. If you'd like me to go over any tapes with you, I'd be happy to. In the meantime, go ahead with it, and get in touch whenever you want to take this up again or to move on to new issues.

If you were the teacher in each of the examples above, your learnings, your feelings, your expectations, your general outlook on supervision, and your teaching might differ considerably from case to case. You might note that in every instance the technical object of study was approximately the same, namely, "patterns of questioning."

As mentioned, it is very difficult to prescribe methodology for preobservation and supervision conferences because of how different they tend to be. Differing issues, different people, different situations, differing value systems, variations in the importance and urgency of issues to be treated, and differences among psychological variables from one instance of supervision to another make it just about impossible to articulate categorical techniques. However, some guiding methodological principles can be stated. In the preobservation conference the supervisor should:

1. Try not to raise questions (offer criticisms, objections, suggestions, and the like) that are likely to undermine the teacher's strategy for the lesson to be observed.
2. Deal in the teacher's terms and conceptual framework rather than in self (supervisor's) or in external, theoretical frames of reference. In other words, if "operant conditioning" is not the framework in which the teacher has conceptualized his or her lesson, the preobservation conference should not be the time to examine it in those terms, precisely for the reasons enunciated in Items 1 and 8 of this list.
3. Avoid supervisory techniques that have proved unsettling to the teacher in the past or might, predictably, be disquieting at the moment. For example, if the teacher has formerly become anxious when you (supervisor) employed inductive techniques to pursue some line of inquiry; or, if the teacher typically seems uncomfortable when supervision follows a pattern of interrogation; or, if the teacher tends to be upset when you use comparison (between the teacher and other teachers or the teacher and self) to demonstrate a point, then such techniques should be deliberately avoided in the preobservation conference.

4. Take special efforts to ensure that communication is clear, that the teacher and supervisor understand each other's meanings precisely.

5. Deliberately control impulses to direct. Give teachers every opportunity to move in their own directions, to set their own issues, to lay things out however they please, to the extent that they are comfortable in doing so or unless they seem to be plunging into deliberations that are likely to work against them.

6. Avoid ritual commitment to the preobservation conference. If strong reasons do not exist for holding it, don't. The same principle applies for every other stage of the supervisory sequence.

7. Incorporate process goals as well as technical ones in planning for the preobservation conference (and also incorporate self-awareness goals when implementing the conference). The preobservation is most likely to succeed if the supervisor is as attentive to its interactional processes as potential sources of incidental learning as he or she is to the business at hand. Our insistence upon this principle is motivated as much by practical concerns as it is by philosophical ones. If the supervisor is not deliberate in the conduct of his behavior, then that behavior can easily operate at direct cross-purposes to the intended outcomes. If my intention is for you to do something adequately but I seem to treat you as though you were totally inadequate, then in all likelihood I am simply spinning my wheels.

8. Avoid introducing novelties in the preobservation conference. Except for small, manageable refinements that the teacher can incorporate easily into the plan (and only the teacher knows, ultimately, what is easy and what is not), new ideas, new goals, and new strategies are not likely to be assimilable or reproducible if they are formulated directly before teaching is to occur.

9. Encourage the teacher not to teach the lesson in question, if the teacher feels unready to teach (perhaps the plans are insufficiently formulated) or for any reason has serious misgivings about the lesson and expects failure. A simple "filler" of some sort is likely to be less disabling for the teacher and less damaging to the pupils than a lesson that fails, if only because the teacher expects it to.

There is nothing easy about functioning according to this model. In many respects, traditions of supervisory behavior and conventions of social behavior work against us: it is neither simply a case of listen-and-talk nor one of "you do what I say." What is most difficult of all for the supervisor to achieve in practice is the multidimensional functioning that we envision. However, by following these nine suggested principles, the supervisor may be better equipped to effect the format suggested earlier. Combined with format, the principles offer the supervisor choices and guidance for a successful preobservation conference.

Let us imagine an ideal supervisor in the preobservation stage. The supervisor must formulate ideas and statements to be used; hear what the teacher is saying and understand the teacher's intended meanings; read the teacher's meanings both at face value and in symbolic terms (that is, be able to read between the lines sufficiently to detect signs of anxiety or any stressful internal condition that is active enough to create interference with intended outcomes); develop responses aimed appropriately at both overt and disguised expressions of ideas and feelings; delimit the range of behavior to keep it consistent with long-range supervisory goals as well as relevant to the immediate problems of supervision; monitor self-feelings, impulses, and motives in order to keep the supervisory work aimed at the teacher's improvement; and make examined, yet almost instantaneous, decisions about what to broach and what not to, what to give, what to withhold, what to reinforce, what to set into special relief by selective emphasis, and so on.

These "musts" are certainly not offered as professional imperatives. Neither do we mean to imply that they should be accepted as doctrinal elements of a supervisory orthodoxy. Instead, they represent a distillation from supervision we have researched and practiced and observed, of techniques that seemed to work and of elements of supervision that seemed to be missing on occasions when, by one measure or another, supervision failed. As such they are guides to be used as the situation and circumstances warrant.

In very simple terms, we have discovered that unsuccessful supervision could be explained, at least partly, by the supervisor's failure to approximate this operational model and that successful supervision has often seemed accountable in just the opposite terms. Although the multidimensional concurrence we envision might be impossible for some to master, except in moments of intense concentration and at the expense of great psychological energy, research suggests that deliberate and prolonged practice which is carefully supervised can begin to make important differences in surprisingly little time. As something to approximate, we have found the model useful, but we do not think of it simply as defining minimum criteria for successful supervisory behavior.

It should probably also be pointed out that this image of highly sophisticated technical behavior is not predicated by the notion that the teacher's behavior and the teacher's success or failure are determined exclusively by the supervisor's behavior — as, for example, in a simple cause-effect paradigm. Nor are we guided by an expectation that teachers are generally fragile. It sometimes seems, erroneously, that clinical supervision operates from such premises, that supervisors hold much power over the teachers, and that should the supervisor zig instead of zag, the teacher will lose control. Hardly. By and large, clinical supervision does not and should not be operated within such premises.

Clinical supervision should not be conceptualized merely as a facilitating practice designed to enable teachers to rise through a developmental sequence of technical competency and professional actualization at a faster pace and in a more thorough and integrated fashion than would be likely to occur without supervision. Although it is true that we (supervisors) have hurt teachers from time to time or, at least, that they have felt hurt by "what we have done to them," we have not done so on purpose and do not think of ourselves doing so. Instead, clinical supervision is conceptualized in a somewhat structured manner because we acknowledge a need *not* to engage in random motions, to be as well organized and efficient as we can in helping the teacher toward goals. In short, examined and deliberately disciplined supervision is preferred because it seems likely to lead toward productive activity, and along the way to generate many positive side effects, not the least of which is the teacher's improved self-awareness and self-control.

PROBLEMS

The sense in which we suspect that the proportions of this book may be misleading is that the most of what exists at present in clinical supervision is its problems. And among the manifold problems it embodies, there is a large subset that we might just as well call its mistakes. One cannot really begin to appreciate where clinical supervision has been or where it is going without a vivid sense of the mistakes it makes and has made and the predicaments that confront its practitioners.

This and other problems sections are intended to bring such elements to life and are motivated by several purposes. Although the point must surely have been demonstrated by our writing thus far, we can think of no better way to drive home the understanding that clinical supervsion, though its future may be bright, is presently no panacea for educational reformers than by showing, candidly, some of the things that go wrong. We hope that one result will be to attract more minds to its development. We also hope to increase other workers' efficiency and to enable them to make better beginnings in this field by proceeding from the assumption that to be forewarned is to be forearmed, even though we are fairly convinced that individual supervisors must inevitaby learn from their own blunders and from the vicissitudes of their own practice.

For the most part, we shall try to limit these examinations to problems that, if they do not actually inhere in clinical supervision, are at least commonly experienced by clinical supervisors. It is hard to distinguish among problems of supervision that antedate the models expressed in this writing — problems that arise, culturally, in almost all instances of human interaction and problems to which our models themselves give rise. Perhaps such distinctions are superfluous, inasmuch as clinical supervisors somehow must cope with many problems, irrespective of their sources. Nonetheless, in this chapter we should like to avoid becoming involved, on the one hand, in inquiries pertaining to fundamental psychological issues in human relationships and in human development (for example, problems of transference and countertransference, problems of identity, problems of authority, and problems of self-definition) as theoretical problems in psychology; and, on the other hand, in problems of school administration and logistics (for example, of rating and formal evaluation, in the economic problems of supervision, in scheduling problems, and so on). Although clinical supervision can be treated academically, we are primarily interested for the moment in taking a concrete and pragmatic approach to this topic and in avoiding treatment that is more theoretical than it has to be in order to project vivid images of the professional lives we lead and the difficulties that confront us in daily practice.

Problems incurred in preobservation may result from supervisor/teacher interaction or noninteraction during any of the activities earlier described in the sample preobservation conference format or from supervisor/teacher activities leading up to preobservation. Included in the latter are any activities that would damage or lessen the teacher/supervisor rapport. Should the rapport have been affected prior to preobservation, problems definitely would occur in preobservation (and for that matter, probably throughout the entire supervision interaction). In the earlier section of this chapter, we suggested various "do's" in conjunction with a sample format of preobservation. Should the supervisor affect the opposite of the suggested do's, the possibility of problems would be enhanced. Let us now discuss some potential problems.

One of the worst mistakes that can occur during the preobservation conference happens to be one that clinical supervisors commonly commit in practice — namely, to unnerve the teacher so badly just before class that the teacher's adequacy becomes impaired and the lesson is weakened. Of all the things that supervisors might do to undermine the teacher's confidence and equanimity before class, one of the most potentially damaging is that of introducing new elements into the teaching plan that are unassimilable in the remaining time or raising questions about the plan when too little time remains for the teacher to implement changes proposed by the questions or suggestions.

It is not difficult to understand the impulses that generate such errors. In some cases, supervisors seem unable to avoid exercising their analytical muscles. Some supervisors, like some artists, do not know when to stop and persist in adding a final stroke that, rather than enhancing their product, muddies it. Some supervisors are unable to resist the impulse to control or to direct and, even when common sense indicates it would be best to leave well enough alone, seem forced to assert their influence without considering the probable consequences. Such behavior seems undesirable, indeed, unwarrantable; nevertheless, it occurs. Proper preservice/in-service programs can help alleviate both the problem and its causes.

Other problems, although they certainly incorporate psychological variables, seem more characteristically to arise from the supervision itself. For example, one feature of supervisory collaboration as we conceptualize it is that supervisors expect to own some measure of the teacher's successes and failures; investing in the teacher's performance, and although not claiming responsibility for it, being able, nevertheless, to rejoice in the teacher's triumphs and to share the teacher's frustrations. With such involvement, it sometimes occurs that supervisors want the teacher's success too badly, so much so that they try to refine the teacher's plans, right up to the finish line. The mistake here is in failing to realize that although last-minute conceptualizations of the lesson may be wonderfully ingenious or creative, supervisors are unlikely to be able to communicate those visions in complete detail in very little time unless unusually great rapport exists. Over and over again, we have observed frustration among supervisors and have experienced the same defeat ourselves, when a beautiful image became distorted by the teacher's implementation and when the principal cause of the distortion proved to be that the teacher never really possessed the same picture as the supervisor. Such discrepancies are much more likely to arise as a result of hurried communication (such as in the preobservation conference) than of the painstaking, careful planning that should take place, if at all, during supervisory conferences.

A related problem is that when for some reason such conferences have not culminated in refined plans, supervisors sometimes feel driven to compensate for yesterday's weak planning by a surge of architectural activity in today's preobservation. A third difficulty, related to these phenomena, is that supervisors sometimes make the wrong decision in relation to whether it would be more useful to protect the teacher from troubles that seem likely to result from the existing plans (such premonitions often occur near the last moment) by attempting to modify them, on the one hand, or leaving things as they are in order not to disturb the teacher's equilibrium, on the other. The problem of calculating these risks and of deciding between them is rarely simple; and although mistaken choices can be forgiven, they may nevertheless be most troublesome.

Another common problem of this stage is that although the teacher has explicit needs that could be satisfied efficiently in the preobservation conference (for example, to practice a series of questions or to test some sequence of activities), the supervisor's own priorities on business supersede them. In such circumstances preobservation may be unsuccessful — not so much because of what the supervisor does but as a consequence of what the supervisor fails to do:

SUPERVISOR: Well, Jim, are you ready for the lesson?

TEACHER: Yeah, I guess so. But I haven't quite determined how to use prepared worksheets during the lesson.

SUPERVISOR: Earlier this morning I just happened to reflect back on my experiences in teaching math and it occurred to me that I always made it a standard practice when using prepared worksheets to . . .

In this example the supervisor is giving the teacher an answer based on personal experience, and Jim at this stage of his development as a teacher needs probably a more indirect type of assistance — something he can work through with the supervisor with meaningful input. The supervisor has misread Jim's asking for help, and his or her own intentions have interfered with a more appropriate response to the teacher's problem at hand.

Sometimes supervisors create unnecessary anxieties by raising last-minute questions which, although they may be valid, generate uncertainty rather than calmness.

SUPERVISOR: Ugh! I just thought of something. I don't think you should be worried that the kids won't understand how to record their results. I mean, that might happen, but we've been through this enough times that I don't think you should really worry about it.

Until the supervisor had expressed all of this, in fact, the teacher had not been anxious.

An occasional error, in the preobservation conference, is for supervisors to prolong discussion at this stage unnecessarily. Experience suggests that perfunctory conversation before observation, followed by some free moments in which the teacher can simply be alone for whatever meditation or activity he or she requires, is more likely to energize the teaching performance than involvement in unessential dialogue with a supervisor. In our own work, we have sometimes felt obliged to conduct a preobservation conference only to discover later that the teacher really should have been using the time we burnt up to run off mimeographed materials needed for the lesson and that the teacher felt inhibited from asserting the need for fear of offending the supervisor or, somehow, of breaking the rules.

A more subtle and profound problem of preobservation is that of separating the supervisor's own optimism or anxieties for the lesson from those of the teacher, who will actually have to conduct it. It sometimes happens that as supervisors our own doubts and fears lead us to assume that the teacher experiences the same feelings with the same intensity as we do, and consequently we become involved in offering gratuitous reassurances and protections that at best waste time and energy and at worst instill unnecessary doubts in the teacher.

More commonly, we observe that supervisors tend to make the opposite mistake, particularly when they feel some special investment in the lesson to be taught — perhaps because of having played an important part in its conceptualization — namely, that their own buoyancy obscures the teacher's doubts; their own optimism becomes projected onto the teacher, with the result that unwitting pressure is put on the teacher to execute a lesson toward which he or she may have serious misgivings and about those whose success he or she feels basically insecure. To state this problem more directly, it seems more usual for teachers and their supervisors to become committed to lessons prematurely, that is, to lessons that the teacher feels unready to teach, than to err in the opposite direction, namely, by delaying a lesson that might actually have been successful. The general tendency to encourage teaching despite justifiable reservations concerning its success is much more prevalent than the strategy that says, in effect, if you don't feel ready, then don't teach it. There seems, somehow, to be a general reluctance to jettison high-risk lessons and a characteristic impatience, among school people, to move on quickly and get the work done, even though such speed may result in bad instruction, whereas free time for the pupils might, at least, have provided something positive in their own experiences. Supervisors are as likely to be trapped by such false economies as anybody. The lure of closure is difficult to resist. Yet this problem can be overcome rather easily. Its solution requires a blend of time and patience. We shall discuss this more fully at the end of the present section.

A problem encountered repeatedly, particularly among neophyte supervisors, is that having become enchanted by the methods of inductive inquiry and by the seeming humanism of nondirective approaches, they use this approach to the exclusion of all others. All things considered, the preobservation conference must include some straight talk, and preobservation is more likely to be the time in which straight talk is the most productive kind of talk than is any other stage of the supervisory sequence. If preobservation is construed as a time for practical assistance rather than as a time for elaborate inquiry, then cherished methods of inquiry may be best reserved for, and implemented in, other stages.

> **TEACHER:** *(with ten minutes left until class time):* Just one thing — do you think it would be better to send the kids to the lab tables by rows, or to tell the whole class to go to their places at the same time?
> **SUPERVISOR:** In what ways is this a problem for you?
> **TEACHER:** Well, I want them to be able to get involved with the equipment right at that moment when their interest in the problem is at its height, and I'm not sure which system would be the most efficient. I guess I'll send them row by row, as fast as I can.
> **SUPERVISOR:** Umm. Something to consider, though, is that by the time the kids in the last row get called, they may have cooled off pretty much.
> **TEACHER:** Yeah, maybe you're right. *(Pause.)* OK, I'll send them all at once.
> **SUPERVISOR:** OK, but then you have to take into consideration that if things get too noisy or out of hand and you have to stop things to discipline them, then that would delay the lab work too.
> **TEACHER:** *(glancing at his watch nervously):* That's true. *(Long pause.)*

Although one should avoid being dogmatic about such things, the efficacy of such analysis is generally lost in preobservation, and such an analysis procedure is much more likely to agitate the teacher at this stage than it would be during the planning time of the regular supervision conference.

If supervisors are reluctant to function directively because the teacher appears to be inordinately dependent upon supervision for advice and directions, we would propose, nevertheless, that some relaxation of "tried and true" autonomy-building strategies can be helpful and appropriate during preobservation. We should make the point clearly that it is not so much a question of abandoning "autonomy" as a supervisory process goal (in preobservation) as it is of softening one's attachment to the methods commonly employed for working toward this condition. One must reckon that, after all, Socratic processes were originally put to use in slow and sunny places and that whereas their adaptability to more frenzied circumstances may be tenable and even advantageous, it does not betray Plato to remember that in just a few minutes a bell will ring. One must steer, somehow, between opposite dangers. On the one hand, as we have tried to say, there are problems of methodological rigidity. On the other, there are always possibilities that a supervisor's behavior in preobservation, particularly when expediency assumes a high priority, will operate at cross-purposes to planned process goals for the supervisee — specifically, for the conference toward which the supervision is moving.

Perhaps the best general solution to this dilemma consists of making supervisory process goals explicit and of being open with one's reasons for behaving as one does. We maintain that teachers should understand explicitly that their sufficiency represents a principal goal of the supervision. Moreover, they should be shown (possibly inductively) that the supervisor will deliberately engage in certain behaviors at certain times, working from the assumption that such behaviors will be more instrumentally effective than others. Then behavioral inconsistencies between relatively directive and economical action in preobservation and more contemplative and analytical behavior in the conference may be less distracting, less dissonant, and more readily reconcilable in the teachers' experience than if the entire business were undertaken unexplicitly.

One further problem, in preobservation, occurs when the supervisor does things that would be better for the teacher to do in order for the teacher to benefit from the rehearsal.

> **TEACHER:** I'm not quite sure how to phrase the question so that it stimulates a lot of discussion. Do you?
>
> **SUPERVISOR:** Well, I think if you ask them how it might be possible for men to build underwater dwellings, and not give them any direct hints and not ask them whether such a thing might be possible, I think that should get them going on it. Let me see, uh, "How could we build . . .?" (and so on).

Supervisors should not mistakenly assume, nor should teachers, that because their own understanding of a technique is articulate and that because they have verbalized their understanding, it follows that the supervisee (or the pupil) understands it too. In this example it may be the case that supervisors' repeated attempts to frame an efficient question for the lesson will be of considerably less utility to teachers than opportunities for trying to frame their own question would be.

Closure is not a necessary prerequisite for the preobservation conference to be successful. In fact, many unnecessary problems result from the supervisor's desire to achieve closure. It must be remembered that the supervision process we envision is an arduous, time-consuming process.

As clinical supervisors, our objective is teacher improvement. Improvement is not an easy task and it is not meant to be. It is not a task of short duration, nor is it meant to be. The rapport of which we speak is important to the clinical supervision process. We suggest therefore that a supervisor cannot risk losing rapport for the sake of reaching closure during preobservation. There will be other opportunities for preobservation conferences, but seldom other opportunities for regaining rapport. Once lost, rapport is most difficult to regain.

It should be noted, finally, that another common deficiency of preobservation conferences is that supervisors lose sight of "contract" or agreement as a central issue of preobservation. In some instances they simply fail to review the supervisory contract in order to make appropriate changes — for example, to omit observation from the current sequence. Even more commonly, they do not trouble to review a complex contract to ensure clarity and mutual understanding. Typically, the first of these errors results in rote practices, which, because they are unessential, create unproductive supervisory sequences. The second error — namely, of working from an ambiguous set of agreements — results at best in wasted time. Supervision grinds to a halt and the participants must repair to recalling exactly what they had decided to do initially — and, more seriously, may result in disappointment, confusion, and frustration, particularly when functions that should have been performed were not performed.

Chapter 6

OBSERVATION

* **Conditions of the Observation**
* **Approaches to Observation**
* **Observation Systems**
* **Modes of Recording**
* **Some Problems of Observation**

We might open this discussion by noting that an effective educational supervisor needs to be a combination of all the marvelous animals whose eyes, ears, antennae, whiskers, tentacles, barbels, feelers, noses, fingers, mouths, tongues, fins, and other sense organs help them to know what is happening in their surroundings, and thereby to be equipped for whatever response will help them to deal with the detected events or conditions. Sometimes labeled by the term *data gathering,* observation is the activity through which a supervisor becomes aware of the events, interactions, physical elements, and other phenomena in a particular place (classroom, laboratory, library, or other environment) during a particular period of time. Were human supervisors as gaudily equipped as our opening sentence proposed, the total of data they might be able to collect would of course be enormous. If their nervous systems were also connected to some sort of a computer (a notion we plan later to explore), so that the almost infinite number of pieces of information could be tirelessly combed for correlations and associations, how useful indeed could such persons be in recounting and in interpreting what actually took place.

Alas, we cannot hope for such splendid resources to become available to instructional supervision; but all the same, we perceive that the excellent sensory organs of the ordinary human being, when connected to that most wondrous of all biological entities on this earth, the human brain, can be put to highly productive use for supervisory purposes. Further, we are aware of various ways for focusing and harnessing such energies, and for exploiting some inorganic resources capable of supplementing, augmenting, and extending them.

70

In clinical supervision, observation is the link between the promise made (in preobservation, to seek answers to the teacher's questions) and the promise kept (in the postobservation conference). It is what a supervisor does in order to be able to test whether answers can in fact be found. It is his or her effort to find out what actually happens in the situations that give birth to the questions in the first place. It is the collecting time, the connecting time, a receiving time, a perceiving time. One's eyes and ears (in particular) are used like Geiger counters, constantly scanning the scene for documentary ore later to be separated and processed. It is a time of inescapable overload, since much more is happening than can possibly be recognized, assessed, labeled, and recorded. It is therefore a time when the receptory and discriminatory powers of the supervisor are rigorously challenged and when accumulated wisdom and experience become immensely useful as a filtering system. Certain trainable skills, to which this chapter will allude at times, also are essential to effective performance in the observer role.

CONDITIONS OF THE OBSERVATION

Some of the decisions that have to be made by the supervisor will have been made jointly with the teacher in the prior conference. Usually, for example, the time of the visit (when to arrive, how long to stay, at what point to leave), the location (the teacher's classroom, a shady spot in the schoolyard, the science lab), the equipment to be brought along (audio or videorecorder, camera), and agreement as to whether or not the supervisor should have any dealings with the students will have been determined in advance. More important, the "contract" provides fairly specific direction with respect to the observer's agenda and focus. If one of the teacher's needs is to understand little Mario better, then the supervisor must be sure that he or she knows which child is Mario, positions himself or herself in the classroom in a place from which "Mario data" can be collected, and utilizes the coding and recording system that is most relevant to the teacher's request.

Depending upon the official role of the supervisor, the presence of that supervisor in the classroom may itself be a condition to take into account. If the supervisor happens also to be the principal, his or her established (to that point) relationship with the teacher, on the one hand, and the students, on the other, might be either a facilitating condition, a disabling condition, or neither. Some scholars in the field of supervision contend that supervisory work is best assigned to persons who are not in a direct authoritative relationship to the teachers, but who rather are in a "staff" role with no responsibility for evaluating, hiring, firing, and the like. Although this argument seems valid in theory, however, the reality is that few school systems make the necessary investment for such purposes, and the great bulk of supervisory assistance available to teachers is provided, for better or worse, by line-officer principals.

Therefore, we must hope that several things will be true when the principal qua supervisor is in the classroom: (1) The teacher over time has come to respect and trust the principal-supervisor and therefore has essentially positive expectations; (2) the principal-supervisor has visited this classroom many times before and is therefore not a novel or unfamiliar element in the experience of the teacher and the children; (3) the children, too, respect and trust the principal-supervisor and sense no discomfort about his or her presence; and (4) the principal-supervisor respects the confidence placed in him or her as a helping professional and behaves accordingly.

Although it may already be implied, one other condition of the observation is that the moment should have no unanticipated negative loadings. Sometimes things go awry between the preobservation conference and the time scheduled for the observation. The teacher, who had planned to have the handout ready by morning, may have had a family crisis with which to deal instead. Mario may have come down with the mumps and will be out for a couple of weeks. The gym teacher may have fallen off the stage and the morning schedule has had to be reworked. The teacher became nervous about the lesson after the preobservation and does not really want to teach it today. The children are jumpier than usual today because Mr. Rasputin chewed them out in the library. Teacher has just learned that Miss Rollins's contract isn't being renewed, and suddenly feels less sure of the principal-supervisor's motives. These and countless other possible developments can cause either the supervisor or the teacher to avoid the observation at this moment in time. Whether to try to go ahead anyway or to wait calls for careful consideration. Sometimes "the show must go on" makes sense; but as a general rule, postponement or cancellation makes more sense than proceeding with an uneasy teacher or a markedly changed situation.

APPROACHES TO OBSERVATION

At least three different kinds of decisions have to be made with respect to procedure or approach. One has to do with prior selection of the items on which to focus, and in this matter the contract if well designed should reduce the problem to manageable proportions. A contract that covers too much of the waterfront will be impossible to handle, and at best the supervisor can select those topics that seem most important and most likely to be illuminated by collectible data. On the other hand, a contract that is sensibly limited in scope and is focused upon matters for which relevant data can easily be gathered gives the supervisor much better guidance.

The next and crucial decision has to do with the methods of data gathering to be employed. In all of the literature of classroom observation (and by the way, it remains a rather primitive and limited body of knowledge and opinion), data collection approaches represent the most widely discussed topic. Whether or not to use one of the available observation instruments and/or systems is one aspect of the decision. What, if any, use to make of "inorganic resources" (audiotape recorder, videotape recorder, other kinds of cameras) is another. Yet another aspect, part of the first, relates to the use to be made of hand-recorded data collection, either as a total approach or in combination with other collection systems. Sometimes supervisors find it helpful to use stop-watches, for example, to measure units of time devoted to teacher talk versus pupil talk, or on-task versus off-task behavior. Later we will deal with data-collection alternatives in greater detail.

The third category of decisions concerns the supervisor's planned behavior while in the classroom. This includes logistical decisions (for example, to sit near to Mario or to be in a strategic corner) and whether to stay in the same place or to occupy several different locations during the observation. It also includes visibility considerations: Should the supervisor seek to be virtually unnoticed, as unobtrusive as it is possible to be, or is it just as well if he or she is an obvious part of the scene? This links with decisions with respect to *interacting* with the children or the teacher. Sometimes it makes sense for the supervisor to ask questions of children ("Do you understand what the directions were?"), or to respond in a matter-of-fact way to any questions or remarks directed by the children toward him or her. It is even possible that the obser-vation plan calls for the supervisor to function part of the time as a coteacher, or assistant teacher, or general "extra hand" at points in the lesson. In a case where children, following the teacher's explanations, are working at tables in small groups, a roving supervisor can not only visit some of the tables to answer queries or check finished work, but also probe for data through chatting with the learners. Most of the time in observation, however, the observer does *not* join in class activity.

OBSERVATION SYSTEMS

The clinical supervision model outlined in this book calls for supervisors to be proficient in each of the following skills: contract building (in preobserva-tion), observing, data collection, data analysis, designing strategy, and con-ferencing. Most of the training progams for educational supervision in this country pay little or no attention to skill building in these areas; and often when they do, they overemphasize one or another of the skill elements (e.g., measuring teacher-pupil interaction by the Flanders instrument) at the expense of other equally significant elements.

In years past the practice in clinical supervision has been to ask teachers what kind of feedback they want and then locate or invent a request target data collection instrument for that purpose. What was observed related often to the current fad (i.e., positive and negative stroking) or to somewhat super-ficial kinds of variables (i.e., body language). Although the state of the art in developing systematic data collection instruments is not very advanced, each year produces new instruments and research adds to our awareness of behaviors that can in fact be classified and measured. In this volume we are a bit hesitant to list, or appear to endorse, those in most common use, because we have seen too many supervisors who have latched on to a particular schema and become its willing prisoners. Furthermore, this is a dynamic field and we suspect that our list could be regrettably incomplete, with some of the newer and better schemes unmentioned.

Cogan[1] in 1973 listed some of the best-known systems, several dating back 30 years. He noted that more instruments are available to measure verbal behavior in the classroom than nonverbal, and our guess is that this remains true in 1980. One healthy trend seems to be that more and more supervisors, or groups of supervisors in school systems, are designing their own instruments and methodologies, sometimes drawing upon ideas contributed by researchers and sometimes drawing on their own experience. These methodologies for data collection fall into categories such as: teacher-pupil interaction, classroom climate, talk flow, verbal analysis, use of space, skill maintenance, nonverbal communication, positive and negative stroking, levels of questioning, body language, and group roles, tasks, and responsibilities.

In recent years, however, because scholars have been able to identify instructional variables that correlate with learning outcomes or to specific teaching models, we are now able to guide the observation and data collection focus toward those practices that appear to matter (i.e., time on task, instructional cues and directives, reinforcement, student participation, and correctives and feedback). Research-based observation makes sense because it not only gives teachers important messages about what makes a difference but also tends to maximize the effectiveness of supervisory observations and to result in behavior reinforcements, modifications, and alterations that may have significant impact on the learning process itself.

One effort at a broader approach, at the in-service level, has recently been developed by Karolyn Snyder. Snyder has adapted Benjamin Bloom's conclusions on quality instruction[2] as a framework for training principals and supervisors in clinical supervision. As one of the programs within Administrators-for-Change Training (ACT),[3] this approach is designed to introduce supervisors (and others) to the nature of Bloom's four variables through observation sequences that, at first, involve looking at videotapes or live segments of actual instruction to discover the nature and the use of each of the four variables. The outcome of this first activity should be skill in recognizing, as it appears, a cue or directive, a reinforcement, participation, and a corrective or feedback.

[1]Morris L. Cogan, *Clinical Supervision* (Boston: Houghton Mifflin, 1973), pp. 134–135.

[2]Benjamin S. Bloom, *Human Characteristics and School Learning* (New York: McGraw-Hill, 1976).

[3]Karolyn J. Snyder, *ACT: Administrator-for-Change Training*, Module Six (Lubbock, Texas: Pedamorphosis, Inc., 1978).

A premise of this particular ACT training program is that since the four Bloom-identified variables do indeed make a significant difference in the quality of the instructional program teachers provide, then supervisor behavior ought to concentrate upon them; and the training of supervisors should equip them for such a concentration.

This argument makes sense to us. At the very least the Bloom categories provide a place to start; and practice in data gathering within the categories and their components provides supervisors with an adequate core framework of observation skills.

Once such skills have been developed through practice (with feedback from the trainer), the next task, again involving looking at teaching segments, is to observe all four of the variables as each occurs within the lesson, in order to identify patterns in the ways (and sequences) that teachers use them. Bloom's findings suggest that in effective learning situations the four variables occur in sequence; that is, cues and directives are followed by reinforcement as learners respond to them, and this leads to participation, which is followed by correctives and feedback. The supervisors-in-training learn to observe whether or not this sequence is followed and thereby to identify either successes or problem areas in the teacher's approach.

Once supervisors have reached a specified level of skill and understanding, the next task is to look at the numerous other ways to identify the many aspects of the four variables. For example, under "cues and directives," data can be collected in the following areas:

- Classroom management procedures
- Social-emotional climate
- Body language
- Relationship of program objectives to learning activities
- Student response to cues
- Use of space

Under "reinforcement," subcategories include:
- Motivation strategies
- On-task/off-task behaviors
- Skill maintenance
- Repetition of learning tasks
- Verbal reinforcements
- Environmental reinforcements
- Student response to reinforcement procedures

For the variable, "participation," these subcategories are examined:
- Teacher-student interaction
- Student-student interaction
- Levels of thinking tasks
- Nature of individual tasks
- Nature of group tasks (large and small)
- Peer learning tasks
- Wait time

- Questioning techniques
- Student participation in planning
- Group roles, tasks, and responsibilities

And finally, under "correctives and feedback" are included:

- Selection of program materials
- Feedback content
- Feedback procedures
- Kinds of correctives
- Relationship between a learning behavior and feedback
- Use of teaching team resources

Yet another approach to observation has emerged with the advent of micro teaching. For example, following Bruce Joyce's[4] recommendation that teachers develop a repertoire of teaching models, at least one for each of four instructional systems, observation becomes model-oriented. If a group of teachers is learning how to teach the "Synectics Model" in the Personal Models, then observation, data collection, feedback, and correctives must be model-specific. Likewise, after a teacher returns to his or her school from successful model adoption, implementing a particular model then would require supervisory reinforcement with appropriate correctives and feedback.

What we are saying is that three approaches to observation are possible today. The first is either totally teacher-initiated and drawn from teacher perceptions of what to look for, or supervisor-initiated, making the teacher aware of the numerous possible options for observation and then jointly select one or several that appear to meet existing teacher concerns most effectively. The second approach is for the supervisor to link his or her perceptions of the teacher's concern to known research and recommend a specific data collection focus or approach that seems best suited for resolving teacher concerns. The third approach, which is quite different from the first two, is predetermined in cases where a teacher is attempting to perform skillfully a particular model of teaching. Whichever approach to observation is selected, prime consideration must be given to the teacher concerned and to his or her professional growth. Master robots are not the goal of clinical supervision, but rather skilled craftspersons who are connoisseurs of their own craft, teaching.

MODES OF RECORDING

Choosing a mode, or combination of modes, for data collection will be easier if there has been adequate attention given, as suggested above, to the purposes of observing. However, "easier" is not the same as "easy"; and one of the most interesting procedural problems in the whole cycle of clinical supervision is

[4]Bruce Joyce and Marsha Weil, *Models of Teaching* (Englewood Cliffs, N.J.: Prentice-Hall, 1972), pp. 24–27.

how best to make a record of the observed events. Among the options are various machines and devices, systems of pencil-and-paper notetaking, and means of gathering in representative materials.

VIDEOTAPE

Even in the hands of a camera crew, capable of making a series of judgments about where to point the video camera and place (or relocate) the microphones, it is not possible for videotape to do as selective a job tuning in to the events of a given lesson as can be done by a supervisor. A person can move his or her head, and especially the eyes, many times more often and more quickly, catching the flow of repartee back and forth within the room, scanning for how many hands are up at a certain moment, looking quickly at the door to see what has suddenly caught the teacher's attention. The problem is that no person can write fast enough or keep sufficient track of everything seen or heard to take full advantage of the selective process that is going on. Furthermore, memory is fallible, and two hours later it is literally impossible to remember *whose* hands went up or what sort of expression was on the teacher's face when he or she looked at the door. On tape, with replay, one can be sure of at least the hands that were in camera range, and study at length the teacher's facial expression, if desired.

In other words, a recording facilitates accurate recall and does not play tricks on its own memory. What is caught on film stays on film, and what the microphone hears can be heard again and again in exact reproduction.

Having several cameras in the room makes it more possible to capture the whole episode than when only one is used, but such procedure also increases the cost and the distraction to teachers and pupils. However, one camera that is aimed at the teacher and another, perhaps in an opposite corner, to focus on the children can in concert provide a two-dimensional view. The combination may well be worth more than twice what one camera can provide for supervisory purposes.

A difficult problem is that microphones, which unlike human ears will pick up *all* sounds indiscriminately, rarely prove as helpful as does the camera. If every child could be equipped with a neck microphone, and if later some electronics engineer could edit the tapes so that only the relevant sounds came onto the master tape, perhaps the art of lesson reconstruction via electronics could be advanced a century or two. However, we seem doomed to long reliance on a few microphones that will only sometimes be picking up the words of the right pupils at the right moment with clarity.

Videotaping, despite some of the problems noted, is an extremely helpful resource in supervision. Often, not only the supervisor but the teacher will replay the tape after a lesson, in preparation for the postobservation conference. Having the tape available during a conference also has great merit, both to verify or correct recollections and to enable additional analysis to occur. In one graduate supervision class, for example, the students went over the same lesson (on tape) in six different class sessions, each time looking at a different type of question and, in the process, discovering that even in the sixth viewing there were surprises to be found.

AUDIOTAPE

Now that audiotape recorders have been miniaturized and are available at very low cost, it would seem that every supervisor ought to carry at least one recorder and a half-dozen tapes with him or her everywhere. Keeping it running during an observation would reduce the pressure on note taking, because one could always fill in the gaps during replay. Being able to put the machine in one corner while sitting in another might extend the range of collectible information. Talking into the machine on the way down the hall, or outside the building, or in the car on the way to another school could double or triple the supervisor's chances of remembering important things. As noted, audio recording does have some serious limitations, but all the same it is a potentially excellent resource.

HAND RECORDING

Notes on paper will ultimately be the resource to which supervisors turn most often, and skill is needed in note taking, not only in words but also in symbols, diagrams, maps, schedules, charts, and other formats. One of the most difficult problems in note taking is that the speed of events and words assaulting our eyes and ears is far greater than the speed of our fingers in recording them. This being the case, it makes sense for supervisors to learn one of the conventional shorthand or speedwriting systems, or at least to invent some system of abbreviation (T for teacher, S^{11} for the student in the first seat of the first row, Q for question, Pr for praise statement, or whatever), and of symbols (arrows for direction of conversation, a square with a T inside, standing for Teacher at his or her desk, and so on). Some supervisors draw a map of the classroom, or part of the classroom involved, early in the visit, with circles representing each child, and then trace the traffic pattern (e.g., back-and-forth movement of the teacher), conversation pattern (e.g., arrow from teacher to pupil X, with Q across the shaft; arrow back to teacher from pupil X, with ? for "doesn't understand"), teacher's focus pattern (dots in each quadrant of room to represent teacher turned in that direction that many times). With respect to the latter, sometimes the data show that teachers regularly pay more attention, at least by body position, to one or another half of the room; one, in particular, hardly ever looked at children in the row next to the window, and it turned out that she had sensitive eyes and was avoiding sun glare unconsciously.

OTHER REPRESENTATIONS OR SAMPLES

Although instant-development still cameras have been available for a long time and movie cameras of the same sort have more recently appeared, it is surprisingly rare for supervisors to make use of these devices. As an adjunct procedure, we think it makes good sense for a supervisor to take a picture or two during the observation, or at least during *some* of the observations that are done. Photographs are, indeed, worth a thousand words at times; and, as in the case of videotape, it is often possible to verify information or augment the analysis or conference when pictorial data are on hand as a reference.

Similarly, it is useful at times to gather up whatever artifacts, exhibits, models, samples, or other memorabilia may become available. Copies of handouts, tests used, student worksheets completed, and other products or resources may themselves warrant evaluation and can be helpful as the analysis and conference stages unfold.

FOR THE FUTURE: SPACE-AGE EQUIPMENT

Finally, in this review of means, we are tempted to mention equipment that does not yet exist but in all probability will be invented and developed in our lifetime. Already, even small children are carrying around pocket calculators with capabilities that would have astonished mathematicians only a few generations back; and with such equipment, insurance salesmen and accountants and lawyers and all sorts of other workers can process and store data in huge quantities and at great speed. In many schools computer-assisted instruction and computer-managed instruction are fast becoming commonplace, and education personnel are beginning to sense the potential of electronic gadgetry for revolutionizing teaching. Why, then, should it not revolutionize supervision?

We imagine a time when the supervisor can carry a machine, perhaps not larger than a portable tape recorder, into the classroom, place one or another instruction disc into the mechanism, and start pushing various buttons (or drawing lines on a pressure-sensitive surface) in order to record what he or she is seeing and hearing. We imagine this machine, or one it connects to later on, eventually producing a display or even a printout that reports the number of times that a certain questioning technique was used, or the number of minutes it took for a certain teaching sequence to be completed, or what the usual teacher-pupil and pupil-pupil interactions are. Connected to a memory bank, we might even be able to tell, with the machine's help, that a certain teacher over the past six months has apparently been loosening her grip on teaching pattern X-3-T and becoming more adept at pattern Y-2-C, as per her stated goals for the year.

In a time when so many people are getting rich in less admirable ways, we would be delighted to see some clever educator take out a patent on such a device and become an instant millionaire.

SOME PROBLEMS OF OBSERVATION

Although various problems have already surfaced in the first part of this chapter, it may be well to consider some of the hazards, difficulties, and puzzles that supervisors encounter as they seek to gather the right kinds of information in the right ways. One of the most important has to do with maintaining an objective stance or perspective.

1. *The Myth of Objectivity in Data Gathering.* Supervisors hold as a value, especially when dealing with data/information/reports about teacher behaviors for purposes of analysis or assessment, that such inputs should be handled "objectively" — that is, uninfluenced by emotion, surmise, personal prejudice, or bias on their part. This is a highly commendable value, and no doubt objectivity should be respected and sought in every possible way. However, it may be dangerous to assume that we have ever achieved the ability to be truly objective, and even more so to base our conclusions on data for the reason that we believe them to be perfectly uncontaminated.

Every time we as observer enter into someone else's experience, what we see and what we hear is inexorably filtered by our past experience, by our values, by our orientation at that moment in time, and by the range of our sensory instruments. Especially in a situation as complex as a classroom, one cannot help perceiving selectively. For one thing, we cannot see everythig, or hear all the sounds, or attend to all the unfolding events before us. If there are several of us in the space at the time, and if an electronic recorder is also soaking up the data, later we may be able to piece together a fair percentage of it all. But even under the most favorable circumstances we can only hope to know at the time *some* of what is happening. Yet history is full of eyewitnesses who sent accused prisoners to jail or worse and whose testimony, however honestly offered at the time, is later shown to be inaccurate. We all discover, in countless ways, that two or three people in the same room often offer radically different versions of a conversation, or an accident, or even of the way people were dressed. Members of observation teams have been known in analysis sessions to place heavy bets on such straightforward things as whether there were six children in the group, or five; on whether the teacher was frowning or smiling at Mario; on the actual phrase the teacher used to chase the stray dog out of the room. Even more tricky have been efforts to decide (if indeed a decision is appropriate) whether the teacher dislikes Mario and is communicating that dislike to him. What, and how much, must we see and hear before we can safely deal "objectively" with such possibilities?

2. *Dangers of the Wrong Mood.* A related problem is that supervisors, like all other humans, are subject to temperamental, emotional, and situational ups and downs. Perceptions, and subsequent interpretations, are inevitably influenced by the momentary mood and condition of the observer. Whether we are conscious of it or not, the mood may be projected into the environment. Feeling happy myself, I tend to see happy people. Feeling tired and cynical, I tend to

see the teacher's fatigue and the pupils' cynicism. Sometimes I see what I want to see — my supervisees demonstrate strong evidence of having learned from me — and sometimes I see what I particularly do not want to see. Sometimes I see more than there really is, and sometimes I see less. It depends on one's frame of reference. What is a little snow to the skier seems like a lot of snow to the motorist.

My perceptions may be clouded by anxiety or confused with wishes. Sometimes I see parts but cannot perceive wholes. And sometimes I generalize too much from single instances and see halos and other global phenomena that are not actually there. What I see is clearly affected by my values and prejudices and biases. Sometimes, too, I do not see anything intelligible because so much goes by so fast. At other times, I fail to see enough because I have only looked for things at which I had some prior intention to look. Often, my perceptual distortions arise from my tendencies to understand events as I have understood events previously. I fit new things into old patterns, even when the fits are poor. I frequently fuse inferences with perceptions and believe that I have seen things that simply do not exist. In sum, where and what I am in a given moment can cause distortion in what I am encountering. When I am observing a teacher, I had best keep that possibility in mind.

3. *Problems of Physical and Psychological Distance.* In the classroom or other setting in which observation occurs, a seldom-examined factor is that the teacher and the supervisor are, by their locations in the room, seeing and hearing two different happenings. Usually the observer sits opposite the teacher, for the good reason that this facilitates watching the teacher at work. As a result, however, he or she sees more of the backs than of the faces of the students. The teacher, in turn, sees the supervisor as one large member of the scene; the supervisor probably has no way of imagining what difference that makes in the teacher's eye movements, feelings, or whatever. A given child's voice may be inaudible to the teacher and clear as a bell to the nearby supervisor. How such distance variables affect their respective recollections of events is a question deserving further study.

Perhaps even more important may be *emotional* distance, as a variable. It is highly desirable for the supervisor to have, and display, some sense of investment and involvement in the teacher's work. Yet at the same time, supervisors need to be free of emotional restraints when they seek to analyze, with such objectivity as possible, what has been observed. Similarly, the teacher's apparent *emotional* distance from a supervisor ("I don't feel too happy about this supervisor's work") could trigger more negative observations than might apparent emotional proximity ("Hey, you're *my* kind of a supervisor!").

4. *Assessing the Effect of the Supervisor's Presence.* An age-old question is how to compensate, if at all, for the fact of the supervisor's presence in the success or failure of a lesson. Although teachers' common apprehensions about observers inhibiting (or exciting) the children seem not to have much basis in

fact, it is admittedly difficult to judge just what does happen that would not have happened in the same classroom unvisited. We think that most pupils, especially those for whom visitors are not a rarity, tend to adjust quickly to the presence of visitors and in fact to "tune them out" very quickly. If the teacher is calm and essentially "normal" in the children's minds, such tuning out is virtually guaranteed. However, an uptight teacher will usually trigger similar discomfort in the children, or at least cause them to realize that the panic button is nearby, and the result can only be an abnormal lesson.

The challenge, then, is for the supervisor to establish, over time and especially in relation to perceived tension or anxiety, that supervision is a helping enterprise and that no threat is intended. This might mean a graceful withdrawal, followed by some rapport-nurturant activities before another visit is planned.

5. *Procedural Gaffes: Inappropriate Participation.* Some common errors committed by clinical supervisors during observation stem from their impulses to engage in behaviors that make them either conspicuous in the classroom or an actual distraction:

(a) Some supervisors cannot resist conversing with fellow observers while a lesson is going on or during a lull in the activity.

(b) Some choose to converse with pupils, sometimes intervening in their work.

(c) Some, with *very* bad manners, will correct a teacher's substantive error in front of the children.

(d) Some get so interested, on the other hand, that they start taking over the class.

6. *Procedural Gaffes: Untoward Behavior.* Common errors involving the supervisor and one or more pupils include the following:

(a) Sometimes it becomes obvious to certain pupils, by the way a supervisor is concentrating upon them, that they are being singled out for study. This can worry, or even anger, a child.

(b) Sometimes supervisors let it be known, by frowns or even audible remarks, that they find certain pupil behaviors amusing or distasteful. Unless reinforcement and punishment has been assigned by the teacher to the supervisor as a legitimate task, the supervisor "should not mix in."

7. *The Other Side of the Coin: Teacher Mistakes.* Sometimes teachers who may be new to the game or who have not been properly coached for observation will deliberately focus attention on the observers before, during and/or after their arrival in the classroom. Excessively elaborate greetings, having the children interrupt their routine in some unexpected way (e.g., sing a song for the visitor, explain last month's mural all over again), engaging in periodic banter with the supervisor, scolding the children because what they are doing will (allegedly) annoy the visitor, or hinting that the observer might have some ultimate punitive power over the children are some examples that come to mind.

8. *Being Equal to the Task.* As any recital of the opportunities and the problems of clinical supervision is bound to confirm, one's success in each stage depends a great deal upon controlling sufficient personal resources. We say or imply a lot in this volume about the importance of a healthy self-concept — in children, in teachers, and in the supervisors of teachers. As we see how important and how difficult the observation stage is, we are reminded of the need to understand, and to have some control over, the values and biases from which our actions spring. In fact, it seems reasonable to demand of all clinical supervisors a commitment to knowing oneself in these terms.

To know what I like and what I dislike, to know what kinds of experiences tend to threaten me, to know something about my problems of distance, and to know, for example, of my tendencies to focus more on teachers than on pupils and to perceive verbal behavior more consciously than nonverbal behavior is necessary to enable me to compensate deliberately for these factors for the sake of reasonably objective recording. To collaborate in observation with another supervisor who knows about himself or herself in analogous terms increases the odds, presumably, that the lesson will be seen fairly and accurately. Especially during one's initial training in clinical supervision, the importance of collaborative observation and rigorous postconference analyses cannot be overstated. In the absence of opportunities for such arrangements, other techniques — for example, role reversals, in which Teacher supervises Supervisor's behavior, or group supervision of some form, by means of which Supervisor may create observational roles for several teachers with whom he or she works in order to create possibilities for multiple observation and for observation of the supervisor's behavior — represent potential methods for coming to grips with these problems.

Some form of process or self-awareness training or counseling — that is, some set of experiences that enhance supervisors' self-knowledge, their capacities for self-monitoring, and their abilities to teach teachers these same capabilities — may be a helpful supplement to supervisor training along the way. Similarly, data-gathering and observation skills ought to be continually updated and refurbished. In fact, supervisors perhaps more than any other category of education professionals need to be perennial and indefatigable students of their craft (or should we say science?). In such a role, supervisors can provide for their teachers an appropriate model of the true professional.

Chapter 7

ANALYSIS
AND STRATEGY
PART I:
Methods

---

* **Methods of Analysis**
* **Methods of Strategy**
* **Implementing
  the Three Criteria:
  Some Specific Methods**

Of all the tasks that confront the supervisor in the course of the clinical observation cycle, probably none makes more demands upon the intellectual resources of the supervisor than the thinking (in Stage 3) that follows an observation and precedes the feedback session with the teacher. As the reader no doubt already appreciates, the preparations in advance of an observation and the activities involved in data gathering are also high-demand tasks that necessitate focused and creative thought. Clinical supervision at *all* stages calls for a mixture of knowledge, experience, intellectuality, and communication talents. It is probably in what we call the "analysis and strategy" stage, however, where cognitive skills are the most necessary. Partly for that reason, and partly because there are so many complexities in the weighting, sifting, and utilization of observation data, we elect in this book to spend considerable time on the topic.

Although we do not want to overwhelm the would-be supervisor with caveats and/or prescriptions, we do seek to explore certain dimensions of this stage in depth. Rather than attempting to contain so much material in one overlong chapter, we have divided the topic into two parts. In this chapter, which focuses on methods, we deal primarily with a general discussion of analysis and strategy. In the following chapter, which deals with problems, we include discussion of goal setting and of elements of strategy, especially those relating to plans for management of the conference.

METHODS OF ANALYSIS

Before we deal directly with techniques and methods of analysis it seems best to establish a conceptual framework for Stage 3 by speaking first of patterns and categories of teaching behavior and second by augmenting previously stated ideas concerning a priori categories of observation and analysis.

Let us begin with a notion that was touched on briefly in the last chapter, namely, that human behavior is patterned — that is, in certain respects it is repetitious — and that, as a subset of general behavior, teaching is also patterned. And if it is true that certain elements of any teacher's behavior tend to be repeated over and over again in his or her teaching, that these teaching patterns on the first day are recapitulated almost every other day, then it follows that the cumulative effects of such patterns are more likely to have consequence for the pupils' learning, for better or for worse, than occasional, isolated elements of teaching whose existence is not incorporated by continuing patterns or whose relationship to such patterns is not immediately apparent.

Whereas it may be that no element of an individual's behavior represents behavior of which that individual is incapable, and that, in effect, every behavior reflects a unique, enduring, underlying "self," it seems true that certain constellations of behavior tend to express a person's quintessential self more than others do. We know an individual principally by salient behavioral patterns, by the manifest style that makes him peculiarly what he or she is.

The teacher's unique identity has special significance in two senses. First, inasmuch as it is most commonly true in teaching (that is, that rather than dealing directly with content most of the time, the students deal with Teacher's representations of that content instead), the quality and character of their substantive learning is affected by Teacher's influences upon the material as it filtered through his or her own sensory, cognitive, and expressive apparatus. Who the teacher is, therefore, inevitably makes differences in how and in what the pupils learn of the material because Teacher's biases, values, distortions, and the like infuse whatever he or she teaches. Teacher becomes subtly, inextricably, and inevitably insinuated into the curriculum.

Second, it is just as necessary to suppose that who the teacher is chiefly determines (along with who the learners are) what incidental learnings will be established. Taken together, these suppositions imply that in relation to both intended curricular outcomes and unintended learnings relating to all sorts of other things that may directly affect conditions of learning, Teacher's salient patterns of behavior count more than anything else about Teacher, for ill or for good. For supervision to have any palatable effects upon the students' lives, it must be aimed at strengthening, extinguishing, or in some other way modifying these saliencies of the teaching performance. Besides the fact that Teacher's patterns fill the air more than anything else about him, one must appreciate how potently learnings resulting from certain stimuli can be reinforced by repetitions of those stimuli and how important this can be either when what is learned makes particularly good sense or when what is learned is nonsense — especially important when such learning is of reasoning processes, personal and role concomitants of learning, self-definition, and of intellectual behavior generally.

In this frame of reference, the clinical supervisor must be committed to center around salient teaching patterns rather than around unusual or relatively superficial variables in teaching. This is not easy to do, because salient characteristics of behavior are more likely to resist change than superficial ones. Also, Teacher manifests certain patterns because they are or they seem to be useful to him or her (even seemingly self-defeating behavior can be useful if what the person needs is to fail). Furthermore, of all the factors tending to rigidify Teacher's patterns, their reinforcement by the pupils, day after day, is among the more significant.

Let us now consider the question of how Supervisor formulates categories of teaching behavior in order to organize data meaningfully. And let us imagine that, in a hypothetical instance of supervision, the Supervisor's contract with Teacher requires observation of the entire lesson and a readiness to broach any issues at all that seem to exist in the teaching.

If the preobservation "contract" has provided a clear sense of the categories of data that Teacher expects Supervisor to collect, then at least some aspects of the analysis will have already taken shape in Supervisor's mind, and the search for patterns within those categories will be facilitated. However, with reference to *other* kinds of data that may have been collected (e.g., data to support "bonus" feedback), Supervisor must organize the data into appropriate categories. To some extent this process requires invention, or at least imaginative treatment of the available data. Much depends upon the conceptual repertoire of Supervisor, and also Supervisor's analytical versatility. Sometimes patterns may be discerned within the data rather easily. It is also important to realize that when Supervisor seems to recognize a pattern in the raw data, he or she may unconsciously "distort" the data or ignore contrary data in order to find comforting support for a particular hypothesis. The extent to which supervisors may in fact allow various biases to interfere with insightful analysis is probably great enough so that safeguards (especially of the self-check variety) are highly desirable. In this connection, research on the powerful effect of first impressions offers some clues: Often even the data collection process is done carelessly once Supervisor has formed impressions upon which he or she feels able to act.

Let us turn now to the actual work of analysis. Imagine that Supervisor has just come from observation and has copious notes, verbatim quotations, timings, and the like from which to develop a design for supervision. The first problem is to create a more streamlined version of what happened than the raw data themselves provide. It is necessary simultaneously to condense the material to a wieldy size and to avoid introducing biases that distort what actually occurred in the lesson. Supervisor wants to wind up with a representation of reality, namely, of the teaching, that is true to life and as economical as it can be — a goal that is never completely possible to reach but is all the same worth pursuing.

Because patterns of teaching behavior, once identified by analysis, generally ought to serve as the substantive content of supervision conferences, it is necessary to search the data for behavioral patterns and to employ certain precautions in the process. A first concern is to ensure that the regularities that are eventually attributed to the teaching are authentic; that is, the identified patterns will really be patterns. A first criterion is that the behavior in question must be repetitious: Whatever its character, the ploy must be repeated from time to time in order to qualify as a teaching pattern. Just as two points, at least, are required to define a line, we can generally assume that some minimum number of repetitions is needed to establish a pattern.

Much of the time the job will be easy because behavioral repetitions will occur within the context of the lesson observed. Sometimes, however, the problem of authenticating patterns becomes more difficult. For example, since their periodicity varies, patterns may occasionally comprise behaviors whose repetitions are thinly distributed. Their rarefaction may make it difficult to recognize their relatedness or tempt one to suppose that some single datum does reflect a behavioral pattern whose attenuation makes empirical documentation impossible or very impractical. In such a case, if it seems important to be able to document a pattern empirically before broaching it with the teacher, Supervisor may be forced to withhold mention of the pattern in question until persuasive evidence can be collected over a cycle, that is, over more than one sequence of supervision.

In hierarchical order, three principles should govern the analysis. Keeping in mind that patterns selected for treatment in supervision will presumably be chosen because they represent teaching behavior that may be significantly related to the pupils' learning, a first choice (all else being equal) will be patterns whose consequences are demonstrable in the data. For example, if Supervisor detected a pattern of sarcasm with which one might confront Teacher for the sake of establishing whether children are getting hurt and are developing unfriendly attitudes toward the school, it is helpful if the data provide several instances in which, immediately after Teacher has thrown a verbal barb, the child reacts in some way (e.g., tearfully or angrily) that is recognizable as an injury. Under such circumstances, Supervisor can present the evidence, which clearly establishes causes and effects. Most of the time, unfortunately, consequences of teaching behavior must generally be inferred because they are not directly visible. All the same, "visibility in the data" is an important selection criterion.

A second test of whether a pattern identified is likely to be of much consequence consists of the question of whether the hypothesis can be supported by theory. In other words, being unable to prove effects directly from the data, the next best possibility is to be able to summon existing theory in support of one's predictions. Let us suppose that Teacher tends to remedy the occasional inattentiveness of his or her 6-year-olds by saying:

> If you don't pay attention, a big dog with pointy teeth will come while you are sleeping and will eat up your arms and legs.

In such a blatant case, it is pretty obvious that educational theory is being violated and Supervisor can feel sufficiently armed to raise tentative questions about this practice during supervision. Again, whenever a child offers a response to one of Teacher's questions and Teacher turns his or her back toward the child, one could probably feel, having some knowledge of operant conditioning, that a sufficiently reasonable basis existed in theory to raise the issue. Most of the enigmas with which supervisors deal will, of course, be related to more complicated theories than these examples provide, however; and to be a good supervisor calls for a very sophisticated command of pedagogical theory. Although some theories are clearly more relevant or more generally accepted than others, almost any theory is better than no theory at all.

Least acceptable as an alternative, albeit one that must be employed from time to time, is to isolate a pattern for examination simply because of hunches one has about it. Failing to have documentary evidence and failing to be cognizant of satisfactorily applicable theory, a supervisor may follow intuitions and address the pattern anyway. It must be recognized in advance, however, that if Teacher is unready to believe, one is least likely to be persuasive on this basis. One is most likely to be wrong (assuming that examined theories have been more rigorously substantiated than hunches); and one runs the risk of teaching, incidentally, that hunching one's way through supervisory analyses represents acceptable practice, when in our framework of clinical supervision it emphatically does not — certainly not as a principal mode for supervision.

At this point it may be helpful to indicate the distinctions between "patterns" and "categories" and explain their relationship to one another. Once a supervisor has unearthed patterns in the data (by methods that will be described shortly), one means for deciding whether or not they are significant and, if so, what specific importance they carry, is to name general categories of teaching into which they may logically fit. For example, if Teacher continually asks many-pronged questions, one could see "questioning" as the relevant category and "multiple questioning" as one of this teacher's salient patterns in that category. Although identification of patterns is represented simply by a sorting and collation of empirical data, the invention of categories and the naming of patterns by reference to them represent processes that enable Supervisor to elevate the data to a level at which they can be understood by theory.

Despite prior awareness of common categories, explicit attention upon categories occurs a posteriori. After the data are in and after their salient patterns have been identified, the next step is to build a paradigm of teaching by constructing a taxonomy to describe it. Having assembled the paradigm, one can move beyond simple descriptive classification to problems of interpretation and meaning — first, by summoning whatever theory is available for a conceptual framework, and second, by shifting to more differential analysis of the patterns in question. In more concrete terms, if a pattern of multiple questioning has been observed, Supervisor draws upon what he or she knows generally about questioning as a component of teaching and examines problems concerning the special importance that a multiple questioning pattern may have in the immediate situation. The analytical focus may shuttle back and forth as Supervisor alternately raises new questions, detects additional patterns, moves from new patterns to new categories, and so forth.

In many instances a given pattern will be incorporable by more than one category. For example, a pattern of multiple questioning, while fitting the category "questioning" might also fit a category "centeredness." Some teachers frame their multiple questions consistently in the first person (a pattern of egocentrism) so that the implicit reason for the pupils to addess the question(s) in the first place is for Teacher's sake: "I want you to tell me how the elements are ordered in the periodic table; can you name the first five for me; can you tell me about their electron structures; why is hydrogen number one? I want you to tell me the difference between atomic weight and atomic number." The very same pattern may have different (plural) qualities of significance depending upon the categories in which it is conceptualized, and its differing qualities may be mutually reinforcing, mutually opposing, mutually canceling, counterbalancing, or mutually irrelevant in the context of the pupils' learning and experience. The fact that a specific pattern has categorical concurrency may be significant in its own right. It often appears that complex patterns of this kind incorporate both strengths and weaknesses simultaneously, either of which could easily be eclipsed if only a single, global category were employed in analysis.

Methodologically, the first move of the supervisor is to peruse the data for easily identifiable patterns. By just scanning the material, for example, it is possible to discover that every other verbalization in the lesson was by Teacher. In this case "teacher-pupil" is the dominant interactional pattern. One may also see at a glance that Teacher heavily outweighs pupils in the ratio of talk: Teacher speaks 50 words for every student's word. It may also be easy to see that whereas 25 children attended class, dialogue involved only seven of them during the lesson and that, of the seven, two had the lion's share. Supervisor may be struck at once by specific words that are repeated frequently, for example, "OK, very good," in which case some kind of stereotyped response may have been unearthed.

Content analysis may reveal that from time to time Teacher imposes his or her own value judgments upon the pupils as, for example, when Teacher tells them that certain problems are harder than others, certain tribes were good Indians but other tribes were bad Indians, and that democracy is best. It may also be that Teacher's values are communicated more implicitly by information included or omitted from his or her exposition (rich people attend the opera; Russian citizens do not criticize the state; poor people are culturally deprived), that Teacher's omissions give rise to factual distortions (all objects can be classified as living or nonliving; all points in a continuous curve will admit of a tangent; America was settled by Europeans fleeing religious persecution), or that, plain and simple, Teacher is communicating incorrect information (Jews never make good soldiers; the earth is flat; the moon is made of green cheese).

It may be that Teacher makes promises and doesn't keep them. Perhaps Teacher uses specialized terminology inconsistently: for example, sometimes he or she calls them "minus numbers" and, at other times, "negative numbers"; sometimes they are "lines," but at other times they are "rays" or "line segments." Teacher's meanings may not always correspond with pupils' meanings, even though conversation proceeds for a time as if there were mutual understanding. For example, it may be clear from Teacher's context that he or she means "independence" to connote fresh, insubordinate behavior, whereas in the pupil's context independence seems a virtue, as in the Declaration of. Or, Teacher's having put the example 333 × 333 on the board, and having asked at one point, "And what do we do now with the three?" it may become clear at once that although Pupil's answer was correct, it was in reference to the wrong three and that, consequently, as Pupil's comments indicate, Teacher's rejection of the answer was confusing to Pupil and seemed unfair.

Sometimes Supervisor finds that Teacher tends to conduct private communications publicly (for example, when he or she reminds Seymour rather audibly that he must take his pill at 11 o'clock) or, in the opposite direction, makes public communications privately (as, for example, by telling Lena that the harmony exercise should both begin and end with a tonic chord), although that information logically should have been directed toward the entire class. In the process of teaching grammar, Teacher might be committing precisely the errors against which he or she is cautioning. Or, on the positive side, it may become apparent that in connection with teaching about inductive reasoning, Teacher is exemplifying such reasoning in his or her own behavior.

In short, by reading the data and asking the question, "What is happening at this point?" sequences of behavior become apparent. Supervisor makes tentative inferences about them, finds out whether the behaviors in question constitute salient patterns in the teaching, reviews inferences and tests them against data and theory, and finds which hunches are supportable and which are not. Withal, Supervisor assembles a collection of patterns and, in effect, a collection of issues among which he or she must sort and perhaps select all over again to develop strategies for the supervision conference. Having found what can be found, as in the examples above, Supervisor next attempts consciously to understand their implications and to deal with them within the values framework and pedagogical assumptions that guide his or her own supervisory behavior and goals.

A challenging problem is how to take into account the children's frames of reference as one basis for deciding in what manner some feature of the teaching is likely or unlikely to be significant. It is difficult to second-guess how specific children or groups of children will experience the teacher's behavior and to be sure that Teacher's behavior is engendering certain feelings and certain attitudes among the pupils. If one were to ask the pupils outright what they feel, their responses might not support one's hypotheses. Nevertheless, when attempting to decide whether a teaching pattern is likely to have important consequences, it is useful to try to imagine that behavior's impact upon a child in the class and to imagine what effects might occur if that behavior should be reenacted throughout the year. Supervisors probably do too little of this sort of analysis. That they should do so is reflected in the fact that many teachers themselves often do not really think much about how things may be experienced by their pupils, and they tend to assume that events in the children's frames of reference will be very much as they see them in their own. For example, as often as not, teachers gauge progress by a measure of what material has been covered. Implicitly they assume that what has been taught has been learned. If not, then why the great thrust to cover Chapter Six by the end of the week? How often have you turned from the end of a lesson feeling it was good, simply because you felt fluent in your teaching and covered, pretty much, what you wanted to? Certainly it seems true that when teachers do think about what class was like for the pupils, their thoughts generally fasten on a very limited sector of the pupils' experience, namely, that sector relating directly to the content being taught. It is unusual to find a teacher who, on a regular basis, thinks explicitly about what else the children may have learned besides chemistry or "the scientific method."

In this vein Supervisor continues to examine teaching patterns in a hypothetical framework of pupil experience (when the data do not provide clues to their real experiences), partly to establish that practice in the teacher's own behavior, even though specific guesses on any occasion may be quite wrong. It seems probable that over long periods of time, with Supervisor's help, Teacher's hypotheses about pupil response will get to be more accurate and more useful.

Most of the time the principal criterion for evaluating patterns is whether or not they helped Teacher to get what he or she was after. Allowing that goals must sometimes be reformulated as a lesson proceeds and taking into account that any lesson may have both long- and short-term objectives, the question can be sharpened: Does the evidence suggest that this pattern helped Teacher to get what he or she wanted at the moment(s) it was manifested? Another question for evaluating patterns is whether, irrespective of Teacher's prior objectives, the outcomes likely to have arisen from their existence, particularly the incidental learnings, seem generally worthwhile or not.

Sometimes the very goals toward which Teacher is aiming may seem untenable or undesirable to the supervisor. Under such circumstances a double analysis can be developed: On the one hand, patterns can be evaluated vis-à-vis Teacher's intentions and, on the other, in relation to alternative goals that Supervisor may favor. Sometimes such conflicts relate to ends. Teacher feels that every student should understand the mechanics of the electoral college, but Supervisor does not. Sometimes they simply relate to means. Teacher and Supervisor agree that the pupils should find pleasure in music but do not agree on how to achieve this end.

After having identified patterns in the data, visually and by analysis of the substantive content, and after having attempted to determine their significance by reference to Teacher's goals and to the pupils' demonstrated or inferred experiences, the final step in analysis is to discover whether the documented patterns can be arranged in some hierarchical order. Some teaching patterns will be more prominent than others. Some patterns will seem more consequential than others — if not in relation to their frequency, then because of the likelihood that they affect particularly important areas of the pupils' learning and development (for example, the degree to which they accept and value themselves). Some patterns will seem to have special importance because of their superordinate relationships to other patterns. For example, if Teacher initiates all questions and directions (category: "origins"), if Teacher performs all evaluations of the pupils' academic progress, if Teacher conducts classes so that pupils never have opportunities for conversing with one another, and if Teacher displays a prominent "I" pattern, then "teacher-centeredness" or "egocentrism" might logically be established as the superordinate pattern in reference to which all other patterns acquire special significance. "Centeredness" may be placed at the top of the hierarchy and may be employed as the organizing principle of the analysis and, subsequently, of the supervision.

Consideration of patterns in a hierarchical arrangement may send Supervisor back to the data to see whether other relevant patterns exist and whether additional evidence exists to confirm or to reject hypotheses already developed, and to take another sounding on whether the hierarchical organization that has been invented rings true in the natural flow of the lesson. Having selected portions of data and having rearranged them according to his view of "what goes together," that is, into arbitrary sequences, Supervisor must take special pains to ensure both now and later (in the conference) that the resulting distortions are justifiable.

METHODS OF STRATEGY

Use of the term *strategy* for the next phase of the supervisor's work sometimes seems overly dramatic, but it tends to emphasize the complex decision-making exercise through which the supervisor must go in order to be properly prepared for postobservation conversation (or other contact) with the teacher. All too often such conversation merely happens — guided, if at all, by spur-of-the-moment gestures and statements and unassisted by careful prior planning and thought. It is perhaps possible to *overplan* for a conference, at the other extreme, but in our experience it is far riskier to neglect planning than it is to jump in cold into the planning process.

Credited to Ernest Steck, of Western Michigan University, is the insightful remark that supervision is essentially a word-picking exercise. Extended to include all the gestures, intonations, body movements, and other dimensions of communication that accompany language, this is a very useful idea for supervisors to keep in mind. Whenever one has visited a teacher's classroom, especially within the context of an observation cycle, the next contact one has with that teacher is inescapably loaded with expectations and questions on the teacher's part. "How did Supervisor feel about what happened? Does he think I accomplished the goals I had in mind? Was he shocked by what I said to Sandra? Why did he seem so displeased when he walked out?" These are only a few examples of what might be on the teacher's mind; and it is obvious that when Teacher next encounters Supervisor, whether by accident in the cafeteria or in the first moments of the scheduled postobservation conference, Teacher will be weighing every word and gesture with great care.

All the more reason, then, for Supervisor to work out a strategy for handling this important encounter, and to be in full control of adequate information that helps him or her to feel comfortable about the strategy that was selected.

There are several levels at which we can conceptualize the activities of this stage. Supervisor makes decisions about what should occur in supervision, what outcomes should result from supervision, and other decisions about how to bring about the events and achieve the results sought. It may be helpful at this point to make a twofold distinction: First, "what and how" is one way to distinguish the ends-means relationship or, in more scholastic language, the "goals-and-procedures" categories into which teaching plans are commonly divided. Second, Supervisor's interest, in this connection, is centered both upon the conference and upon events that will occur after the conference in future teaching, in future cycles of supervision and, generally, in the future development of Teacher's professional behavior. In short, Strategy incorporates decisions relating to means and ends, presently and for the future.

Having analyzed his or her observation notes and having isolated various patterns of teaching behavior from the data, Supervisor must decide which issues to select for the conference. This means, in effect, that goals must be set in relation to which he or she can formulate selection criteria. Supervisory goals are generally conceptualized in a multidimensional framework — that is, in the context of issues and problems deriving from several overlapping frames of reference.

Some goals are generated by the data. The supervisor can take his or her leads from features of the teaching that stand out in particularly sharp relief; from patterns of teaching which, for one reason or another, attract his or her special attention. Catch as catch can, it is almost always true that certain patterns of teaching seem to carry special significance as one analyzes observational data. Of course, the tendency to isolate specific teaching patterns may simply reflect Supervisor's perceptual or professional biases rather than any measure of their objective importance, and this is one problem that must, of course, be carefully considered.

Instead of beginning from the press of data, Supervisor may define goals in reference to continuing problems with which he or she and Teacher have been working. In other words, from a framework of already existing supervisory issues Supervisor may select elements of data that, to the casual observer, might not seem particularly important for supervisory treatment. Indeed, should certain issues take precedence because of earlier priorities, and should it happen that no material from the current data is germane, Supervisor might deliberately elect to ignore the immediate lesson or to defer its analysis in order to stay engaged in lines of inquiry that require extension or culmination or closure. Ideally, it is best to determine that observation would be gratuitous beforehand, in time to avoid it, but in many cases one cannot be sure about such things in advance.

Another basis for determining goals might exist in Supervisor's conceptualization of some sequence of problems that should represent a long-range design for supervision. He or she might, for example, have decided that certain categories of teaching should be examined in some logical, sequential order according to a model that suggests, in effect, that development of a particular teaching technique requires certain technical competencies to be established in order for other dependent competencies to be establishable: in simple terms, a technical model that prescribes first things first. Neither will every such sequence be equally valid or useful nor, in all probability, is there any specific sequence that can have equal validity for all teachers. In any event, Supervisor's goals for a particular conference might be generated by a "master plan," in which case his or her selection of issues for treatment (and of relevant data) could appear quite different from those of another supervisor who takes leads directly from the raw data.

These examples suggest that Supervisor's goals and rationales for supervision may come from different places at the same time. Indeed, as we examined methods for preobservation earlier, we saw that sometimes the goals will have been stipulated beforehand in the contract, at the beginning of a sequence of supervision. It is unnecessary to place such frameworks for goal setting in any order of value. Let us simply recognize that a plurality of contexts for defining goals exists, that the few examples given above do not represent an exhaustive collection of possibilities, and that, in common practice, multiple frames of reference can operate concurrently as Supervisor tries to decide what he or she is after.

The foregoing mentions of Supervisor were offered only for simplicity's sake. It would be a mistake to suppose that these examples are meant to imply that the supervisor should make decisions unilaterally or that his or her rationales for goal setting should be kept secret from the teacher. On the contrary, clinical supervision attaches very high priorities to collaborative goal setting, to the adoption of supervisory goals deriving from Teacher's own system of priorities, and to the practice of making Supervisor's goals explicit and of reaching agreement on them in instances when his or her goals set the directions for supervision. Implicitly, in other words, the press of data and references to a long-range supervisory plan might each be incorporated by an even larger system of meaning (namely, by Teacher's frame of reference) to the degree that Supervisor can understand it. Even though Supervisor must often review notes, perform analyses of the teaching, and formulate strategies for supervision, he or she should, nevertheless, function as Teacher's advocate during these stages — not, necessarily, as an advocate of what Teacher has done — and should take pains later on to establish whether or not he or she anticipated Teacher's requirements accurately.

We have raised the question of goal setting, assuming that Supervisor needs goals in order to decide which teaching patterns to select for supervisory treatment. It could equally well be argued that Supervisor needs analyzed data in order to formulate goals. Goals are to data as chickens are to eggs, and no simple solution to the problem of which comes first is likely to be sufficient. In practice, Supervisor generally engages in a process of shifting back and forth between his or her observation notes and other frames of reference in trying to lay plans for the next step. There is no single correct sequence for handling this task. It is no more correct to begin with goals than to begin with data, and operationally it is often impossible to make such distinctions. Indeed, one must avoid blinding oneself to either dimension of the problem or allowing oneself to adopt either approach exclusively.

As long as it does not matter, theoretically, where one starts, we can begin by discussing some general methods for selecting patterns of teaching for supervision. We may assume that Supervisor works from certain a priori goals, and that these goals have been and will continue to be formulated in a context of priorities that derives largely from Teacher's own frame of reference. Moreover, according to this model of clinical supervision, we can anticipate that Supervisor will define both technical goals and process goals. Methods for structuring such goals will be examined below.

In general, how does Supervisor select specific patterns with which to deal?

In general, three principles serve as selection criteria for material to be addressed in supervision. The teaching patterns (and associated issues) discussed should be salient, few in number, and — as well as can be judged beforehand — intellectually and emotionally accessible to the teacher for analysis and treatment. Before dealing directly with specific techniques employing these criteria, let us spend a moment to describe the clinical supervisor's reasons for adopting them.

REASONS FOR SALIENCY

One set of reasons for "saliency" has already been offered above in the section on analysis. It has been argued, essentially, that salient patterns will probably have the greatest effects upon the pupils' learning. A second rationale can be expressed by the proposition that even though there may sometimes be discomfort associated with treatment of prominent teaching patterns, Teacher's confidence in supervision, incentives for supervision, and rewards from supervision are likely to pale if, in his or her perception, supervision is merely a quibble, a string of equivocations, an obsession with superficialities. Teacher's morale will depreciate if supervision merely wastes his or her time. For supervision to be important and for it to seem important, it must deal with issues that *are* important, and salient features of the teaching are more likely to satisfy this condition than peripheral ones.

A third reason is that it is generally easier to establish the significance of ancillary patterns by reference to salient patterns than vice versa. That is to say, prominent patterns of teaching can more readily serve as organizing principles for the data than lesser elements. A fourth reason is that Teacher can generally recognize saliencies in his own behavior more easily than superficialities, partly because they express more of his style and partly because, by definition, more data are available to document salient patterns. Although one occasionally encounters defensive flights into superficiality or a teacher's apparent inability to recognize prominent regularities of his own behavior, such cases represent exceptions (or reflect Supervisor's failure to have predicted "treatability" accurately). We will deal with this subject later on.

REASONS FOR FEWNESS

A common error is that of saturating supervision conferences with so many issues of such great significance that not even the spongiest teacher could be expected to assimilate all of them. "Few" is usually better than "many" in much the same sense that silence is golden. First, the time available for any supervision conference is not infinite, although such conferences occasionally seem endless. Second, even in infinite time, Teacher does not have infinite patience or an infinite capacity for assimilating ideas or generating them. Anyhow, assimilation is only an intermediate goal at best: The real goal is to develop reasons, strategies, and techniques for working on the patterns considered, something considerably more difficult and complex than simply recognizing their existence.

REASONS FOR "TREATABILITY"

We suspect that reasons for this criterion are self-evident. We might say that even after supervision has become an old shoe, Supervisor sometimes guesses wrong about the psychological accessibility of certain issues and, when he or she compounds this error by persevering in their treatment, generally winds up having squandered the conference. At best, it has been a waste of time. At worst, if this sort of thing happens repeatedly, Teacher may reject supervision altogether.

IMPLEMENTING THE THREE CRITERIA: SOME SPECIFIC METHODS

In the larger context of methods for strategy, one might say, recalling the "what-how" distinction made earlier, that the very decision to choose on these criteria is an element of method. The next methodological question is how to do so.

SALIENCY

How can Supervisor determine whether any given pattern of teaching is salient? What referents are germane?

The most easily satisfied condition for saliency is probably that the pattern in question should appear frequently in the teaching. Frequency and abundance are generally simple to detect. There is always the possibility, however, that frequency alone is not a sufficient condition for establishing saliency for supervisory purposes. If it happened, for example, that every time a pupil responded to Teacher's questions or statements, Teacher gently scratched his ear, "ear-scratching," despite its frequency, might not be worth troubling with in supervision. Unless, because the pupils had caught on to this flection's relationship to their own behavior and were deliberately attempting to condition Teacher to tear his ear off, Supervisor could establish the pattern's special significance for them, he would probably not give it any second thoughts.

Thus it would seem that "frequency" must be joined with "significance" in order to establish useful definitions of saliency. One might, in fact, attribute saliency to a pattern because of the clarity of its demonstrable effects upon the student, irrespective of its frequency in the teaching. If Teacher only made

Roger cry once during the lesson, but if it were easy to show that he cried because of something Teacher did to him, then however it was that Teacher behaved might seem salient in the context of that lesson, certainly in the context of Roger's experience. In any event, frequency has been the handiest and most useful index of saliency in our practice of clinical supervision thus far.

As was suggested in our earlier discussion of analysis, some teaching patterns will seem to be highly important, even when their effects upon the children are not directly demonstrable. Such patterns might seem significant beause of their ostensible emotional effects or, perhaps more commonly, because of their intellectual character: They might, for example, seem very appropriate or completely inappropriate to the children's actual levels of cognitive functioning. The point is that Supervisor may justifiably elect to deal with some pattern of teaching because it seems to be salient in relation to theory. Learning theory, developmental theories, and personality theories serve us most commonly in this connection. Should many teaching patterns seem to have theoretical saliency, then frequency might be taken as the determining factor for selection.

Some patterns derive saliency from their relationships to other patterns. It sometimes occurs that although analysis has unearthed a dozen patterns and although each such pattern may seem significant enough to warrant treatment in supervision, some single pattern or pair of patterns occupies a superordinate relationship to the others. Under such circumstances, Supervisor may select that single pattern that most thoroughly expresses the others' significance and may choose to grade saliency in this manner. Once a superpattern has been examined in the supervision conference, it is often possible to introduce its subordinate patterns rapidly, as examples, and without elaborate analysis.

Another sense of saliency is represented by an instance in which, although Teacher manifested many inherently strong teaching patterns, B, C, and D, their potential effectiveness was lost because of weaknesses in architectonic pattern, A. For example, Teacher's initial directions were ambiguous (category: direction giving; pattern: ambiguous directions), but once the children had been set to work, her manner of circulating among them, accepting their questions, and rendering individual assistance was exemplary. It might nevertheless be demonstrable that the degree to which they required individual clarifications and the degree of redundancy characterizing Teacher's remarks to individual students betrayed the initial weakness.

Or, similarly, saliency might be attributed to patterns resulting in broken sequences, in missing links that undermined an otherwise successful lesson. In one example, Teacher's directions were perfectly clear, the children's tasks were clearly defined and seemed acceptable to them, and the teaching incorporated a hundred other virtues, but at certain critical moments the lesson broke down because, when the time came for using laboratory equipment, the children were uncertain of which apparatus to select and discovered that there was not enough material to go around. Then Teacher's failure to muster appropriate equipment beforehand, his faulty pattern — "failure to provide appropriate materials," or "failure to identify relevant items of equipment," or "failure to prepare the children to deal with ambiguities and shortages beforehand" — might justifiably be considered salient and be isolated for supervision. In short, saliency can sometimes be defined in relationship to weak keystones or to missing pieces in otherwise cogent structures.

Saliency may also be construed in normative terms, that is, in relation to commonalities among teachers. In a departmentalized secondary school, for example, in which children are instructed by many teachers in a normal day, certain teaching patterns that do not seem particularly significant in the context of any single teacher's performance may nevertheless acquire a collective saliency that (we hypothesize) has important cumulative effects upon the students. Should it become apparent that all teachers, B–Z, employ didactic instructional approaches in which all questions and directions are formulated for the pupils, and should it occur that Teacher A manifests this same tendency, then, in view of the children's total experience under such teaching, Supervisor might justifiably elect to address these patterns in A's teaching (or in anyone else's). Whereas a varied diet of instructional methodology might easily provide for such teaching in certain instances, an unvaried regimen of didactic teaching would fail to provide important intellectual opportunities for the learners. Saliency, therefore, may be related to the surrounding scholastic environment and may be situationally determined.

We might close this inventory with the suggestion that saliency may be defined in relationship to what Teacher feels is important. Specific problems or teaching patterns that have been isolated in earlier supervision and upon which Teacher is deliberately working, or categories of teaching in relation to which Teacher has expressed special concern during Stage 1, can generally be placed at the top of the list of things to be considered in supervision. Relevant patterns disclosed by analysis automatically achieve a status of saliency. This is one sense of what is meant by references to "Teacher's frame of reference."

This method can be adopted in simple or in complex strategies. In the simplest manner, Supervisor may select patterns for the conference that Teacher has named in advance: "I want you to keep track of my verbal rewards to the children." Supervisor detaches reward patterns from the data and examines them with Teacher in the conference. In a somewhat more complex strategy, Supervisor may decide that certain patterns are salient, not so much because Teacher has named them explicitly beforehand but rather because he suspects that there are significant relationships between such patterns and special problems in which Teacher is interested. Using the same example, if Teacher's rewards happen to be highly responsive to idiosyncracies among the children's behavior, and if, in other dimensions of her teaching, Teacher also displays great sensitivity to individual differences (for example, in the problems she assigns, in the assignments she makes, and in the questions she asks), Supervisor might reasonably cite patterns of questioning, assignment giving, and the like in order to demonstrate that in addition to mastering "good" reward patterns,

Teacher's teaching, overall, constitutes a composite of patterns in which responsive behavior is pervasive. Or, to use a negative example, if Teacher's rewards are stereotyped, and if stereotypy is also evident in other categories of her teaching, then patterns belonging to such categories could be cited along with reward patterns in order to identify the broader phenomenon.

In summary, some methods for selecting patterns on a criterion of saliency are to examine them in connection with:

1. Their frequency and abundance in the data.
2. The existence of demonstrable effects upon the students.
3. Their theoretical significance.
4. Their structural importance in the lesson.
5. Their commonality among teachers.
6. Their known or predictable significance in Teacher's already existing professional frame of reference.

Because fewness is a criterion that Supervisor generally employs after he or she has selected on saliency and accessibility, we shall change the order of things at this point, examining some methods for deciding accessibility and saving fewness for last.

ACCESSIBILITY OF PATTERNS FOR TREATMENT

There are certain complexities that inhere in clinical supervisory practice, and it is important to acknowledge them. Supervision sometimes collapses because supervisors exercise poor judgment in selecting issues for treatment, and in many cases it has become apparent, later on, that their faulty judgments arose from simplistic thinking or from an absence of thinking about the emotions likely to be associated with examination of certain behavioral patterns for certain teachers.

One of the mistakes often made by neophyte supervisors is to underestimate — or to fail to estimate — the emotional significance of supervisory behavior for the teacher. Fascination with technical problems and with substantive issues often tends to make one rush through elaborate analyses of this pattern and that pattern as though one were explaining the derivation of a statistical formula. Such behaviors would send teachers scurrying into broom closets. Similarly, supervisors can overwhelm teachers with overly elaborate displays of data, or complicated analyses filled with jargon, or — even worse — forays into the psychotherapeutic realm. At the other extreme, the apparent reluctance of supervisors to deal directly with issues, revealed through innocuous and unproductive chitchat or other evasive behaviors, can be disturbing to teachers. It is important for supervisors to collect such data as they can with respect to their own tendencies of this sort, and consciously to correct them.

Before broaching methodological techniques in more detail, there are some general questions to be examined pertaining to clinical competencies required of clinical supervisors. Such questions are particularly germane because we have reached the point, in this hypothetical sequence, where Supervisor must make predictions about the emotional loading that specific issues are likely to have for Teacher and must employ such predictions in deciding which patterns to select for the conference.

We confront the sticky problem of how much psychological sophistication Supervisor needs, of whether, in fact, he must know what a well-trained clinical psychologist knows in order to deal with emotional variables — even to think about them — in the teacher's existence. Granting that Supervisor's conceptualization of Teacher — his or her interpretations, "diagnostic" constructs, and basic conceptual framework — may be substantially different from Psychologist's, what can be said about supervisors generally, that is, about clinical supervisors who have not had concentrated psychological training? What kind of understanding should Supervisor be able to bring to the notion of "emotional loading"? Without being made into a beard-and-couch psychoanalyst, what can the supervisor be taught in his or her professional training that will provide a grasp on emotional factors?

It is probably enough for Supervisor to be able to read internal and external signals of anxiety (that is, of his own and of Teacher's), to be able to determine whether experienced anxiety is of immobilizing intensity, and to be able to recognize some common patterns of defensive behavior.

Experience suggests that with appropriate training and with some supervised practice, most supervisors are able to recognize expressions of anxiety, to alter their strategies responsively in the face of such symptoms, and to appreciate reasons for maintaining sensitivity in this context of supervision. Some supervisors, after a time, have also proved capable of monitoring their own feelings in supervision, of reading their own distress signals, and of making appropriate decisions about what and what not to do when such signals flash during supervision conferences.

As one might guess, psychologically untrained supervisors often speak in untechnical language about emotional interference and about emotional factors generally. They speak of being nervous, of feeling upset, of seeming tense, and the like, and it has never seemed particularly important for them to use more clinically precise terminology. Where Psychologist may conceptualize anxiety in theoretical terms, Supervisor is more likely to regard such phenomena in behavioral terms and to think about them empirically. While Psychologist may have reason to be concerned with the unconscious sources of anxiety and his treatment strategies may depend, in some measure, upon diagnosis at that level, Supervisor tends more to deal with manifest anxiety and to "treat" it operationally. An especially sharp distinction between these specialists is generally that whereas Psychologist may have to contend with the antecedent, personal experiences in which the patient's present anxiety may have originated, it may be sufficient in most cases — this is one of clinical supervision's most difficult questions — for Supervisor to focus upon situational determinants. These determinants include elements in the immediate scholastic environment that trigger anxiety responses and possibilities existing in the immediate situation for managing anxiety, for coping with it, for deintensifying it if that seems necessary, and for converting it into forms of productive energy.

It is most important to note that in certain senses Supervisor's job, in this connection, is not intellectually or technically easier than Psychologist's. His problems of understanding and of treatment are likely to be extremely complex. The point is rather that Supervisor's clinical functioning may not demand the same background of substantive knowledge as Psychologist's.

Some examples of the serious difficulties with which the supervisor is confronted are: (1) those difficulties associated with determining the intensity of expressed anxiety and the question of what it should imply: to stop, to go on, to deal with feelings directly, to depersonalize the issues being addressed — that is, of what differences such anxiety should make, if any, for supervision; (2) those difficulties of identifying which of the manifold stimuli operating at any moment in supervision are affecting Teacher's anxiety; (3) those difficulties related to recognizing whether one's own behavior is being governed rationally or by psychological stress at any particular moment; and (4) the difficulties of separating one's own feelings from the supervisee's — of determining, in other words, whether the teacher's apparent tension or its absence is what it appears to be or is a projection of the supervisor's own mental condition instead.

As in the therapist's case, Supervisor must be able to handle the problem of how to translate moment-to-moment "diagnostic" insights into appropriate supervisory behavior. Again, it seems true that while Supervisor's interpretations and techniques are somewhat different from Psychologist's, they are nevertheless technically difficult to master. Although it may be different, it must certainly be as complicated for Supervisor to focus upon how Teacher is responding to him, qua Supervisor, as it would be for Therapist to deal with how the patient relates to him, qua "father."

The purpose here in comparing psychological and supervisory practice in these terms stems primarily from assumptions made by many supervision students in the past, namely, that because supervision is "superficial" (in comparison to psychotherapy, for example), it is consequently an easy clinical profession. Not so. If clinical supervision is superficial in any real sense, that is the sense in which it deals chiefly with current experience rather than with archaic childhood experiences, it is more committed to phenomenological models of behavior than to Freudian ones, and, in a majority of cases, supervisees manifest the problems of mentally healthy people (they are no more nor less crazy than the rest of us) rather than problems of pathological intensity. When all is said, however, those problems of existence left to supervision are rarely simple ones, and supervisors would be mistaken to view their practice, their requirements of knowledge and technical proficiency, or themselves as something elementary and uncomplicated. If anything, Supervisor's work may be harder than Therapist's because of the paucity in his or her training of theoretical models by which to make human behavior intelligible and because of certain self-imposed professional limits. By and large, Supervisor's clientele stops short at the threshold of emotional disorder. It behooves the clinical supervisor to concentrate on basically strong, intelligent, and well-functioning teachers, instead of attempting to "save" professionally marginal personnel. Supervisor's successes will be relatively undramatic compared to those of the hospital psychiatrist.

It was originally conceived that because clinical supervisors would not ordinarily be trained in psychological counseling, and because clinical supervision has a unique disciplinary identity and is something different fom counseling, and because, in any event, supervision cannot ordinarily provide the protections of counseling, it should therefore be employed to treat superficial behaviors and to treat on a superficial level. That is, supervision should only attempt to modify surface behaviors, which predictably would be amenable to change, and should not attempt to affect Teacher's "underlying identity" despite the certainty that no matter how seemingly superficial, all behaviors are expressions of that identity. The only touble with these precepts is that the supervision they generate fails to work in most cases, and the assumptions they incorporate about human behavior and human change are substantially false. It is, incidentally, interesting to observe that because of their fear and abhorrence of any practice that smacks of "amateur psychologizing," some of clinical supervision's chief proponents persevere in this belief (in superficial supervision of superficial behaviors) despite overwhelming evidence that it is untenable.

Experience has confirmed that supervision cannot live by substance alone, that its success is every bit as contingent upon the manner in which it operates as it is upon the issues it includes. It is just not enough in most cases to tell Teacher what is wrong and what is right in his or her teaching and what to do about it (as if anyone were really likely to know such things). When all supervision does is to focus upon specific technical elements of the teaching performance, its effects often do not change the overall quality of the teaching. What generally happens is that one "symptom" gets exchanged for another; as one faulty pattern is brought under control, another emerges to take its place, and the general character of the teaching does not change significantly. What we have learned is that it is not enough for the supervisor to be right, and that it is often self-defeating, as already noted, to treat teaching as though it were somehow disembodied and independent of the teacher doing it.

Sometimes Supervisor becomes involved in futile relationships. Most of the time, although he has established useful relationships, the problems of teaching and learning and understanding and modifying behavior with which he must deal are awesomely complex, and, in either case, if Supervisor is likely to constitute any kind of menace, it is when he takes an uncomplicated view of himself and of his practice.

Let us turn now to the question of method, namely, of general techniques for selecting patterns for treatment. How does Supervisor decide which teaching patterns are likely to be treatable and which are likely to be refractory to supervision? One elegantly straightforward method is to ask. Although one can readily imagine many problems in this method, Supervisor may, nevertheless, invite Teacher to choose among issues with which the Supervisor is prepared to deal as a result of analysis and planning. This technique, incidentally, represents one possible strategy for "full analysis," a special variation of the basic model of clinical supervision that we will examine later on.

For the present, let us imagine a sequence of supervision in which, for one reason or another, Supervisor has the primary responsibility for planning what to treat, so that we can glimpse some of the methods available. Perhaps the first step should be to estimate whether a given problem (embodied by a specific pattern or set of patterns) is likely to be too hard, intellectually, for Teacher to comprehend. One tends, in time, to develop a feeling for the level of conceptual complexity at which Teacher generally treats problems of practice and an afterimage of the species of past problems that have been handled productively and those that have not. This is not to suggest that one should not deliberately aim to strengthen Teacher's capacity for conceptualizing tough problems or that supervisors should steer clear of issues that seemed intellectually unmanageable in the past. It is to say that of all the predictions that Supervisor must make in order to judge "accessibility," those relating to whether a problem is too hard or not will probably be the most valid. Subjectively, at least, it has seemed that way.

Particularly in the early days of a supervisory relationship, before Supervisor has been able to collect many data or to form strong impressions of this kind, "shotgunning" can simplify selection on his criterion. Supervisor may, in other words, risk introducing a problem because even though he cannot predict, precisely, the conceptual level at which Teacher will treat it, he determines, nevertheless, that the problem permits conceptualization at various levels, almost any one of which could be useful for supervisory purposes. In this context, "method" is, first of all, an active awareness of selection on a criterion of logical complexity and, second, the acts of (1) analyzing the pattern (problem, issue) itself in such terms; (2) analyzing one's collected perceptions of Teacher, in these terms; and (3) estimating whether problem and Teacher seem made for each other, with as much precision as possible. Given that high-level precision is unlikely, Supervisor will generally deal in probabilities — namely, the probability that Teacher's range of conceptual behavior and the problem's range of productive conceptualizations will overlap.

The less stereotyped Supervisor's impressions of Teacher's intellectual behavior are, and the more versatile he is in understanding the significance of teaching patterns at multiple levels of complexity, the more likely is Supervisor to confront Teacher with issues on which he may get some mileage. Intuition obviously represents a large element of Supervisor's work in this connection, but experience suggests that intuitive processes can be sharpened and educated to some degree by deliberate effort and practice.

Having decided that in the absence of emotional interference, some pattern will probably not be too difficult for Teacher to handle, Supervisor moves on to other considerations. He may try to ascertain the quality and degree of emotional loading that the pattern in question or that the process of examining that pattern may have for Teacher, if any. His assessments of emotional loading will generally be in relationship to anxiety — that is, to his predictions of whether a problem is likely to produce "too much" anxiety for Teacher to be effectively treatable at the moment. From a more positive perspective, he may also select patterns that, he predicts, will provide emotional income for Teacher to treat, patterns whose identification and treatment are likely to be rewarding. Although it is more easily said than done, another process in which Supervisor may engage at this stage is to scan his own feelings and motives for selecting any pattern in particular and his own tendencies to choose or to avoid, to reward, or to punish, and to rationalize his decisions.

Most of the time, Supervisor operates from empirical data. He recalls, in effect, past instances of Teacher's apparent anxiety in supervision and tries to discover similarities and differences between the substantive content and supervisory processes that occurred in former incidents and those that would occur if he broached the pattern in question in the forthcoming conference. He tries to recall whether similar problems or processes have forced Teacher into defensive behavior in the past.

As he makes decisions about issues to address, especially delicate ones, Supervisor must examine his own motives: "Do I want to punish this guy for doing something I disapprove of (in which case I will deliberately raise issues that I know will upset him)? Do I want to avoid this issue because I am afraid to be confronted by anxiety? Do I fasten on this issue because, somehow or other, Teacher's behavior sets off some strong, personal discomfort in me? Have I good reasons to believe that Teacher's ability to modify this pattern is greater now than it seemed before? Am I likely to be kidding myself when I rationalize that although this issue could upset Teacher, nevertheless his ultimate reward will be very great indeed if he discovers his ability to overcome his anxiety and to master a difficult change in his teaching behavior?"

To predict emotional loading, Supervisor might also refer to normative data, that is, to his past experiences in supervising many teachers. He might recall, for example, that on almost every occasion when he confronted teachers with evidence of sarcastic behavior toward students, they either registered expressions of surprised hurt; or claimed that they were only joking and meant no harm; or claimed that although such behavior might seem like sarcasm to an outsider, the pupils had become accustomed to it and accepted it; or claimed that among adolescents, sarcasm was an accepted mode of expressing affection and respect; or enunciated some other, equally hopeful, denial. If past experience of this kind suggested that the issue almost always provoked anxiety and defensive behavior in supervision, Supervisor might reasonably expect the same quality of response (although not necessarily) from his present supervisee, even in the absence of relevant data from their particular relationship.

As a more familiar example, if teachers generally have displayed anxiety when Supervisor has questioned their mastery of the substantive content they were teaching, he might logically anticipate similar responses in the future. In such a case, Supervisor would not have to be thinking in psychologically elaborate terms in order to have picked up such signals. His empirical data and the generalizations they generated might be relatively innocent of theory. This is not to say, of course, that recourse to theory would not be helpful.

In a somewhat more complicated manner, Supervisor must often decide among patterns that incorporate strengths and weaknesses simultaneously and toward which Teacher's feelings are likely to be ambivalent. The existence of bivariate patterns sometimes introduces great difficulty and confusion into the task of selecting on a criterion of emotional loading and into the supervisor's attempts to predict which stimuli will be anxiety-producing. Supervisor's general approach, in this context, is to employ whatever empirical, normative, or theoretical information is at his disposal to predict how threatening any given confrontation is likely to be to Teacher, what quality and measure of emotional support Teacher might require to deal constructively with the issues involved, and then to decide whether he is competent to provide such support should it seem urgent to address hot issues.

Prior assessments of this kind should focus upon what Supervisor already knows about Teacher, about their previous supervisory interactions, and about himself, in relevant terms. Predictions may arise from both experiential and theoretical knowledge. Even without extensive experience in supervision, Supervisor can frequently predict what will repel or attract or hurt or scare on the basis of his examined, personal experience of human beings. In this sense, Supervisor's personal history may represent a potential resource rather than simply a set of behavioral patterns that must be overridden.

In similar fashion, history of experience as a supervisor — we have already noted that past experience can generate blinding stereotypes — may sensitize Supervisor to forms of defensive behavior that arise commonly among supervisees who, especially when they are new to clinical supervision, are likely to feel threatened by it. One simply picks up images of defensive "types," that is, of common defensive ploys, that seem to be perfectly valid. Of course, one problem with stereotypes generally is that supervisees really *do* feel that way. Another problem is that one tends to assume implicitly that similar stimuli require similar responses, and it can easily follow that Supervisor begins to treat metaphors instead of people. Nevertheless, one feature of Supervisor's method for planning what to do (or not to do) with potentially threatening material consists of consulting past experiences with similar dilemmas. Another is to consult his or her "catalog" of defensive behaviors that have emerged in other supervisory relationships. Here are some examples:

1. Teacher A agrees with everything Supervisor says. In fact, Teacher agrees so readily that it is possible to turn Teacher about through diametrically opposed positions.
    SUPERVISOR: . . . so one thing to consider is whether the kids understood your directions. . . .
    TEACHER: Yes, I'm sure that my directions were perfectly clear.
    SUPERVISOR: But when you asked, "Are there any questions about what to do?" almost all of the children raised their hands.
    TEACHER: Yes, they seemed confused; they didn't understand.
    SUPERVISOR: But then you said, "Hands down!" and the children apparently were able to get to work without any trouble.
    TEACHER: Yes, I'm sure they understood.

2. Teacher B consistently disagrees with almost everything and continually attempts to attribute problems to Supervisor.
    SUPERVISOR: . . . and I was worried that so much noise and disorder might be hazardous, you know, if it were a real fire instead of just a drill.
    TEACHER: Well, didn't you tell me yesterday that one of the things wrong with my teaching is that I give all the directions and the children don't make enough of their own decisions? I thought that's what you wanted.
    SUPERVISOR: Yes, but . . .

3. Teacher C throws up a verbal barrage talking so much about so many things that there is rarely enough time to address specific problems thoroughly.

4. Teacher D, in a similar manner, introduces red herrings; problems that seem urgent but which, because they are always focused away from the Teacher's own behavior, effectively preclude supervision of salient teaching behavior.
    SUPERVISOR: . . . so we might try to put ourselves in Margaret's place and ask, well, uh, how would you feel if you had prepared a long report like that and had cut out pictures from magazines and drawn diagrams — and then, when you presented this, the teacher sat at the desk filling out the register and the children were whispering and not paying attention and . . .
    TEACHER: Yes, uh — just before I forget, you know — I just don't know what I'm going to do about the acoustics in that room. It's really terrible! The chairs and desks all squeak, and that metal ceiling makes it like teaching in a barrel. Even when they're quiet, there's a lot of noise going on.

5. Teacher E, a professional old-timer, tries to put Supervisor on the defensive.

   TEACHER: Um, yes. Uh, by the way — I'm curious — have you ever done any classroom teaching?

6. Before anything else can happen, Teacher F begins to deprecate self and teaching in every possible manner. Supervisor is disarmed and not only abandons the issues he or she planned to treat, but offers reassurances and flatteries in spite of the fact that, in his or her judgment, the teaching in question was not very successful. Some supervisors are able to resist this approach. With them, Teacher F does not waste words, but merely cries silently. Should Supervisor be able to resist even this degree of heartrending behavior he or she will shortly develop a reputation of being a monster.

By developing and consulting a catalog of such behaviors. Supervisor accumulates an ever-expanding bank of manifestations of anxiety and defensiveness in supervision, both generally and in relation to specific teachers with whom he works. Supervisor must take care, on the one hand, to resist stereotyping leading to the same expectations of all teachers who display similar behavioral patterns. It might be true, for example, that while Teacher A's rapid, breathless talking reflects pronounced anxiety and represents a means for avoiding supervisory analysis, Teacher B's abundant verbal activity reflects unusual fluency and intellectual energy and, if it expresses anxiety at all, derives from a relatively superficial and easily overridden anxiety associated with periods of silence during conversation.

On the other hand, in this context his catalog of memories should serve Supervisor by sensitizing him to the symptomatic meaning that supervisory behavior may carry. In other words, such experience should correct assessments of human behavior that record only at face value and that fail to detect implicit feelings that are being expressed: Supervisor should develop some special capacity for sensing discomfort. By collecting and examining such experiences, Supervisor should become progressively less susceptible to disarmament by defensive novelties in his supervisees' behavior and less likely to be toppled into defensive postures of his own because he is surprised or frightened or confused by what Teacher does. By the same token, his repertoire of supportive and useful responses should be enriched by such experiences. Although we have stressed anxiety, these thoughts are equally applicable to the problem of sensing positive emotions. Supervisor should know what kinds of experiences have spelled success and mastery and pleasure for Teacher previously in order to amplify present and future opportunities for Teacher to collect positive rewards.

He must at least recognize, as he selects patterns for supervision, that when Teacher is hurting enough or is angry enough, Supervisor is not likely to succeed in any constructive purpose if he blithely ignores Teacher's condition and continues to follow his plan at all costs. He must believe that emotional interference can easily obscure substantive technical issues and can obstruct rational thinking. Consequently, Supervisor must alert himself to emotional valences at the strategy stage even though he might prefer not to.

He must recognize, pragmatically, that to persevere insensitively in the prosecution of "important" issues may be self-defeating if Teacher learns incidentally, as a result of Supervisor's behavior, that Supervisor is punishing and that supervision is hurtful. Once such a process has begun, it becomes progressively more difficult to reverse it and increasingly unlikely that Teacher will gain the technical proficiency that Supervisor wishes for him. In some cases it has appeared that teachers modified their behavior primarily to get rid of supervisors they hated. To get Supervisor off one's back, however, is an incentive that seems inherently damaging and evidence of supervisory failure.

Depending on his background of study and training, Supervisor may also make predictions of emotional loading based upon general theories of human behavior. For example, he might generally suspect that because human beings so frequently experience conflict in relation to hostile feelings, examination of teachers' expressions (and repressions) of hostility toward their pupils would probably evoke considerable feeling in supervision. Or, given that "authority relationships" present emotional difficulties so often in our culture, Supervisor might anticipate that to treat Teacher's role qua "authority figure" in the classroom, or his own (Supervisor's) role of authority in supervision would probably not be emotionally innocuous.

It should not be surprising to discover that feelings of anxiety often accompany explicit attention to such issues as personal coldness or aloofness, tendencies to infantilize pupils, tendencies to mother them, tendencies to insult them, seductive teaching behavior, scapegoating, favoritism, and the like, simply because of how psychologically basic the feelings that underlie such behavior are likely to be. In other words, one might reasonably suppose that when the issue in question incorporates feelings and behaviors that occupy prominent places in Teacher's personality or carry moral connotations or seem, somehow, related to taboos of the culture or of the scholastic subculture, Teacher's response (though perfectly normal) may involve substantial emotional labor and may generate palpable anxiety.

At this point, let us recapitulate some of the methods available to Supervisor for selecting patterns on the criterion of emotional loading. In short, he or she should determine as far as possible whether an issue (or process) is likely to be so threatening that Teacher will become too anxious to work effectively or will spend himself in defensive behavior instead of analysis and planning for the next episode of teaching. He or she should, additionally, recognize teaching patterns whose examination would probably contribute to Teacher's real and experienced success. As a supervisor, one should also give some attention to one's own motives for selecting or rejecting the pattern in question and one's readiness to deal with its emotional consequences, in either direction.

To make such predictions, Supervisor will consult his past experiences with Teacher. This past represents his first source of data under most circumstances. He may also refer to his general experiences in supervision, to his general knowledge of human beings, and to whatever relevant theory he knows. He may also review the history of his personal responses to Teacher and may try to identify motives to treat or not to treat anything in particular that arises principally from his own past pleasures and frustrations in that relationship. After having examined teaching patterns in this fashion, Supervisor should consciously formulate rationales for introducing specific patterns and, particularly when such patterns are likely to have a high "anxiety quotient," should scrutinize his rationales as objectively as possible. Such rationales, incidentally, will generally be related to supervisory goals.

Supervisor should, additionally, be sensitive to Teacher's overall psychological condition, that is, irrespective of emotional loadings attached to specific teaching patterns. One tends to have good days and bad days (or months or seasons); periods in which one is strong and periods in which one feels fragile; periods of depression, of heightened energy, of fatigue, of ambitiousness, of dullness, of alertness, of uncertainty; small, but often decisive temperamental shifts, any of which may arise from circumstances of living that have no direct relationship to professional supervision but can, nonetheless, generate propitious or unfavorable conditions for supervision. Such sensitivity should be primarily for the sake of making better guesses about whether any given issue is likely at this point in time to get off the ground or not, for deciding problems of pacing, or even for deciding whether supervision should be undertaken at all.

Analogously, a good coach must be able to recognize when his player is in a slump or when he is hung over, in order to regulate his regimen of training appropriately. Overpractice can be dangerous, while underpractice is usually ineffective. Under ordinary circumstances it is neither appropriate nor necessary for Coach to begin an inquiry on the effects of Slugger's childhood deprivations. While Teacher's marital adjustment may be none of Supervisor's business, it is very much his business to sense any degree of hopelessness arising from that context that may be psychologically pervasive and may undermine Teacher's general morale. Some of us compartmentalize emotions less effectively than others.

Again, it does not necessarily follow that because Teacher is perceived to be in a slump he or she ought to be left alone, treated gently, or not supervised at all. Sometimes, tender loving care will turn the trick and will recover Teacher for supervisory purposes. At other times and with other individuals, work that is harder than ever seems more therapeutic than soft music. Supervisor must get to know, largely by cautious trial and error, who his customers are and how individual supervisees are likely to be affected by various approaches during troubled periods. Supervisor can neither ignore the facts of Teacher's life nor employ categorical, surefire remedies for all spiritual ailments.

Teacher's expressed desires to deal or not to deal with specific patterns or problems should also figure in Supervisor's determination of whether specific issues are accessible for treatment or not. Unless positive reasons exist for employing other strategies, a good rule is to treat what Teacher wants to treat and avoid what Teacher wants to avoid. Should Supervisor elect to treat some problem that Teacher has explicitly rejected, then he must, ordinarily, work on Teacher's feelings about the thing before moving into the problem directly. No matter how strongly Supervisor may feel about it, if Teacher isn't also turned on to it, then Supervisor might just as well talk to himself. When Supervisor feels obliged to select some pattern for treatment that Teacher has formerly vetoed, he must also recognize Teacher's negative feelings, his resistance, as a prior problem and must understand the consequences that follow for strategy — namely, that it must include plans for working through Teacher's feelings.

Finally, in simple terms, Supervisor should be able to predict whether any given pattern is likely to seem essentially technical or essentially personal in Teacher's frame of reference. When Teacher has proved to be the kind of person for whom everything seems highly personal, then Supervisor must decide whether he will be able to separate technical issues from their personal concomitants in any substantial measure or, if not, whether he is capable of examining the whole ball of wax in order to achieve technical refinements. In some cases this might even become a problem of whether clinical supervision is possible at all.

This does not mean that in order to be supervised, Teacher must, somehow, be able to separate himself from his products and to treat his patterns of professional behavior as though they were someone else's. Nor does clinical supervision aim simply to modify behaviors as though they were disembodied. On the contrary, it is a supervision of whole and integrated people. It sometimes seems, however, that if Teacher is psychologically incapable of any momentary separation (that is, if he cannot muster any functional objectivity worth noting and if, in effect, every question, every criticism, and every expressed doubt feels like an attack upon his soul), then there is probably not much hope for supervision, as we generally conceptualize it, to be of much use. Problems of this kind will be illustrated later.

FEWNESS

Once sifting has yielded a residue of salient and supposedly treatable patterns, it often happens that too much remains to include in any single supervision conference. In such cases, how can Supervisor decide what to discard, at least for the time being?

The following principles of selection, presented here in an essentially random order, may be useful. It should be noted that, depending upon the specific contingencies in any situation, any number of hierarchical arrangements are possible among them. You will notice that some of these criteria have already been examined in the contexts of saliency and accessibility:

Principle of data
Principle of subsumption
Principle of sameness or difference
Principle of loading
Principle of time
Principle of energy
Principle of sequence

Principle of data

If Supervisor has clearer or more abundant data to document some patterns than others, he may select those patterns for treatment, all other things being equal. Especially when specific patterns are very clear in the data, when the effects of such patterns are clearly demonstrable, and when, consequently, it becomes relatively unnecessary for Supervisor to authenticate their existence or to explain their effect lengthily, it can represent a real economy for such patterns to be selected in favor of more ambiguous ones.

Principle of subsumption

Supervisor may select those patterns (Class I) that subsume other patterns (Class II) either in the sense that Class II patterns represent behavioral components of Class I patterns or in the sense that the presumed significance of the latter class is incorporated by the broader significance of the former. On some occasions, this method can be reversed — namely, when Supervisor's strategy is to build from small pieces to large mosaics, that is, from patterns of lesser significance toward a synthesis of relatively greater significance. In concrete terms, if Teacher's style seems massively egocentric, Supervisor may attempt to arrive at that construction by identifying specific patterns of egocentric teaching and by developing the pertinent generalization by his own effort. Or if Teacher's style is essentially charismatic, Supervisor may focus on short illustrative episodes from the teaching in order to give Teacher similar opportunities.

The basic reasoning for such an approach could be that Teacher is more likely to accept the existence of small, specific elements of his behavior than that of large, pervasive characteristics. Or Teacher might, predictably, feel less overwhelmed or threatened by examination of small parts than by that of large ones. Or it might seem more manageable, operationally, for Teacher to work on modifying specific teaching patterns than for him to grapple with pervasive stylistic tendencies.

Subsumptive relationships, in other words, can be used in either direction. Logical considerations might indicate selection of superordinate patterns: psychological considerations might indicate an opposite approach. Generally, unless special reasons exist for beginning with secondary patterns, it is most efficient to employ the principle of subsumption to isolate incorporative patterns for treatment. Supervisor must be ready, however, to relinquish his logical model in order to make psychological accommodations that may be necessary for clinical effectiveness.

Principle of Sameness or Difference

For any given supervision conference, Supervisor may select patterns relating to some common category of teaching (for example, all patterns concerning classroom logistics) or may deliberately select patterns from different categories (for example, logistics, questioning, and rewards). Sameness may be desirable if Supervisor wants to develop a concentrated focus on some single dimension of Teacher's behavior. Difference may be desirable if Supervisor wants, deliberately, to broaden the base of discussion or to prevent an overemphasis of supervision in any specific category.

Sometimes it seems best to keep things open. Sometimes it seems best to home in, microscopically, with the sharpest possible degree of resolution. Sometimes Teacher needs relief and gets relief by shifting about from one set of problems to another. Sometimes Teacher feels disoriented or frustrated by such shifting and prefers to deal with one thing at a time, until he feels mastery in its connection. Sometimes Teacher functions best when he has choices to make. At other times he feels best not to be bothered by choices. Sometimes specific patterns achieve special clarity when they are treated together with related patterns. Sometimes problems become individually clearer when they are treated concurrently with very different problems.

Decisions of this order must generally be altered from teacher to teacher and in Teacher's supervision from time to time. Even though one cannot prescribe, categorically, either sameness or difference as a better principle of selection, the principle itself, used flexibly, is a very handy one.

Principle of Loading

Depending on Teacher, patterns may be selected or rejected either because of their predicted emotional loading or in spite of it. It is usually best to avoid treating anything that seems likely to make Teacher very anxious. Sometimes, however, one might purposely attempt to jolt him or her into a quantum leap toward greater involvement or lesser certainty or higher energy. Sometimes — especially when there are strong reasons for predicting successful outcomes — one can deliberately open an emotion-laden issue because Teacher seems right on the verge of resolving it and just ready to reap some reward. If it seems that such loading would interfere with technical progress, reject the pattern in question. If the opposite seems likely, include it. Supervisor's problem is not so much to eschew strong feelings as it is to recognize when emotionality can serve Teacher's interests in supervision and when it is likely to operate against them. Certainly there must be legitimate opportunities in supervision to rejoice, and joy is something to be felt, not simply analyzed. And certainly there must be room in such a complicated business as teaching, to experience frustration; and, as we know from personal experience, that can either be good or bad.

In any event, although such generalizations are never completely valid, one intuits a relationship between loading and fewness, namely, that fewness may not accomplish its objective — the purpose is to avoid saturation — if each of the few patterns selected is fraught with stressful feeling for Teacher. After patterns have been screened on saliency and accessibility, good or bad decisions on fewness can tell the story. Emotionally significant issues that might have been treated productively can be irretrievably lost if they are lumped together in the same conference in too great a number or in an unfelicitous sequence.

Principle of Time

Supervisor should have some reasonable idea of how long it will take to treat specific patterns in the conference. Among the factors that can be used to determine the amount of time that should be set aside to deal with it are: (1) whether or not Teacher has expressed positive or negative motives to deal with a particular pattern, (2) how fluent Supervisor feels in his ability to explicate the pattern, (3) how fluently Teacher is likely to address it, (4) how logically or emotionally complex or simple the pattern seems to be, (5) how sharply or distractedly Teacher happens to be functioning at the moment, (6) how rewarding or innocuous or threatening the pattern may prove to be, and (7) how many data will be required to illustrate the pattern in question.

Common sense tells us that fewness, being a relative thing, can turn out to be manyness if the few patterns selected are each too time-consuming to be handled together in a single conference. Although supervisory issues tend to carry over from sequence to sequence of supervision, it often seems that some points are better than others for terminating a conference. It sometimes appears that even intermediate closure should occur at some special juncture of inquiry, not just anyplace. One problem, consequently, in selecting on the criterion fewness, is to project times and to make decisions accordingly.

Lest this seem altogether magical, we can think of parallel examples from teaching. It may be that the children are engaged in some social studies unit that spans several weeks. Nevertheless, Teacher is likely to consider timing as he plans each day's activity. He is likely, in other words, to plan his lessons so that the pupils formulate some question by the end of Tuesday's work, and discover some set of generalizations on Thursday, and define some relevant problems during Friday's session for which they will prepare problem-solving strategies to present on Monday. Such planning need not be rigid or homogeneous and, without these defects, might spell the difference in whether the pupils experience sufficient structure to maintain focus or not. Similarly, good planning in the use of conference time can spell the difference in benefits to the teacher.

Principle of Energy

Logical complexity, emotional loading, clarity of data, and the like will influence the amount of mental energy required to prosecute specific issues in supervision. Recognizing this variable, Supervisor should avoid the likelihood that either member will become prematurely fatigued, as he selects on fewness. Once again, past experiences supervising Teacher represent the best index for judging outcomes of this kind.

Principle of Sequence

Whether or not the purposes of fewness are achieved can depend upon the order in which selected patterns are broached in the conference. The general idea in this regard is that if, for example, patterns are ordered so that clear, logical transitions can be made from one context to the next, then, because such a conference should prove less exhausting and take less time than if such transitions were nonexistent, the goals of fewness might be more readily achieved in one sequence than in another.

Supervisory transitions or the organizing principles behind sequences need not necessarily be substantive. They might, for example, be qualitative, progressing from essentially weak patterns to basically strong ones. In any event, we find that in most instances it is helpful to tell Teacher at the outset whether the sequence of issues to be broached in the conference is ordered randomly or according to some deliberate organizational rationale, to free him or her from the necessity of having to guess about such things. Such a simple statement as "There are a few things I thought we might get into, and it doesn't make any difference in what order we examine them" can save Teacher whatever energy might otherwise have been spent trying to sense the direction in which the conference was moving.

In this chapter, our principal question has been related to how Supervisor reduces his or her complete analysis of the observational data by selecting specific patterns to treat in the conference. Our discussion has proceeded as though Supervisor's strategy was being dictated primarily by the press of data, rather than by general goals. Given an analyzed body of behavioral data, we have suggested that selections should be based upon criteria of saliency, psychological accessibility, and fewness; we have offered some rationales for this model and some indication of how, generally, supervisors can perform for the work involved, that is, some description, at least, of what kinds of things they might think about when attempting to make such decisions. In the next chapter there will be included a discussion of goal setting and other bases for the decisions that are in fact made.

Chapter 8

ANALYSIS AND STRATEGY PART II: Problems and Elements

* **Problems of Analysis**
* **Problems of Strategy**
* **Setting Goals for the Selection of Supervisory Issues**
* **Additional Elements of Strategy**
* **Summary of Chapters 7 and 8**

PROBLEMS OF ANALYSIS

There is often no sharp distinction between problems of observation, which we reviewed in Chapter 6, and those of analysis. In fact, the latter frequently arise from the former. If, for the most part, observational problems tend to emanate from unconscious biases and perceptual selectivity, then problems of analysis are more likely to be errors of logical reasoning, errors based in cognitive activity consisting of erroneous assumptions, invalidly construed relationships, superficial organization of data, and plain bad guesses, particularly in relation to the children's actual experiences. We have already referred in Chapter 7 to a number of key problems of analysis, some of which need to be amplified. There are two principal problem areas in the context that generally overlap in relation to any given teaching pattern: problems of categorization and problems of evaluation.

We have noted that even after rigorous measures have been taken to protect the observer's objectivity, their effectiveness may be lost by the manner in which the data are treated. Reviewing some earlier statements, we recall that most processes of categorization are partly subjective, that categories are human inventions, and that people tend to reify various categories, especially those to which they have become accustomed. Some descriptive categories seem more amenable to objective application than others. For example, much of the time the classification of an element of teaching by the category "questioning" requires only an observation of grammatical structure. "Rewards" is somewhat more problematical: Definitions of "rewards" may vary and, irrespective of definition, the term itself is likely to carry implicit qualitative connotations that influence one's classificatory process. To employ categorical definitions of "positive" and "negative" rewards may represent a partial solution, but this is easier to adopt than to implement because we may tend to favor positive examples and to overlook negative ones.

It is sometimes hard to know whether one has discovered a behavioral pattern or not. One problem is that the supervisor may simply fail to recognize significant patterns in the teaching and consequently may wind up centering supervision on relatively unimportant issues. Failure to identify critical patterns may stem from their attenuation, from an absence of relevant constructs in the supervisor's professional frame of reference, from the possibility that supervisors perceive only tangential regularities rather than central ones, and so on. We may find parts without recognizing their relationships to more significant wholes. For example, supervisors may develop analyses of teaching in which they isolate "I" patterns (that is, patterns of teaching in the first person) but in which they fail to make a fundamental distinction: between "I's" that might incidentally have suggested unfortunate role definitions and "I's" that were perfectly appropriate because Teacher had been describing a personal experience (a language teacher's trip to a foreign country) that was completely relevant to the lesson.

One's appetite for closure and for answers often interferes with categorization by prompting one to stop thinking about a pattern once it has been classified and, in that manner, results in premature dismissal of patterns that might have been understood more significantly in connection with multiple categories. A similar problem consists of the tendency to discover likenesses and to generalize from such discoveries that what was found existing in certain instances truly exists in all instances.

Another issue requiring study is that distinctions between categorization and evaluation are frequently blurred in practice. When we find that each time a pupil has offered a response and the teacher replies, "Yes, thank you; very good," we may call this pattern "stereotyped" and may classify such examples under "stereotyped rewards." Almost certainly, however, that very classification implies a value judgment as well as an application of certain formal criteria. In connection with such an example, we generally do not advance to the next step of analysis by asking whether, in the case before us, the existence of such stereotyping was good or bad.

One's appetites for closure, uniformity, and simplicity also create tendencies to evaluate teaching patterns in one dimension. One typically avoids ambiguous classifications and value judgments, and variables in the teaching performance tend to be regarded as strong or weak, good or bad, but not commonly enough as strong-and-weak, or good-and-bad — that is, as $\pm$ patterns. Many supervisors tend, additionally, to avoid reverse interpretations and to avoid playing devil's advocate to themselves except at special moments when they set out consciously to do so. One effect of this condition, to which we have already referred, is that supervisors generally hang with a value judgment once it has been formulated and commonly do not consider contrasting interpretations after their shutter has clicked initially.

And again, recognition behavior seems more prevalent than creative, synthesizing behavior; and supervisors seem to project known configurations onto ambiguous data more naturally than to discover novelties or unique patterns among them. We generally take normative views of human behavior and employ normative strategies for modifying it. In analysis of observational data, one tends to find what one has found previously; one tends to recognize patterns one has encountered before; one tends to classify the data by categories with which one is familiar. Being neither good nor bad, such behavior simply reflects laws of the mind without whose existence the mental apparatus could hardly function.

One often relies on consensus for ensuring the validity of interpretations, that is, upon agreement among a jury of analysts; and although consensual validation undoubtedly does provide some measure of safety, we cannot even then be sure we have correctly identifed the pattern. At critical moments in analysis and in the remaining stages of the supervisory sequence, it is almost always more reasonable to concede uncertainties than to assert truths, despite the feeling of conviction by which certainties are generally accompanied.

If it is likely that analyses are affected by projective processes and by prior sets, then it is a certainty that the data are distorted by any process of condensation. We must be careful when we reduce or contract our data: the final product may be unrecognizable because of differences in scale. For example, we think of the earth as a rough-hewn, oblate lump whose complexion is marred by high mountains and deep trenches, rather like an ugly fruit. We are told, however, that if a model of the earth were constructed to correspond to the size of a billiard ball, and if every surface feature were reduced proportionally, the resulting object would be virtually as smooth as a billiard ball. To make matters even more complicated, the reductions of clinical analysis are more like sculpting than like shrinking. Supervisor streamlines his or her data by eliminating factors from them. We are reminded of the conundrum:

QUESTION: How do you sculpt an elephant?
ANSWER: You take a stone and carve away everything that does not look like an elephant.

The "stone" with which Supervisor begins — namely, raw data — will certainly be transformed by analysis. The problem is how closely the material will resemble itself when the analysis is done. Will it still be characteristic of the lesson originally observed, or will it look more like an elephant?

Decisions affecting which data included in the final analysis and which are not arise partly from judgments that Supervisor makes concerning what is important and partly from his or her perceptual capacities. One cannot include patterns that one cannot see. Since parts of the teaching will be examined in the conference rather than the whole lesson, it is sufficient to preserve parts of the data as perfectly as possible. Addtionally, it is good practice to keep even the discarded parts near at hand (namely, the full observation notes) during the conference. This can be good insurance against teachers' protests that supervisors' analyses are invalid because they treat components that have been "taken out of context." In the opposite direction, teachers and their supervisors often sense, correctly, that although the lesson, as a totality, failed to achieve its intended purposes, it nevertheless included episodes of teaching that were technically potent and momentarily effective, vis à vis those same purposes. Keeping the notes for a while will help to confirm that sense.

Many problems of analysis revolve around ontological questions, problems of knowing what truly exists. To deal with them, supervisors must summon all the more energy to examine themselves, to maintain objectivity, and to compensate for whatever cosmic or personal interference operates to undermine the integrity of their work. Several administrative and logistical strategies exist to fortify professionl self-discipline — for example, team teaching, in which group supervision may be undertaken — and these can be very helpful. However, in the end our success depends on the magnitude of commitment and skill and energy manifested by its *individual* practitioners. Good clinical supervision represents a way of living, professionally, and a state of mind that one either values or does not value. We value it, and we believe that those who also do will manifest such skills and commitment.

PROBLEMS OF STRATEGY

Besides employing such criteria as saliency, fewness, and the like, and following such methodological guidelines as we have considered, clinical supervisors operate within a broader framework of objectives. In addition to selecting substantive issues and establishing significant relationships among them, we as supervisors also consider a range of supervisory processes as we plan the conference, and work toward ends determined by what Teacher wants, does, and is, in certain respects, and by Teacher's own system of professional values. As we have noted, clinical supervisors aim for both technical and process goals. Our problem: What are such goals like, and how are they formulated?

SETTING GOALS FOR THE SELECTION OF SUPERVISORY ISSUES

Our clinical supervision will have a substantive technical content — though not necessarily at every point in a cycle — and consequently it is appropriate for us to frame content goals for the conference. Ideally, such goals will be stated in three sets of terms: as the new or sharpened concepts that Teacher should acquire in supervision (cognitive outcomes); as the new or sharpened behaviors that Teacher should manifest as a result of supervision (behavioral outcomes); and as the specific level of mastery (criterion behavior) at which Teacher should perform in order for supervision to have achieved at least minimum success.

For example, in an observed lesson Teacher exhibited a pattern of naming specific pupils before asking a question: "Johnny, what is four times seven? Marlene, what happens when we round off this number to the nearest ten?" Having noted that every time Teacher called a name some of the other children proceeded to do other work even though the lesson was arithmetic, Supervisor decided that the class's attentiveness could be more certainly assured if Teacher reversed the sequence and asked the question before calling on any specific child to respond. The reasoning: "If the kids realize that they may be called upon anytime, then they'll be more likely to pay attention to questions than if they know in advance that the teacher won't call on them." The technical goal, in this case, is formulated as follows:

Conceptual Outcome. Teacher will understand why it might make better sense to state questions before identifying students to respond than after.
Behavioral outcome. Teacher will enunciate this reasoning during the conference and, in subsequent teaching, probably will demonstrate the technical modification in question.
Criterion Behavior. The frequency of today's questioning pattern in a subsequent lesson (assuming that lesson will be structured in essentially the same manner) will be sharply reduced. Since, in today's teaching, "pupil first" occurred in 70 percent of questions asked, that pattern will gradually decrease to a lower percent of the questions asked. (In other words, we decide, in this case, that when a certain degree of quantitative change is observed, this technical issue can be eliminated from further consideration in supervision. We may also decide that Teacher should determine the quantitative criterion for which to strive.)

Recognizing that Teacher is more than a computer and, for that reason, is likely to learn more from the supervision than the specific technical information being considered, we will formulate other goals relating to nontechnical learning outcomes that should result in the conference. Employing the notion of incidental learnings as we do in analyzing Teacher's teaching, we should plan our own behavior with an eye toward incidental effects it is likely to have upon Teacher. Rather than simply making sure that the agenda of technical points is covered in the conference, without concerning ourselves with the specific behaviors in which to engage to make them, we should formulate our strategy upon the premise that how we get where we're going is at least as important as what substantive learnings are achieved and that, in all likelihood, the quality of substantive learning will itself be partly a function of the supervisory processes we employ. Our strategy arises from the presuppositions that the supervisory processes employed (1) will affect the quality of Teacher's substantive technical learning and (2) may also affect Teacher's ideas and feelings about self, teaching, supervision, and the supervisor, for better or worse. Rather than leaving such learning to chance we attempt to bring what otherwise might be incidental learnings under deliberate control and, toward this end, formulate a set of process goals in addition to our content goals.

In either teaching or supervision, process goals can be conceptualized in the same terms as any other goals — namely, as cognitive outcomes, as behavioral outcomes, and in reference to some minimally acceptable criteria of mastery. In one sense, the process goals we formulate during Strategy will pertain to our own behavioral processes in the conference. Our process goals will pertain to intellectual and behavioral processes that ought to be established or refined or extinguished in the teacher's future practice.

Let us take a hypothetical example of how process goals may be stated. Having worked through several sequences of supervision with Teacher, we have begun to develop the impression that although Teacher has been generally alert and receptive, has seemingly understood the technical issue discussed, and has strengthened and extinguished various positive and negative teaching patterns respectively, he or she has generally moved in directions set in supervision rather than in self-directions. But in so doing, Teacher is also becoming — or has already become — an essentially dependent person. Instead of initiating his or her own issues and questions in supervision, Teacher waits expectantly for us to do so. This form of passivity is hardly surprising, for we have taught Teacher to behave this way. We have raised issues and have observed Teacher treat our issues, and the evidence seems to suggest that we have taught Teacher to expect that our job would be to teach and his or her job would be to learn — that Supervisor would be the active agent and Teacher the reactive agent in the supervisory process.

This disturbs us. As supervisors, we should help teachers to function more autonomously and not to increase their dependencies upon us. Supervision should not be a follow-the-leader type of exercise. Therefore we must try to reverse the pattern. This may not be an easy task, for it soon becomes clear that having never examined his or her own teaching systematically or developed skills for doing so, Teacher's ideas about what kinds of things to tackle and what lines of inquiry to follow are, initially, somewhat sparse. Should we let teachers set their own pace in supervision? Perhaps not. Since the supervisory process requires getting used to, teachers could learn new modes of behavior in supervision after the supervision has acquired some substance. We decide to lead in the early stages and then undertake the development of new supervisor-supervisee roles and relationships later on. Beef up the collection of working concepts first, and then do some worrying about our processes after we have become conceptually rich.

Even the most studiously calculated approaches in supervision can be tainted by rationalization and, knowing that, we should keep a constant weather eye on our motives, particularly in connection to decisions of the order that we are presently considering. Thus, perhaps in a majority of cases it is best to begin supervision with process goals, lest points of no return are passed before they are recognized.

Then we can begin letting go, begin reversing the proportions of initiative that we have exercised with Teacher. The process goal "self-initiated inquiry" can be formulated as follows:

Conceptual Outcome. Teacher will understand and accept self-initiation as a supervisory goal.

Behavioral Outcome. Teacher will take the initiative for structuring supervision conferences and for mapping the goals and methods for future sequences of supervision.

Criterion Behavior. Teacher will initiate some self-issues in supervision and progressively will set more problems and tasks until his or her command of the course we steer will be clearly established.

Let us try stating another process goal, "analytical tool skills":

Conceptual Outcome. Teacher will learn a prolific assortment of techniques for analyzing teaching behavior.

Behavioral Outcome. Teacher will demonstrate analytical versatility by identifying patterns in teaching, extrapolating issues from the observational data (audio or video tapes; observation notes), arranging problems in order of importance, urgency, treatability, and the like.

Criterion Behavior. Teacher's analyses will have logical consistency, will be based upon tenable hypotheses and interpretations, will consider contradictions in the data, will incorporate reasonable inferences, and will be susceptible to validation by the consensus of other competent analysts.

Note the absence of exactitude in the definitions of criterion behaviors above. Had our goal been for Teacher to learn to perform certain mathematical operations under certain, specified conditions, then in less ambiguous terms the evaluation criterion could have been expressed precisely as a test score — assuming, of course, that the test simulated those conditions under which the learner (Teacher) was originally supposed to have been able to perform the operations in question. Because the test of Teacher's learning in supervision is performance in subsequent teaching, it is difficult to conceptualize standard tests that could measure Teacher's learning with mathematical precision. Unlike simple mathematical problems, problems of instructional practice rarely, if ever, have solutions that are clearly right or wrong. Yet, recent research with observational analysis points us in certain directions that indicate those certain teaching behaviors/patterns that are more effective/conclusive to learning than others.

Experience suggests that criterion behavior is a tenable concept in supervision and that, even failing mathematical precision, criteria of mastery are enunciable and usable. In our first illustration, "behavioral outcome" names the kind of behavior in which the teacher should engage. The criterion behavior introduces quantitative considerations ("progressively . . . more") that, though lacking precision, at least incorporate a criterion of increasing frequency. In the second illustration, although quantitative increases may be implicit, what distinguishes the statement of criterion behavior from that of behavioral outcomes is that whereas the latter describes categories of behavior that should appear, the former introduces value judgments (for example, "logical, tenable, reasonable, rich") relating to such behavior and validation by a professional. If disagreements can arise over quantitative outcomes, then disputes over quality are even more probable. Consensus can be established for the wrong reasons and failure to achieve consensus can exist for good reasons, and so on. Although such criteria may lack experimental rigor, they are nevertheless valuable in that at least they define evaluative contexts in which productive inquiry and professional incentives may arise.

In either case, that is, when either qualitative or quantitative criteria are employed, Supervisor and Teacher must have some means for judging how much change is enough, what degree of frequency or what level of quality suffices. Sometimes "enough" can be determined by testing. If some teaching pattern is seemingly associated with some mean level of achievement by the pupils (or by the achievement level of some specific pupil) and if that pattern's modification can be correlated with improved pupil scores, then even though it might be impossible to prove a direct cause-effect relationship between the modified teaching and the pupils' performance, the logical or theoretical probability of some such connection might justify an assumption of cause, at least for the time being. Should future events appear contradictory, then future opportunities may be exploited for experimentation in which the modified teaching pattern is held constant and other variables are manipulated.

Sometimes the sufficiency of change can be determined by testing the pupils and sometimes not. When testing is germane, its reliability and degree of relevancy will vary. Criterion behaviors must frequently be defined by other considerations. When the postulated effects of a teaching pattern are evident in the pupil's behavior and are susceptible to recording by an observer, then the criterion behavior may be specified in relationship to changes among the pupils, for example, *"Criterion behavior:* Teacher will pause long enough, when beginning new lessons, for all of the pupils to give their attention."

Once content or process goals have been formulated behaviorally, then criterion behaviors, that is, degrees of change in the teaching, will often be determined by what seems realistically possible for the teacher to achieve in the time available in a cycle of supervision. Even though large, long-range modifications are sometimes adopted as supervisory goals, it is generally best to work at developing incremental approximations of such outcomes in order for small momentary gains to be appreciable (and reinforceable) in day-to-day supervision. Sometimes estimations of what is immediately feasible for Teacher must serve as the exclusive determinants of a criterion behavior, especially when no ideal degree of modification can be specified, when any change would seem better than neglecting to modify the pattern at all, and when the pattern and the changes in question are particularly difficult or seem that way to Teacher. In this connection, criterion behaviors must sometimes be set intuitively. In another sense, definitions of minimal sufficiency depend upon the importance, the significance, or the urgencies associated with the pattern to be modified. Should the pattern, although it is salient in some manner, be relatively superficial in terms of its hypothesized effects upon the children, for example, then criterion behaviors might be stipulated more modestly than if the pattern seemed to produce profound effects.

In short, the formulation of criterion behavior will generally involve some combination of the factors: how readily able Teacher is to achieve (certain increments of) the changes in question; how important the pattern's effects are likely to be on the children; possibilities for testing the effects of change; possibilities of observing the effects of change (in the pupils' behavior, in the teacher's supervisory behavior, and the like); by objective, quantitative variables when possible and by examined intuitive reasoning when simple, quantitative testing is unfeasible.

Despite the ambiguities involved in formulating criterion behaviors for content and process goals in supervision, and sometimes, even, in stating such goals in behavioral terms, we strongly advocate this practice for the following reasons:

1. Unless desired outcomes can be stated behaviorally, there is some chance that the outcomes in question are merely figmental (in this respect, it may represent good reality testing for Supervisor and Teacher to test their prospective goals against the possibility of formulating them in behavioral terms.

2. Unless supervisory goals can be stated behaviorally, there is little chance to observe whether or not they have been achieved (because only behavioral outcomes

are visible and inferences can easily run rampant and wishfully in relation to desired but invisible outcomes).

3. Opportunities for Supervisor and Teacher to evaluate achievement of desired change, to make progress, and to define required tasks are most favorable when their "contract" specifies minimally acceptable outcomes as clearly as possible (successes are apt to feel more secure and rewards more certain than if outcomes are defined very generally).

4. If we can demonstrate goal setting that satisfies these conditions — namely, that goals shall be stated behaviorally, that conditions for exhibiting the desired behavior shall be specified, and that criterion behaviors shall be defined in advance — then by turning Teacher's attention to the existence of these conventions in supervision we may provide concrete examples of instructional planning that should serve Teacher well in working with pupils.

Consider some decisions that we might make concerning supervisory processes. Among other things, we must generally decide whether our approach in the conference should be essentially didactic. This means, more concretely, that we must decide whether we will present data (patterns) in relation to which Teacher will construct interpretations, perform an analysis, and develop strategies for future work inductively or whether, instead, we will present our own interpretations of teaching patterns and then recommend strategies for effecting desirable changes in techniques involving deductions from principles of theory (for example, "Since we know that children of this age are more likely to learn visually, kinesthetically, and from tactile experience than from exclusively verbal teaching, it follows that your choice of Stern Blocks as the medium of learning in this unit is a sound one") and methods by which the significance of selected patterns is developed by some meaningful synthesis of empirical observations ("So what might you be ready to conclude, having observed that most of the children arranged the blocks in serial order even though, in the absence of any cues from you, they were unable to say what they had done in words that conveyed abstract understanding of serialization?").

Similarly, we may decide whether Teacher should initiate the issues to be treated in supervision or whether we should initiate them. Once again, our basis for such decision making consists principally of our knowledge of what has worked before with Teacher or, in the absence of sufficient data from that relationship, of what has generally worked before with teachers. If we favor practice in which inductive inquiry and teacher-initiated issues take precedence, we may proceed by trial and error, that is, by employing essentially inductive modes at first and then turning to more didactic methods, perhaps, if the first approach seems unproductive.

By now, we have pieced together a picture of Strategy, and more particularly, of methods of strategy, whose principal elements are that (1) we as supervisors will formulate content and process goals on two levels: one pertaining to the structure of the teacher's own teaching and one relating to the conduct of supervision; (2) content and process goals should be defined as cognitive outcomes and behavioral outcomes, and in reference to criterion behaviors; (3)

we should select patterns from the observational data on the criteria "saliency," "fewness," and "treatability"; and (4) a dynamic relationship exists between such methods of selection and the specific goals motivating any given sequence of supervision.

This last thought is intended to convey the expectation that, for example, saliency may be determined by the specific goals because any such episode may be generated by salient teaching patterns found in the current data.

ADDITIONAL ELEMENTS OF STRATEGY

Besides selecting specific teaching patterns for treatment and formulating or reformulating supervisor goals, we as supervisors have other decisions to make during Strategy relating to management of the conference. Some common questions to decide are:

1. Should we undertake a full or partial analysis of the data?
2. In what order should the issues of this conference be examined?
3. Should we deal primarily with strengths or weaknesses in the teaching; to what degree, if any, should "pluses" and "minuses" be balanced?
4. Are there specific junctures at which we should test Teacher's comprehension by engaging in role playing or by asking Teacher to paraphrase a line of reasoning we have presented?
5. Under what circumstances should we be ready to abandon our own analysis of this lesson in favor of other approaches?
6. What balance should exist between considerations of the past (analysis), the present (supervisory processes), and the future (planning future lessons)?
7. What method of recording, if any, should be employed for this conference?
8. Should Teacher be given carte blanche for structuring this conference; should he or she be offered specific options; should we hold him or her to the analysis we have prepared?
9. What quantity of data should we present to document the patterns we have selected?
10. Should our "contract" be reviewed at the outset; what changes, if any, should be made in our contract?
11. At what point should the conference end?

If we decide to build certain decision points into the conference, points at which Teacher might select among specific lines of inquiry to follow, then, in most instances, we should prepare multiple, branching strategies in advance. In other words, we should be technically and conceptually ready to move in Teacher's directions, particularly if we have named the available choices in advance. Under circumstances in which supervision is being undertaken by more than one person at a time (for example, in team situations), Strategy should also incorporate explicit decisions for regulating each member's participation in the conference. Very elaborate plans can be made for governing group supervision — pertaining, for example, to questions of what material should be treated by which members, who should lead at what moments, who should collect data for postobservation analysis, and what kinds of verbal and nonverbal signals should be exchanged for altering the order of events or for asking permission to disagree or for deciding it is time to quit or for shifting leadership, and the like. At least such a strategy should dictate which member has overall responsibility for management and, in everyone's interests, should specify agreements (or no agreements) to disagree, with appropriate qualifications.

We shall now take the questions listed above in order.

1. *Should we undertake a full or partial analysis of the data?*

Ordinarily, this question would have been decided before we selected specific teaching patterns for treatment. If we decided in favor of "full analysis," then it would be gratuitous to labor over selections, except under special circumstances.

Full analysis can be construed several ways. By any definition, however, its chief method is to present Teacher with a more complete collection of data or a less abridged analysis of the data than would ordinarily be offered as a result of selection on the criteria "salient," "few," and "treatable." We might, for example, spend the time available for Strategy transcribing our observation notes into some readable form in order to present the complete data to Teacher. Our strategy, under these conditions, might be to begin the conference by saying, "Here are the notes. Shall we see what we can find that may be important?" Another variation of full analysis is for us to present the complete data along with all of the patterns he or she identified during Stage 3, instead of a selected group of such patterns. According to this strategy, we might or might not include evaluative comments in the presentation of patterns.

Two general disadvantages of full analysis are: (1) It tends to be uneconomical of time and often creates the problem of having spent so much time in analysis of past teaching that Supervisor and Teacher are unable to proceed to planning future teaching, and (2) it overwhelms Teacher to be confronted by so much material, either because there is simply too much to assimilate or because there is too much emotional involvement. The latter is particularly significant. Most teachers cannot handle so much in such a short period of time — nor should they be expected to.

We should decide during Strategy whether the potential virtues of full analysis are likely to offset its problems for the individual teacher we are about to supervise. In general, this approach seems indicated under two conditions: (1) when Teacher is unusually resilient, unusually energetic, and demonstrates unusual capacities for analyzing copious data efficiently, or (2) when Teacher seems particularly threatened by fantasies of what goes on in our mind as we peruse our notes, of what we are holding back from the analysis, and, in group supervision, of what types of things have been said about the teacher during Stage 3. In short, full analysis may work with strong teachers because they are strong and also with frightened teachers who worry about damage to their reputations in supervisory analyses from which they are excluded.

One might reasonably employ full analysis for a somewhat different purpose — that is, to show teachers whose previous work in supervision has been adequate new techniques for analyzing classroom data. Such supervision might be intended to heighten Teacher's ability to undertake systematic self-analysis or to prepare Teacher for undertaking the supervision of fellow team members and colleagues. Perhaps the greatest advantage, for all teachers, of an occasional full analysis is that it tends to demystify supervisory procedures that take place in their absence. But full analysis must be used with caution, for it can be overwhelming for teachers — and potentially damaging.

2. *In what order should the issues of this conference be examined?*

Particularly when unrelated teaching patterns are to be treated, the order in which they are broached can make important psychological differences in the conference. We must bear in mind that although such patterns may be unrelated in the sense that they belong to different categories of teaching behavior, Teacher is integrated and responds as a complete personality to every impinging stimulus. It is impossible to prescribe categorically in this context because of individual differences among teachers that determine whether any specific method will be effective or not. We can, however, describe methodological rationales that may work, depending upon surrounding circumstances.

We might, for example, begin with conceptually difficult issues in order to direct Teacher's interest toward them before fatigue sets in. Or we might start off with simple matters, as a form of pump priming. We might begin with "strengths" in order to establish feelings of success against which Teacher may borrow, emotionally, when attention is turned subsequently to "weaknesses." Or we might begin with weaknesses in order to alleviate anticipatory anxiety quickly and to be able to close on a positive note. We might begin by treating issues in which Teacher has expressed a special interest in order to satisfy his or her hungers as early in the conference as possible. Or we might elect to get other things out of the way first as a means of eliminating distractions from the serious work. If we have found it useful in the past to deal with Teacher's feelings about supervision, then we might at least think about whether such treatment has generally seemed more productive before substantive dialogue commenced or after supervisory issues had been opened.

"Order" then, is something about which we should think explicitly as we plan what to do in the conference. One way to begin is by asking, "Even though the patterns to be treated are substantively unrelated, does my experience with Teacher suggest that the order in which they are examined is likely to make any important difference?"

3. *Should we deal primarily with strengths or weaknesses in the teaching; to what degree, if any, should pluses and minuses be balanced?*

Let us start with the realization that a great number — perhaps a majority — of teaching patterns are $\pm$ rather than clearly $+$ or $-$. This is to say that after analysis is complete, it generally appears that almost any teaching pattern embodies both advantages and disadvantages, for all the pupils, or for some pupils, at one time or another. Also, it should not sound as if Teacher does not participate in determining the value (or nonvalue) of his or her own instructional patterns. Pluses and minuses are not, as a rule, determined a priori by the time a conference begins.

Nevertheless, as we examine the observation notes, we do not magically suspend our values and force ourselves to assume that nothing is good and nothing is bad until Teacher has joined us in determining so. On the contrary, not only do the patterns uncovered often feel distinctly positive or negative, but according to this model of supervision, they often seem likely to be emotionally plus or minus for Teacher to consider, and we must recognize such possibilities as we estimate whether individual patterns are accessible for treatment. We may consult our intuitions concerning good and bad features of the teaching and may consider our predictions of which patterns, if any, are likely to provoke difficult feelings in supervision. Our tentative assignment of $+$'s and $-$'s and $\pm$'s is for the purpose of designing a supervisory strategy rather than being an expression of necessarily foregone evaluative conclusions.

An additional possible misconception when discussing pluses and minuses attaches to the word "balance." If in our analysis we offer three strengths and three weaknesses of the teaching episode, we cannot assume that Teacher will break even emotionally.

Our most valuable single source of information for planning in this context consists of knowledge gained in previous sequences of supervision with Teacher. Based on past experiences, we may be able to predict, with greater or lesser accuracy, the emotional valences that are likely to attach to specific substantive issues or to result from specific supervisory processes. In other words, our cumulative impressions of Teacher's tolerances, saturation points, and ability to accept (or tendencies to reject) analysis should provide us with at least a rudimentary set of parameters for estimating what will be experienced as giving and what will be experienced as taking.

Although one aim of clinical supervision is to counteract teachers' and supervisors' tendencies to create halos around teaching by differentiating specific elements of teaching in analysis, another is to create positive incentives for supervision by enabling Teacher to achieve relevant rewards. Although Teacher would be mistaken to evaluate instructional practice in global terms, he or she should nonetheless be able to conclude supervision conferences with basically positive feelings about self, about supervision, and about the future. It behooves us, consequently, to consider subjective balance realistically beforehand, avoiding simpleminded cause-effect construction as we do so.

Given that teaching is complex, ambiguous, and demanding, perhaps the most important capacity for us to develop is that of being able to treat ambiguities and failures productively — that is, in a manner that permits shrewdly examined failures (weaknesses, or minuses) to generate successful modifications in the teaching. One critical element of Teacher's outlook on clinical supervision must be an expectation of failures, but an optimistic rather than a fearful one. To be a rational educator, one must expect to encounter inevitable failures. For teachers, or for any clinical practitioners, some strength must be developed, not only for tolerating mistakes but for seeking them out and for positively rejoicing in their discovery and successful treatment. We propose that, in teaching, the only grievous mistake is the one that remains undetected.

Balance becomes an important concept, perhaps a key concept, for creating a supervision conference in which, although weaknesses are addressed, their identification and treatment energizes and motivates a teacher. Whether or not examinations of failures were productive often seems to depend upon the emotional residues that remain after a conference has ended.

4. *Are there specific junctures at which we should test teacher's comprehension through either role playing or presented paraphrasing lines of reasoning?*

It is generally wise, at Stage 3, for supervisors to adopt strategies for protecting the effectiveness of conference communication — that is, for ensuring that Teacher will understand that communication. In the same fashion, we should plan measures to assure our own comprehension of ideas and feelings that Teacher will be attempting to communicate. Let us just deal with the former.

One problem that exists for all teachers and supervisors is the seemingly universal tendency to confuse one's own fluency (either real or imagined) with the quality of other people's understanding of one's words. We are more likely than not to assume that because we expressed ourself well, our ideas will have been understood consistently with our intended meanings. If, however, Teacher's mind was on other things, we more than likely deceive ourselves by such an assumption. Our chances for deception are multiplied if the teacher offers nonverbal implications of understanding as well.

Presumably, when either Teacher or Supervisor raises a question or defines a problem or expresses a value or reports a feeling, a measure of importance is attached to it. Rather than its being sufficient for agreeable conversation to take place emptily, as at a cocktail party, under such circumstances it may be crucial for talk to be the carrier of substantive ideas and to exist principally for that purpose. A pertinent conceptual exchange must take place. And how do we test for this?

One of the most effective tests is to contrive a role-playing situation in which Teacher has the opportunity to demonstrate the behavior in question. Similarly, a good way to be sure that we understand what Teacher is saying is to try to say it back, one way or another, in some form that will get agreement. Such communication methods are doubly virtuous in that they provide chances to correct misinterpretations as well as opportunities to assure consensus.

It follows that one task, for clinical supervisors, is to establish this convention early in supervisory relationships; to teach Teacher to tolerate playbacks and role playing and to demonstrate our own decision to press for clarity by engaging in like behaviors.

At the strategy stage, it is often useful for supervisors to plan, in advance, special moments at which playback should be particularly valuable during the conference. When might playback be particularly appropriate? Perhaps in connection with an unusually subtle or very complex concept or with an idea that can be understood in various senses, some of which capture the intended point and others of which miss it, or perhaps in relation to an issue about which Teacher is likely to feel ambivalent or resistant. Note such moments in advance to ensure your remembering to employ playback, if it becomes appropriate to do so, before the opportunity has slipped away. Paraphrasing Teacher's verbalized ideas ought to become an almost automatic reflex at moments when we become confused by what Teacher is saying.

One caution, however, "too much of a good thing" represents one peril associated with these techniques. Nevertheless, their advantages tend to outweigh their disadvantages. Role playing, especially, seems to reinforce what supervision is really after: behavioral modifications. It generally seems more useful and rewarding in supervision for Teacher to do whatever it is that he or she wants to do in addition to simply verbalizing understanding of and knowing how to do it. Although some "doing" cannot be simulated without the children's presence, there are a surprising number of techniques that Teacher can rehearse in supervision and that, once they have been mastered, should be performable even in stress situations.

5. *Under what circumstances should we be ready to abandon our own analysis of this lesson in favor of other approaches?*

Once a decision has been made to deal with selected patterns, rather than to perform a full analysis, we should always be prepared to abandon our strategy in response to contingencies arising in the conference. In this respect it seems important to note the frame of mind in which we should regard this strategy, even if it is not possible to suggest specific methods to be employed in this connection at Stage 3. Clinical supervisors must also be sufficiently resilient to overcome a feeling of investment in formulated plans, perhaps with great effort, if it should turn out that Teacher experiences a sense of urgency to deal with other matters.

If certain issues have assumed emotional primacy for Teacher, it is almost certain that he or she will be distracted from other issues that we prefer to examine unless deliberate steps are taken to reduce the tension surrounding them. It particularly behooves us to treat problems Teacher identified beforehand (in Stage 1), if only to put them aside temporarily, should no pertinent data have been generated during the lesson.

6. *What balance should exist between considerations of the past (analysis), the present (supervisory processes), and the future (planning future lessons)?*

Decisions on this question often determine the success or failure of a conference, particularly in regard to how Teacher feels about it, more than any other single factor of strategy. Concretely, the question is really that of how much time to spend, respectively, in analyzing the teaching, in examining processes operating at the moment in supervision, and in planning future sequences of teaching.

In earlier clinical supervision practices, conferences often consisted of little more than complex analyses of the observed teaching. This was fine for supervisors, but teachers were often put out because of having had to endure what seemed to be an essentially time-wasting exercise in which critical dissections of their teaching were performed without apparent purpose.

Soon our work was directed toward planning for future lessons to be examined during the existing supervision cycle. We discovered that teachers felt most helped by supervision when it left them with something concrete in hand; something to symbolize real accomplishments; something that would have functional utility "tomorrow" — namely, a lesson plan for tomorrow. We resolved, consequently, that supervision conferences should culminate in the creation of such a plan.

This approach was not, however, problem-free. For one thing, it proved difficult to control teachers' growing dependencies upon supervisors to invent lesson plans for them. For another, plans created by supervisors were sometimes distorted badly in the next day's teaching, partly because of invisible misunderstandings that existed yesterday and partly because of fear of the procedure. It also became clear that although past and future had begun to exist in some reasonably productive balance, there never seemed to be time enough for dealing with problems of the present — for example, with such problems as the dependencies to which we have just referred — that were blooming in some supervisory relationships.

Supervision that stays too much in the past soon begins to feel abrasive, and it is generally not enough to hope that if supervision focuses principally upon completed teaching and performs mainly analytical functions, Teacher will make appropriate applications to his or her own teaching in his or her own good time. More often then not, that approach simply will not succeed.

Certain methods, involving some degree of compromise, help to create a relatively successful and satisfying cycle of supervision. Indeed, the principal strategy for achieving reasonable balance is to think of supervision distributed over cycles instead of aiming, somehow, to crowd everything into any given supervisory sequence. The way in which to allocate time should be decided at the beginning of a cycle, during the "contract" stage. Decisions about what to do first should be based upon Supervisor's and Teacher's ideas about what Teacher needs the most and wants the most.

Cycle sequencing may depend on any number of variables: supervisor/teacher rapport, lesson to be taught, impasse situations, and the like. If time is short for conferences and if it appears that no single conference can incorporate a satisfatory balance among the variables in question, then by formulating an appropriate strategy and by agreeing to appropriate compromises, an overall feeling of productive balance and propitious closure may be achieved for any cycle.

From time to time we encounter problems whose solution requires attenuated cycles of supervision, sometimes spanning weeks and months (though, in most cases, not on a daily basis). We may sometimes, for example, need to spend weeks dealing with process — Teacher doesn't trust us, is very anxious about being observed, feels severely constrained by analysis — but eventually we are able to join Teacher in planning that he or she will deem as helpful. If we stop supervision prematurely, Teacher may never learn to take advantage of clinical analysis and consequently might not experience the rewards attainable by that practice.

7. *What method of recording, if any, should be employed for this conference?*

What should be recorded? What reasons favor recording? The easiest records for clinical supervisors to compile consist of the observation notes they record in any event, which can easily enough be dropped into files after each supervisory sequence. To have such records available enables Teacher or Supervisor to capture a view of changes that have occurred in the teaching, particularly among the salient teaching patterns upon which supervision has focused, at moments when looking backward may be particularly reinforcing or useful in some other manner. Keeping longitudinal records of analysis is especially useful when supervision is operating toward long-range developmental goals and when it is frequently difficult to remember clearly how things have gone in the past.

Tapes are most valuable for use in the training of supervisors and as material for research in clinical supervision. In practice, tapes and observation notes are frequently useful when we enlist the services of another supervisor, need independent interpretations of a problem, require some specialized knowledge in the supervision that neither Teacher nor we possess, or need help to plan strategies for Teacher's future supervision.

Some teachers and supervisors find note taking distracting or inconvenient during conferences and follow the practice of listening to their own tapes after the conference and noting whatever they want to during the playback. Listening to tapes of conferences has been particulary useful during periods of supervision in which the major focus has been aimed at supervisory processes, that is, at the quality of interactions between the supervision and teacher. Instead of confronting teachers with our impressions of their behavior, we ought to have simply listened to tapes of supervision conferences. Obstacles seem to pass more effectively when Teacher is able to perceive his or her own defensive maneuvers than when we tell him or her about them. While our telling often, self-defeatingly, makes Teacher even more defensive than before, if we employ a strategy in which Teacher is given the chance to identify self-behavior by listening to tapes, and using the opportunity successfully, the achievement of appropriate insights is likely to occur more efficiently.

As supervisors we must consider what effects recording, by any method, is likely to have on the conference. Even when a tradition of tape-recording has been established in Teacher's supervision, we should remain alert to the chance that on any given occasion the presence of an audio- or a video-recording machine may create tension. During Strategy, consequently, we should decide, first, whether reasons exist for recording the conference; second, whether past experiences with Teacher indicate that recording is likely to be acceptable; and, finally, whether any momentary evidence suggests that on this particular occasion it might be best to let recording go. Decisions of this kind may always be tentative, particularly if recording equipment is present and ready to be activated at any moment during the conference. The balance to decide, in any event, is between persuasive reasons to record and the price that recording may exact.

8. *Should teacher be given carte blanche for structuring this conference, be offered specific options, or be held to the analysis prepared?*

This is not quite the same question as whether or not to employ full analysis or as that of judging the likelihood that reasons will arise in the conference to abandon Supervisor's a priori strategy, although these issues clearly overlap. In certain respects this question is more inclusive in that it suggests the possibility that Teacher can elect to do anything he or she pleases with the conference (for example, to discuss philosophies of education); to talk, exclusively, about the lesson that was observed; to ignore the lesson and to talk only about future directions in teaching; to discuss relatively personal issues that pertain somehow to professional functioning; to discuss a student; to discuss irrelevancies; or to cancel the conference altogether.

What reasons could justify such complete freedom to manage supervisory time? Once again, as with the full analysis, this strategy (which could be called the "open conference") has seemed most sensible to employ either with unusually strong teachers or with inordinately anxious ones.

A teacher's personal identification with work (ego involvement in professional performance) can generate a powerful commitment to technical learning and a positive joy in self-evaluation and self-directed training under favorable conditions, just as it can generate anxiety and defensive resistance under unfavorable ones. In the former case it is usual to find Teacher providing the motive energy and psychological drive for supervision. For us to be most useful to such a teacher, we must learn, at least, how to avoid distracting this individual from self-defined tasks — how, in effect, to keep out of the way. Analogously to the training of a virtuoso pianist or of a great painter, our role evolves, after a time, into that of coach. We become less a teacher of technique and author of assigned exercises and more a critical dialectician; a mirror; an occasional collaborator in invention; a handmaiden, primarily to the teacher's own strategies; a traveling companion through whatever directions the teacher pursues. More prominently, perhaps, than in any other phase of supervision, our principal commitments, at this final level, are to perform whatever functions can help Teacher most to accomplish what he or she wants to. It is not difficult to imagine that after substantial experience with clinical supervision, many teachers gain expertise in analyzing behavioral data and charting strategies for modifying their teaching patterns. Some, in fact, may even surpass their supervisors' skills after a time, particularly in connection with understanding and transforming their own instructional behavior.

It is not difficult to sense the appropriateness of open conferences at this level of supervision. It seems that as a teacher becomes more skillful, the threat of observation and analysis is diminished and the teacher tends to be more receptive to supervision.

For such teachers, consequently, some rationales for open conferences are: (a) with Teacher direction, supervision may better meet Teacher's felt (and actual) needs; (b) we can provide direction by request rather than by default; and (c) self-initiated supervision becomes more likely and desirable. The decision for an open conference should be made as early as possible in a sequence of supervision, so that Teacher will have needed time for preparing strategies (if desired). It is particularly important for Teacher to have enough time to examine observation data or to listen to a tape of the lesson before the conference to perform a full or limited analysis of the lesson.

Open conferences may also have some utility, especially early in supervision, with very anxious teachers. The major problem involved in using this technique with uninitiated teachers is that they may squander an open conference on superficialities or on peripheral or irrelevant issues. We can solve this by stipulating in advance that although the contract calls for carte blanche, we reserve the prerogative of examining the conference's success, retroactively, with Teacher.

When the open-conference technique has been adopted, it becomes particularly important for us to recognize that many gradations exist along the "open-directed" continuum and that more directed analysis can be developed by small degrees over successive cycles of supervision. An honest and effective approach, generally, is to be perfectly open and explicit with Teacher in reaching agreements that enable us to begin to introduce his or her issues and interpretations into supervision. We should attempt to work, by small steps, into cycles of conventional clinical supervision in order to train Teacher in the analytical and self-directed treatment techniques required to pass, ultimately, to a level of supervision at which Teacher may take the major initiative.

The open technique may have other objectives and advantages:

(a) It is sometimes useful to reduce the intensity of concentration and effort which can become quite strong in cycles of clinical supervision. Trying too hard to regulate some pattern of teaching or to master some element of technique often reaches diminishing returns; the very intensity that Teacher brings to his or her task precludes sufficient relaxation to perform the technique in question. An open conference may serve to untighten Teacher on such occasions.

(b) In much the same manner, it sometimes appears that, once Teacher has gained conceptual control over a technique but is experiencing difficulty in its execution, a truer economy can be enjoyed when Teacher turns to other issues temporarily. It is not uncommon to discover that teachers can master technical problems with relatively little difficulty after a period of ignoring them or that, having begun to struggle with a technique and then having turned to other problems, the answer comes spontaneously, without any focused conscious effort to get it there.

(c) An open conference or a cycle of such conferences can enable Teacher to find his or her own stride and may generate cues to guide our regulation of the tempo thereafter. We may discover, for example, that the average number of patterns with which Teacher elects to deal in any given session is greater or smaller than when we made such choices. We may discover some propensity for working in certain categories of teaching behavior more than in others, or for working in a plurality of categories concurrently, or for avoidance of specific categories.

We may find that, left to his or her own initiative, Teacher tends to define problems of practice more complexly or more superficially than we do. We may find that Teacher tends to polarize value judgments so that specific patterns generally seem either good or bad, or we may discover that Teacher is more subtle in detecting simultaneous strengths and weaknesses incorporated by such patterns. We may find that Teacher tends to jump the gun on evaluating the effectiveness or shortcomings of various techniques, defers judgment until reasonable evidence can be collected, or positively avoids committing self to value judgments, no matter what.

We may find confirmation in Teacher's self-initiated behavior for strategies that we have been employing; we may find contraindications for such strategies; and we may discover productive lines of inquiry that would not have occurred to us had Teacher not been given freedom to take intellectual control.

(d) The open conference can be ideal for "diagnostic" purposes insofar as Teacher can be observed in a natural condition, rather than in one that has somehow been imposed, and can provide strong signals for directing future supervision.

(e) The open conference may, additionally, provide Teacher time to deal with residual issues (that is, with bits and pieces that have spilled over from past cycles of supervision), and with the chance to initiate ancillary activities that, although they may not represent elements of direct clinical supervision, may nevertheless be consistent with supervisory aims. For example, conference time can be used to engage the supervisors in designing a professional research project or in planning some technical experiment or in studying supervisory problems and methods in order to develop specialized competencies for use in supervision to be initiated with teaching colleagues.

As for the rest of this question of strategy, we should decide how important it might be to hold Teacher to some specific analysis or to offer limited choices among alternative analyses we have prepared. Often, unless negative indications emerge spontaneously during the conference, it seems best to stick with the planned analysis in order to pin down certain issues that have previously been ambiguous but are now illustrated clearly by the present data or because it seems necessary to follow through on specific patterns that were introduced during an earlier sequence of supervision. Sometimes it seems best to engage Teacher in making decisions about which course, among several specified courses, to follow.

One reason for limiting choices rather than providing an open field may be to ensure that we will be adequately prepared and adequately fluent to function efficiently in the conference. In any event we should recognize that multiple models of clinical supervision do exist and that the model employed for any given sequence should reflect conscious decisions rather than habituation to some general procedure. Indeed, our own creativity in using clinical supervision models is an important ingredient of successful supervision.

9. *What quantity of data should be presented to document the patterns we have selected?*

It is easiest to broach this question by stating the problem that motivates it When we summon too few data to document a teaching pattern whose features may be subtle or complex, we risk confusing the teacher, who — though nodding cooperatively — may have little idea of what we are talking about. The opposite danger is that we may produce such a large amount of data to document a pattern already recognized by Teacher that Teacher may begin to feel humiliated.

Previous experiences with Teacher should provide us with some notion of how much documentation is enough. Specific patterns may be judged with regard to their logical and behavioral complexity, their likely emotional significance, and the like, for selecting appropriate quantities of supporting material. Some general rules of thumb are:

> have too many data available rather than too few
> select the clearest examples from the data rather than obscure or ambiguous examples
> select well-defined patterns in favor of subtle ones — unless, of course, special urgency attaches to some subtle teaching pattern
> defer treating nebulous patterns until some later sequence, during which it is hoped that they will emerge more clearly
> when in doubt concerning how much documentation is necessary, test Teacher's comprehension by playback or role-playing techniques.

There is no rule, incidentally, that says we must present all of the supporting observational data. In fact, there are likely to be positive advantages connected to having Teacher peruse the data to find material relevant to the "contract" or "agreement." Data should serve a purpose; (that is, there should be a need to know on the part of Teacher) if we are to present data to Teacher. Further the data should reflect "contract" or "agreement" items. If we wish to be indirect, we may even ask Teacher to scan the data.

10. *Should our "contract" or "agreement" be reviewed at the outset; what changes, if any, should be made in our contract?*

To the first part of this question: Yes, if not at the *very* outset, certainly at an early point. It is always a good idea for us to keep an eye on the agreements by which we and Teacher maintain direction. It becomes embarrassing to discover, late in the game, that agreements we thought existed implicitly did not, in fact, exist at all. Experience has taught us to assume, as a rule, that unexplicit contractual understandings are likely to be simple figments of the supervisor's imagination or projections of wishes.

Contract changes depend on many variables. As supervisors we must be aware of these variables and react accordingly. Contract changes are sometimes desirable and sometimes necessary for effective supervision to occur.

11. *At what point should the conference end?*

One element of strategy consists or technical and process goals that we formulate for the conference. One way to envision the ending, consequently, would be that point at which such goals seem satisfactorily accomplished. Unfortunately, unexpected contingencies and the general condition that only so much time is available for supervision conferences create many situations in which, for one reason or another, a conference must be terminated before its goals have been met. It is also frequently true that while we may hope to achieve certain short-term outcomes during a single conference, we are also working toward complex developmental objectives in relation to which closure, if it occurs at all, results as a cumulative effect of many conferences and of long-range supervisory work.

It is easy to imagine all kinds of unpropitious endings that might result when time runs out for supervision:

> many data have been unearthed, but the patterns they comprise have not been defined
>
> several patterns have been identified, but their significance has not been established
>
> some weaknesses have been examined, but accompanying strengths have not been discussed, or vice versa
>
> certain technical problems have been defined, but strategies (plans) for their solution have not been formulated
>
> the teacher has raised an issue of urgency, but there has not been enough time to develop the reassuring evidence or the methods of attack that are required. When the bell has already begun to ring, Teacher sometimes finds what has really been troubling him or her or just begins to show signs of crystallizing a concept around which supervision has been struggling.

Experience suggests that we are generally better advised to consider felicitous stopping points in advance. Although other considerations might generate a model incorporating some other sequence of issues for the conference, when the question is simply about economical distribution of time and about when to quit, certain elementary guidelines may be employed. For example, in the absence of opposing reasons, we might arrange to broach hard things first and to save easy issues for the end, if there is time left. "Hard" things might be defined as issues that are conceptually complex or emotionally difficult to handle or so ambiguous that, predictably, it will take considerable time to develop relationships among the supporting data.

If we plan to invite Teacher to raise problems as well as to introduce concerns of our own, we are wise to give Teacher the opening time. Once we have noted favorable stopping points at the strategy stage, we should also plan to provide time, at the end of the conference, for developing some kind of transition into the next sequence of supervision. We might, for example, point out to Teacher that certain issues have not been covered, and may take time either toward the end of the conference to discuss whether or not such residual issues should be brought over into the next sequence of supervision along with, or instead of, new business that is likely to arise in the new sequence.

As in other sectors of activity, it is generally best to quit when one is ahead. It represents good practice, consequently, for us to think in advance about the moments at which Teacher is likely to experience success, according to his or her strategy for the conference; to think about such moments as possible termination points; and to remain sensitive to Teacher's feelings, in this regard, during the conference. No degree of prior calculation can substitute for being alert to Teacher's actual experiences, although such calculation can heighten one's awareness of existing feelings. Despite our wishes, Teacher will not necessarily feel the success that our efforts were designed to produce. It follows that our method should include deliberate scanning, once the conference is under way, for logical and psychologically favorable stopping points.

SUMMARY OF CHAPTERS 7 AND 8

Methods of strategy have been viewed in these chapters primarily as decisions for us as supervisors to make, as principles and guidelines for decision making, and as elements (issues, problems, variables) to be kept in mind throughout the conference planning stage. Perhaps the first of our decisions is whether or not to plan an a priori strategy for the forthcoming conference. Should we decide affirmatively, we must then consider whether to present a full analysis, a selected analysis, an open conference, or some other type of analysis. In each case we should formulate *technical* and *process* goals, which should be stated in cognitive terms, as behavioral outcomes, and in relation to criterion behaviors. In connection with selected analysis or with strategies that offer specific options from which Teacher may choose, we select teaching patterns on the criteria "saliency," "fewness," and "accessibility for treatment." Saliency of patterns is determined by reference to such factors as frequency, demonstrable effects, theoretical significance, structural importance in the lesson, commonality, and priorities assigned by Teacher. Accessibility is estimated principally in relation to logical complexity and emotional loading, which in turn are predicted on the basis of our past experience with Teacher, past experiences with other teachers, relevant theoretical knowledge, and, sometimes, professional intuitions.

Self-examination, particularly in reference to our motives for selecting specific patterns and specific supervisory processes, is a major element of strategy. "Fewness" is guided by such factors as clarity (in the data), subsumption, sameness or difference among patterns, affective loading, time energy, and sequence. Additional decisions must often be made in relation to objective balance among strengths and weaknesses and subjective balances likely to arise in Teacher's frame of reference, in conjunction with selected patterns: the use of playback and role-playing techniques for clarification and rehearsal; alternative strategies to accommodate contingencies arising unpredictably in the conference; temporal balance, that is, distribution of conference time over past, present, and future issues in the teaching and supervision; recording; quantities of documentary data; examination and possible revision of the supervisory contract; and termination points.

Chapter 9

THE
SUPERVISORY
CONFERENCE

---

* Interval Behavior
* Conference Conditions
* Choices of Words
* Problems

All of the energy and thought expended by Supervisor in the three prior stages (preobservation conference, observation, and analysis and strategy) has been invested in order that the next and crucial stage (the supervisory conference) may result in the intended benefits for Teacher. However, the best prior preparation that can be imagined can go to waste, either entirely or in major part, if the conference itself is not expertly managed. We therefore turn to detailed examination of the conference, in the hope that such examination will cause all prior advice and assertions to fall comfortably into place.

The supervisory conference has among its purposes, the following:

1. provision of lesson feedback for improving future teaching.
2. provision of adult rewards and satisfactions.
3. definition and authentication of issues in teaching.
4. provision of didactic help.
5. provision of training in techniques of teacher self-improvement.
6. development of incentives for professional self-analysis.

As you read this chapter, we trust that you will appreciate the importance of these purposes and their implications for a successful and rewarding experience by both supervisor and supervisee.

In *Looking in Classrooms*, Tom Good and Jere Brophy noted:

Teachers, like everyone else, are sometimes unwilling to examine their own behavior and engage in self-evaluation. Is this because teachers are not committed to their professions or are unwilling to engage in this extra work necessary to improve their existing skills? Is it because they feel that they are already functioning at optimum effectiveness? We doubt it. We think teachers will seek opportunities to evaluate and improve their teaching if acceptable and useful methods are available.[1]

Teachers generally feel that they do not receive sufficient support or services necessary for pursuing instructional improvement. Most studies that probe supervisory services corroborate their feelings. Lovell and Phelps recently reported that of those teachers surveyed in Tennessee, more than 80 percent reported that they had experienced no observations by, or conferences with, a supervisor. Of those reporting that they were observed by, and had conferences with, a supervisor, many said the conferences were less than ten minutes in length.[2] Other studies show similar results.

The central purpose of the postobservation conference is to carry out the strategy for providing Teacher with constructive feedback on the lesson taught with the hope of effecting improvement in Teacher's performance. The conference is itself an observable example of supervisory behavior. It is a function that is readily observable by Teacher and one by which Teacher decides whether or not Supervisor is capable of offering the supervision necessary for Teacher's instructional improvement. Through it, Supervisor reveals to Teacher how well the analysis and strategy stage has equipped him or her to be of help, and Teacher has only this observable act to determine whether or not Supervisor actually knows what he or she is doing. Should the conference be less than effective (as viewed by the teacher), then Teacher may assume that other parts of the cycle may have been less than effective as well. The fact that Supervisor may have conducted the preobservation conference well, observed well, and analyzed and strategized well may be to no avail if the conference is a disaster or nearly so.

The disaster, it might be noted, could be caused by factors beyond Supervisor's control. Consider the following case:

Situation. The setting is the fifth-grade pod of an elementary school, separated from the other pods and from the main building by connecting outside walkways. Four teachers comprise the total teaching team for the fifth grade. Two of those teachers are team teaching in the social sciences, and the room in which they teach has a dividing curtain between their respective classrooms. When they team-teach social sciences, the room divider is always open so that they have the physical space of two classrooms. The teachers have taught with

[1]Thomas L. Good and Jere E. Brophy, *Looking in Classrooms* (New York: Harper & Row, 1973), pp. 344–345.

[2]John T. Lovell and Margaret S. Phelps, "Supervision in Tennessee as Perceived by Teachers, Principals, and Supervisors," *Educational Leadership* 35 (December 1977), 226–228.

each other in these rooms for the past six years and complement each other quite well. One teacher is somewhat stronger than the other, but they work well together. The students enjoy the teaming system for social sciences and perform well for the teachers.

The supervisor has observed a lesson, videotaped parts of it, and performed a Flanders interaction observational analysis of the lesson for each teacher. Analysis and strategy have been completed. The supervisor had worked informally with the teachers for the past several months and was aware that they were quite effective. On this particular lesson, however, their effectiveness was not very apparent. Pursuant to analysis and strategy, the supervisor's plan was to be somewhat indirect in the conference. When the teachers arrived for the conference, they seemed a bit more nervous than normal; and the supervisor tried to be as supportive as possible in setting the stage for a very positive and fruitful conference. The tape of the lesson was shown to the teachers. During the viewing the supervisor stopped the tape from time to time, pointing out positive aspects of the lesson to the teachers and praising them for their interaction skills, but the teachers seemed unwilling to react to the comments. After the teachers viewed the tape the supervisor asked their opinions of the lesson. They responded with such comments as "this was an excellent lesson," and "we are well pleased with it."

The supervisor, sensing that all was not well, decided to depart from the planned strategy and asked if they wished to view again any part of the lesson tape. They declined. The supervisor, being somewhat perplexed by this turn of events, then attempted to bring out several more positive aspects of the teaching but again met with little or no success in soliciting teacher response. Rather than going into analysis of each teacher's part in the lesson from the Flanders analysis matrices, the supervisor shifted gears. Noting that time was slipping away and being confused over the teachers' seeming nonacceptance of conference strategy, the supervisor suggested they end the conference for that afternoon and perhaps look at certain aspects of the taped lesson again tomorrow. At first the teachers were reluctant to accept this suggestion but finally they agreed. The supervisor was still in a state of bewilderment but planned later for the next day's conference.

The next day at the agreed-upon time the supervisor met with the teachers again. One of the teachers initiated the conference by stating, "You know, we had very little, if any, sleep last night. We had previously heard that you were down here observing at our school to determine which two teachers were to be fired. We didn't want to be the two and that's why we didn't react to you very much yesterday. As we talked with each other and with our husbands almost all night last night, we finally reached the decision that what we were told could not have been true, judging from the way you worked with us yesterday. We are now ready to begin the analysis of our session in earnest." The foregoing case illustrates, among other things, the need for the supervisor to be flexible, both procedurally and emotionally.

As stated, the central purpose of the conference is to provide constructive feedback to the teacher and thereby promote improvement of future teaching. The goals of any conference will have been predetermined, for the most part, by the happenings of the stages of clinical supervision leading up to the conference and by the relationship between the supervisor and teacher. The burden for ensuring that the goals are reached, for maintaining the pace of the conference, for coping with problems that arise, and for deciding when to depart from the planned strategy (earlier decided upon in the analysis and strategy stage) if the strategy fails or deciding when to terminate the conference rests primarily with Supervisor. In fact, Supervisor should accept these responsibilities as part and parcel of the clinical supervision process.

In the example, Supervisor clearly accepted these responsibilities. Instead of pursuing in the initial conference what was rapidly becoming a defensive struggle, Supervisor decided to cut short the discussion and suggested it be pursued again the following day, hoping that during the intervening time period renewed planning and reflection would be helpful. This approach was successful since the teachers themselves were persuaded during the intervening time period that Supervisor's motives and manner of working with them discounted their earlier fears.

It is important to recognize that no two conferences are precisely the same, just as no two strategies are ever likely to be identical; consequently, anything we might say about conference methodology is meant only to be suggestive. One sometimes develops the impression that against almost any method one might recommend, another worker could levy criticisms. It does not require a mischievous temperament to raise questions about almost any supervisory ploy. What works with a particular teacher today may not work at all tomorrow — or perhaps with any other teacher, ever. Every move that Supervisor makes is something of a gamble, and in retrospect might well seemed flawed in some way. The seasoned and skillful supervisor, however, draws upon experience, including knowledge of Teacher and remembrances of prior similar situations, every time a move is made.

Training in conference technology — for example, of the sort provided in graduate schools for guidance counselors — can be helpful to educational supervisors; and some of the theories and technologies that are applied to counseling have been profitably adapted to their work. We would caution, however, against blind addiction to one or more technical systems that come in and out of fashion in the counseling world. It is better, we believe, to be aware of the many options that are available and to learn how and under what circumstances it is best to use them.

Overcommitment to particular systems, especially those that advocate specialized conventions of technical behavior, can reduce the counselor's or supervisor's ability to function in a more intelligent, responsive, or creative manner. When stereotyped technical behavior dominates one's approach, in other words, the process can become rigid and mechanical. Training programs therefore should avoid instilling automatic technical patterns in the trainees, and the supervision of counselors and supervisors in the field should monitor any tendencies of the supervisors to fall into habitual patterns.

In the early phases of their training, counselors conventionally are taught rationales and methods for beginning treatment relationships and, more specifically, for conducting initial interviews. Some counseling students concentrate on individual interviews; others examine techniques for group counseling. Counseling students are exposed to various models of initial interviews and learn certain general procedural conventions: The client is greeted; various kinds of "structuring" are begun; confidentiality is explained; use of the tape recorder (video and/or audio) is discussed; counselor's remarks are designed to stimulate the client's spontaneous behavior, for diagnostic purposes; a schedule of future meetings may be arranged; and the like. Depending on their theoretical orientations, the counselors-in-training employ various methods for building rapport, establishing trust, developing relationship, and, in varying degrees, learn how to offer certain kinds of questions, interpretations, and reflections of the client's feelings.

In such training, especially in role-playing situations, there is an omnipresent danger that despite changing characters, the play may vary too little. Although some students maintain a sensitivity and responsiveness to their individual "clients," by and large they may tend to perform the same technical litany, irrespective of idiosyncratic differences among them. What may happen, then, is a simple recapitulation of technique, a stereotyped learning, a rote application of procedures whose appropriateness or necessity is not questioned or adjusted to fit clients' varying individual requirements. In some cases it even seems that the counselor's automaton-like behavior interferes with intelligent and sensitive responses that might be more usef--l and obscures individual differences, which in some cases could prove critical to recognize and to treat. Ironically, some of the counselors who most resemble wind-up toys in these role plays are the most fluent in enunciating Rogerian concepts having to do with understanding the client's frame of reference and the world of objects and feelings as it exists in his or her experience.

Our supposition is that, unless we are careful, the training afforded clinical supervisors can produce the same type of behavior. We trust that most training for counselors, supervisors, or teachers is not conducted in that manner, but unfortunately, however, some supervisory and preservice teacher training is flawed in such respects. Automaton-like behavior can pervade many of our actions, both in our jobs and in other activities in which we engage, professional or nonprofessional. Furthermore, in most cases we have little indication or awareness that this behavior is occurring; and even when we are made aware of the fact that this behavior is occurring, it may be difficult for us to change the behavior, even if we know it would be in our (and our clients') best interests to change it.

If it is true that behavior is difficult to change, and if many of our habitual tendencies are unknown even to ourselves, then we need to take advantage of all sorts of experiences that might be helpful in identifying and modifying them. Supervisors, no less than the teachers with whom they work, need to receive feedback on their behavior patterns. This can happen in both the school district setting and other contexts. In the following example, we see how an outside interest proved professionally helpful to a counselor.

Most cities have an organization known as Toastmasters International whose defined mission is to promote self-improvement in leadership and communications. At each meeting, members deliver speeches, which are then critically reviewed. The speaker in one such meeting was a member who is a counselor in a correctional institution. As he delivered the speech, his voice was a monotone, his appearance and mannerisms were client-oriented, and his speaking style was like that of a counselor working with a client during a normal day's activity. Later, during the evaluation of the speech, some of these problems were mentioned. The speaker then asked both the evaluator and the group for advice to remedy that particular set of problems. He related that he had been a Toastmaster for six years, and during that time has had these same recurring problems with his speeches. "What can I do?" he asked. The evaluator and others told him that in his speeches he was acting and reacting as he normally would in the daily course of his job and that he needed to break away from that pattern while speaking, and further, must discipline himself to do it.

The above example has some interesting implications for clinical supervision and, in particular, for the conference. A Toastmaster Club group normally meets every week (and has approximately 10–25 members). The meeting follows a program format that regularly includes speeches and evaluations. Speeches are delivered with specific objectives as delineated in the toastmaster's manual (each manual, beginners' and advanced, has listed objectives for each of the speeches the person is to make over a period of time and the objectives are well defined) and evaluated within those objectives. The topic of the speech and the content thereof (except for suggestions for the latter within the stated objectives) remain the prerogative of the speaker. Roles are different for each meeting so that over time every member receives experiences as speaker, evaluator, and other roles.

In the meeting each speech is evaluated by a member designated by the general evaluator of the day's meeting. In all meetings, that evaluation is presented verbally to the group; in some meetings, as in this case, the speaker has the opportunity to interact verbally with the evaluator during the meeting and may also choose to elicit further comments and evaluation from other club members and/or suggestions they may offer for improvement. Normally the evaluations are quite direct in manner, as might well be the case in a typical clinical supervision conference. The process of speaking and then being evaluated is quite similar to that in the observation cycle of clinical supervision.

In fact, persons in clinical supervision positions, or persons aspiring to such positions, would probably find the Toastmaster experience an excellent form of in-service training. One of the most important aspects of the Toastmaster training pattern, which deserves emphasis in supervision training as well, is that evaluation is welcomed and great pains are taken by all members to provide and maintain a threat-free atmosphere. Being a voluntary activity in which each member's goal is self-improvement and the sharpening of speaking skills, Toastmasters of course provides a different kind of setting than is normally possible in the schools; but all the same its program represents something to strive for. In addition to signaling the value of a supportive atmosphere, the Toastmasters pattern illustrates the importance of role delineation and of rapport.

A necessary condition for proper clinical supervision to occur and for the resulting improvement of instruction is for both Teacher and Supervisor to understand and accept their respective roles. The teacher must understand the role of Teacher and must understand and accept Supervisor's role as Supervisor. Just as important is Supervisor's understanding of the role as Supervisor and Teacher's role as Teacher, and both must understand their interactive role. However, once roles are established and both Teacher and Supervisor feel comfortable and confident within their roles, Supervisor might safely experiment with some role interchange in the conference — in somewhat the same pattern experienced in Toastmasters. Further, it is Supervisor's responsibility to decide which roles are to be assumed and for what time period — flexibility being an important consideration.

With practice, roles may be better effected by both parties and, in so doing, their own real roles as Supervisor and Teacher may be strengthened, both in conference and in general applications in their respective responsibilities as Teacher and Supervisor. Successful applications of this procedure can lead toward the threat-free atmosphere that is desired since both parties can learn to accept, appreciate, and understand the implications and responsibilities of each other's role. For Teacher, defense mechanisms may become less pronounced through this process; for Supervisor, the understanding of hows and whys of Teacher's defense mechanisms may take on new and added meaning and lead to improving Supervisor's ability to successfully cope with these mechanisms.

INTERVAL BEHAVIOR

Events in the interval between our observation and the moment of conferencing can become, whether accidentally or by design, either a help or a hindrance to the total process.

Earlier we touched briefly on some of the problems faced by Supervisor as he or she prepares for the conference, especially with respect to encountering Teacher in some unexpected face-to-face context and having to control one's words and facial expressions so as not to give an inappropriate message to the anxious teacher. If such an encounter occurs after the analysis-strategy thinking has been completed, but at a time when neither party is able to proceed immediately into the conference, the supervisor is probably better prepared to invent a suitable on-the-spot message than if his or her homework still has to be completed. However, in either case there are certain potential risks, as well as possible advantages, of which Supervisor should be aware.

The interval actually begins at the moment Supervisor takes leave of the classroom. If, while walking out, Supervisor is feeling very negative about the episode and perhaps even muttering to himself under his breath, an observant teacher will almost certainly sense Supervisor's feelings, and therefore be all the more sensitive to whatever Supervisor may say, either then or at noon in the lunchroom or in the parking lot during the fire drill.

Aware of this possibility, some supervisors seek to avoid any contacts with teachers in the interval, while others actually plan certain interval behavior (words, gestures, dropping off of notes, and so forth) as part of their communication strategy. It would be difficult to set down any general rules one way or another, but it is certainly important for Supervisor to realize that interval behavior is a potential positive or negative factor in dealing with the observed teacher.

One interesting question has to do with the optimum length of the interval itself. Usually, in the preobservation conference both parties can consult their schedules and agree that the supervisory conference will be held at X o'clock this afternoon (or tomorrow morning or whatever). A general rule is that the conference ought to be held as soon as possible after the observed event; but sometimes it is apparent to both persons even in advance that a longer time may be needed for the supervisor to digest the data or for Teacher to be psychologically ready for the discussion. In the interval, different feelings and/or perceptions could develop, in which case an effort may be made by one or the other party to renegotiate the appointment time. Teacher, for example, may want to get the discomfort over with, and so he or she pops into the office to ask, "Could you talk with me now?" Less likely, but all the same possible, is that Supervisor may be the eager one, and so he or she pops into the classroom with the same question.

On the other hand, the appointed hour could arrive with one or the other party still unprepared for it. Teacher arrives at the office to discover that Supervisor, obviously uncomfortable, wants to postpone the event. The reasons could be totally unrelated to the anticipated difficulty of the conference (had to take an injured child to the hospital; called to the main office for an emergency budget meeting; had forgotten about the two-hour ceremony at the mayor's office) or, on the other hand, they could have to do with Supervisor's failure to come up with a graceful way to say what needs saying. Or perhaps Supervisor is ready and waiting, and Teacher fails to show up, or sends a brief message over the intercom, or appears and asks to be excused.

Such possibilities are real; and therefore the length of the interval may in fact differ from what was originally expected. All the more reason, we believe, for Supervisor to be alert during all stages of the observation cycle, to the extreme importance of what is communicated (said and done).

We might offer up a few general guidelines with respect to interval behavior.

1. In the preobservation conference, try to anticipate some of the problems that might arise in the interval, and perhaps even include in the agreement some understandings about how to deal with accidental or similar contacts.
2. Take care when departing from an observation not to communicate any unintended messages of approval or disapproval.
3. Discipline yourself to follow the pattern upon which you have decided with respect to interval contacts. (One way to avoid an accidental hallroom encounter is to stay out of the hallway.)
4. Consciously develop a repertoire of interval behaviors to achieve certain objectives; for example,
   (a) gentle phrases to fend off a premature conference.
   (b) neutral phrases of the small-talk variety, to use during routine or accidental encounters.
   (c) encouraging phrases, to signal to a teacher that the conference will probably be reinforcing.
   (d) phrases designed to intimate that something less than reinforcement is in store.
5. In all cases, never lose sight of the importance of rapport, and recognize that interval behaviors are by their nature potentially hazardous to, or nurturant of, rapport maintenance.

CONFERENCE CONDITIONS

Recently a group of experienced teachers in a graduate supervision class was discussing conference technology, and a question was raised: "What are some of the things that should *always* be true about a supervisory conference?" Their discussion probably will be of interest to others:

TEACHER A: I want for it to be in a comfortable place: comfortable chairs, good lighting, temperature bearable, even some niceties such as pleasant drapes and a rug.

TEACHER B: Well yes, but even more important for me is the *location:* it should be convenient for me to get there . . . not too far from my classroom.

TEACHER C: The supervisor's office?

TEACHER B: Only if it's nearby.

TEACHER A: Not me. I'd rather it *would* be in her office. She has a nice, quiet, comfortable, private place.

TEACHER C: Yes, privacy is important. In your classroom you never know who's going to interrupt you.

TEACHER D: I think it's important that the conference should be a real sharing experience, not just a one-way message from on high.

TEACHER C: Amen. And let's add: it should be free of evaluation. Maybe sometimes it can include evaluation, but I see the supervisory conference, especially in the 0 cycle, as a *helping* activity.

TEACHER A: . . . characterized by mutual respect.

TEACHER C: Yes. And based on needs that *I* have, not so much the supervisor's.

TEACHER D: Our supervisor tries to arrange the chairs so that no one is in a dominant physical relationship to the other person.

TEACHER A: How's that done?

TEACHER D: Well, she places two similar chairs next to each other, with a small coffee table between.

TEACHER E: I'd worry more about the available time. He can sit on a throne as far as I'm concerned, but I hate it when he rushes me through the discussion.

TEACHER B: Yeah. Time's important. Time pressure can really prevent the conference from reaching its goals, a comfortable closure.

TEACHER G: I'd also argue that the conference shouldn't happen just by itself.

TEACHER A: What does that mean?

TEACHER G: Well, it shouldn't be the only one. There should be a regular history, and this one is just Chapter 6, let's say, in a ten-chapter book.

TEACHER C: Book-of-the-month?

TEACHER G: Well, yes, in a way. Book-of-the-year, maybe. What I meant is that it's a continuous — or ongoing — kind of thing. I don't want just *one* conference to be all that important.

By way of summary, these teachers saw as important certain physical considerations (comfortable, private space, well located, furniture well arranged), the availability of adequate time, the existence of a helping and sharing relationship, the absence of evaluation pressures, and, in the same vein, a relationship of mutual acceptance and respect. Teacher G hit on another crucial idea, that of each conference being part of a longitudinal sequence.

It may be appropriate at this point to include some general suggestions, including a few already mentioned, concerning optimal conference conditions. Time factors to be considered are:

1. Time interval after observation before conference is held
2. Time during the day to hold the conference
3. Length of time to allow for the conference
4. Time to allow for follow-up conference — that is, when to hold it and for how long.

Logistic factors are equally important and among those to be considered are:

1. Where to have the conference
2. What seating arrangements are to be made for the room

3. How to protect against distractions (e.g., asking secretary that you not be interrupted, choosing a room where distractions would be minimized, arranging for positive body language conditions as furniture and room conditions permit, choosing a pleasing aesthetic surrounding, seating arrangements, and the like)
4. What equipment to have available (video- or audio-tape player, pupil records, sample materials, observation analysis data and instrumentation)
5. What to add to facilitate conference rapport. Refreshments?

Some of these conference variables will have been decided upon in the preobservation session and may even have been included in the contract, such as when to meet and where. The choice may have been made by Teacher or Supervisor or both. Decisions concerning equipment may also have been decided upon at that time. If not, then Supervisor may have made such decisions during the analysis and strategy session.

CHOICES OF WORDS

Teachers in the foregoing discussion would probably agree that the verbal (and related nonverbal) behaviors of Supervisor play a very important role in conferences; and ideally Supervisor should over time develop a varied and extensive repertoire of words, phrases, and related schemes for the accomplishment of various intended messages. Although the word sometimes carries with it the suggestion of trickery or outwitting an opponent, we like to use the word *ploy* as a categorical term for the various approaches that might be devised and consciously utilized.

There are at least three events along the way in which a series of alternative ploys ought to be available for selection. One is what we call the *opening ploy:* words and actions that are (intentionally) used by Supervisor in the first few moments or minutes of the conference. Another is the *transitional ploy:* schemes used in order to signal that Supervisor is now about to move to another phase or part of the conference. *Closing ploys* would be an obvious third category; and the reader will recall that in our discussion of interval behavior there were references to other situations for which we recommended that supervisors develop some communication strategies.

THE OPENING PLOY

The strategic importance of Supervisor's actions in the early moments of conference makes it absolutely essential to base them upon some deliberate plan. Such a plan includes anticipating how Teacher will react to a given action, and having a standby plan ready in order to cope with each possible response. One ploy, frequently used, is to open the conference by asking the teacher how he or she felt about the lesson. Supervisor in choosing such a ploy must be prepared for such responses as:

1. Oh, I thought it was terrible. Did you, too?
2. I feel just great — one of the best lessons I've taught. Right?
3. I'm all confused. I couldn't possibly evaluate it without your help.
4. Hey, wait a minute. It's *your* job to tell *me* what you think!
5. I feel the way I usually do after a supervisor has been in the room.
6. The kids really spoiled it for me. Henrietta never did that before.

. . . and so on. If Supervisor felt that it was a good lesson and was hoping that Teacher did, too, then Response 2 offers one kind of an opportunity, but Responses 1, 3, and 6 offer quite another kind. Response 5, at least, requires clarification, and Response 4 creates some tension that might have been avoided with another ploy.

A second kind of ploy is to ask for additional data. "What happened in the class after I left? I'm curious to know. Did Jimmy actually finish his project? How did the kids do on the test?" This ploy is useful if Supervisor needs some extra information to support an emerging hypothesis or recommendation. It may also have the effect of reducing some of Teacher's tensions or at least of creating a moment when she or he can volunteer some information, even beyond what was requested.

A third ploy, orderly and businesslike, is to start the conference by recapping the preobservation agreement and then to deal, one by one and in the order in which they came up, with data pertaining to each question. The agreement reached in the preobservation conference helps determine what activities need be conducted in the postobservation conference. Normally, the more structured and complete the preobservation conference can be, the easier it is to plan for the postobservation conference.

A somewhat related ploy is to plunge directly into the data, presenting whatever charts, diagrams, or other visual materials are available and letting some of the conclusions or implications grow out of them. Supervisor may in such an instance wait for teacher questions and/or interpretations to emerge before discussing his or her own assessments.

Sometimes, as a version of the foregoing approach, Supervisor replays part or all of a videotape or audiotape, enabling Teacher to review certain of the events that, during analysis, emerge in Supervisor's mind as particularly pregnant with supervisory implications. A version of this approach, which in some schools is actually standard procedure, is to have Teacher review the tape in the interval, so that he or she can also have done some analysis in preparation for the conference.

What to do when Supervisor perceives that the data convey mostly negative messages? Is one of the above-mentioned ploys likely to be more successful than others, in creating an atmosphere within which Teacher can, with least embarrassment, face reality? Unfortunately, no certain responses to these questions are available. In general, however, it seems important to use an opening strategy that accomplishes both (1) reassurance to Teacher that Supervisor is still a friend and supporter and (2) an opportunity for Teacher to get, and deal with, the message in a businesslike and matter-of-fact way. For Supervisor to wring his or her hands in despair, or overkill, or otherwise dramatize the problem beyond Teacher's ability to cope with the news is obviously inappropriate.

When Supervisor perceives that the message is basically positive, determination of an opening ploy is obviously less difficult. However, positive overkill is also possible, and for a conference to end with Teacher shouting down the hallway, "I'm number one!" would also be obviously inappropriate.

In most situations, especially if the original contract or agreement made some kind of sense with respect to Teacher's development, the conference will deal with a mixture of "good news and bad news." ("Bad" is too strong a term, but the phrase is very popular and all the jokes about "I've got some good news and some bad news" serve to remind us of the difference it makes as to which news is mentioned first). Starting with the good news, which is a very popular opening ploy with most supervisors (after all, the king didn't kill the good-news messenger!), helps get the conference off on a positive note; but we must remember that when we start that way, most teachers perceive it as a time filler while Supervisor is screwing up the courage to come out with what really (in teacher's apprehensive mind) is the verdict.

Ending with the more sobering news does, on the other hand, have at least one virtue, mainly that it tends to remain fresher in Teacher's mind when the conference has ended. Some strategists prefer, however, to start with such news and then to switch to the happier messages so that the conference ends in smiles.

We might well imagine, or remember, another dozen or so ploys. Further, we realize that those so far mentioned could lead in many more directions, and have more or less value in various imaginable circumstances, than we have mentioned. Classes in clinical supervision could, in fact, spend hours examining such possibilities, and we hope that this book will prompt such excursions.

What we suspect, with regret, is that all too often supervisors fail to consider the opening ploy in advance and by default they simply let the conference happen. Laissez-faire, in our view, is not very often an acceptable type of strategy. However, there are perhaps some ways for Supervisor to effect a laissez-faire approach that may be defensible.

Sometimes Supervisors elect to have a series of conferences following an observation rather than just one, holding part of the conference on one day and the remaining part on another day. Both conferences can focus on only several items of the lesson. This is best done by prior arrangement, although where Supervisor feels that there is too much to be handled, he or she may elect this option so as not to overwhelm the teacher.

Opening techniques depend to a great degree on Supervisor's working relationship with Teacher. Determining the opening ploy is a more important consideration in the early working stages of the supervisor-teacher relationship than it is likely to be after Supervisor has worked with Teacher over a period of time. After Supervisor has established trust and has conducted many conferences, the issues of how Teacher is likely to deal with tension-inducing questions, react to supervisory strategies, and the like become more manageable. Yet Supervisor must *always* be conscious of (and thoroughly plan for) the opening ploy; in fact, in some cases the opening ploy decision is more important *after* Supervisor is well acquainted with Teacher.

TRANSITIONAL PLOYS

Another intriguing question, to which again we refer groups of readers for brainstorming, is how best to shift, at some point in the conference, from one sort of discussion to another. Particularly, what are some ways that a supervisor who opened with good news can set the stage for the less-than-good news? Here are a few sentences taken out of conference transcripts:

S1: Well, I'm glad there were so many strong points we could discuss. Now *(pause)* . . . um . . . I'm afraid there is some other stuff we'll have to look at.

S2: I don't quite know how to tell you this Ernie, but . . . well . . . on the questions business the data are . . . well, negative.

S3: Now, then . . . would you like to talk about some of the *problems* that I found with your lesson?

S4: Jim, you're such a nifty teacher that improvement may seem impossible *(chuckle)*, but, well, let's look at some areas of possible improvement.

S5: In the body language area you asked me to examine, did *you* realize that one of your mannerisms is . . .?

S6: OK, so much for the warm fuzzies. Now do you feel up to a criticism or two?

S1: (again): I'm afraid not all of the news I have for you is that good.

S7: How did *you* feel about the game you gave the kids? We saw some problems with it.

S8: Do you mind if we look at a kind of a tough problem?

The reader may perceive that some of the statements don't really seem like transitions, and most of them are merely examples rather than models. Over time, each reader is urged to put together a list of exemplary transitional ploys. The same goes for ploys that might be used to *conclude* a conference.

How does Teacher deal with a Supervisor who is apparently reluctant or unprepared to deal with sensitive issues? Here are a few sentences, again from transcripts, to which supervisors found it necessary to respond toward the closing of conferences:

T1: You really haven't told me everything, have you?

T2: I expected more criticism. Didn't you think I could handle it?

T3: Aren't you going to tell me how you felt about my warmth?

T4: This whole discussion seemed tippy-toe. Why aren't you leveling with me?

T5: You haven't really told me what you thought, have you?

Sometimes teachers make statements like these because they are really frustrated, and although they may not desire to receive negative news, they are annoyed if they think such news was withheld from them. On the other hand, we have often heard teachers who don't quite trust all the good news ask such questions just to push Supervisor into an additional "warm fuzzy."

The interchanges in conferences are, to say the least, fascinating to study — and to learn from.

OTHER DIMENSIONS OF CONFERENCING

The events of the first few minutes of a conference can often be controlled to some extent by Supervisor, especially if Supervisor has been skillful in the analysis and has selected appropriate opening-ploy behavior for launching the discussion. In short, being well prepared helps to guard against situations that might be awkward or difficult and enables Supervisor to pursue the purposes of the conference with less risk of failure. This is probably less likely to be true in the early stages in a supervisor-teacher relationship, during which the participants have less information about each other and a more tentative professional friendship, but even in a first-ever conference, good planning can bear healthy fruit.

Not only good planning, but a strong commitment to the helping (as contrasted with the *evaluating*) role of supervisors can help Supervisor to succeed. Behaving as any good teacher should, Supervisor seeks in the conference to respond to Teacher's apparent morale and state of mind, to recognize and deal with signs of confusion or misunderstanding, to offer as much reinforcement as is appropriate and possible, to provide data that bear upon the questions and concerns of Teacher, to keep the conference discussion within boundaries that make sense at that moment for that teacher, and (perhaps above all) to nurture and encourage Teacher's own capacity for professional self-analysis and self-supervision.

Again at this point, the clarity and the appropriateness of the "contract" or agreement that grew out of the preobservation conference can become a major factor for either good or ill. If Teacher posed problems or questions that are really authentic (i.e., genuine concerns, growing out of needs for improved professional performance), and if Supervisor had a good understanding of how he or she might collect data relevant to those concerns, both parties are likely to approach the conference more eagerly than if there were ambiguity, triviality, or irrelevancy in the contract.

Even under apparently favorable predisposing conditions, however, things can go wrong. Sometimes the opening ploy, while acceptable in most respects, can generate some new problems or lead down some unproductive paths. Sometimes it is the transitional statements that suddenly turn things around the wrong way. Sometimes time runs out or an unfortunate interruption occurs. Various problems develop. Therefore, the next and largest section of this chapter addresses them.

PROBLEMS

Many different kinds of problems will arise in the course of conferences. Some of these occur frequently, and over the years we have developed some sense of how to deal with at least some of them. Other problems do not occur so frequently, and when they arise we may find them to be either manageable within our experience framework or extremely complex and difficult. Many of these problems grow out of errors made in prior events — for example, careless listening in the preobservation conference or inadequate data gathering and analysis. Some grow out of the interpersonal or other problems Supervisor and Teacher have not yet examined and corrected. Many stem from the different perspectives brought to the conference by the participants: The teacher's orientation to the classroom and the children may be dramatically different from that of the supervisor. When Supervisor and Teacher occupy two very different psychological worlds, and especially if Supervisor seems to Teacher to be out of touch with the reality that Teacher perceives, or vice versa, then interaction is bound to be adversely affected.

Some other problems grow out of habits and relationships that have a long history in the schools. Traditionally, as well as in our own time, teachers and supervisors have been separated by hierarchical distance, by frequently conflicting objectives, and by differences in professional focus that have tended to keep supervisors aloof from classroom teaching while the teachers have been constantly up to their ears in it. Not infrequently, their differences have been tantamount to class struggle, as exists classically between labor and management, despite each group's tendencies to define itself as a professional discipline. Besides losing sight of teachers' lives because of their increasing distance from them, we suspect that supervisors have tended, progressively, to meet with distrust when they attempted to redefine their professional relationships more constructively, empathically, and intimately. One of the most common problems we encounter among teachers experiencing clinical supervision for the first time — sometimes this persists indefinitely — is that they seemingly cannot believe or trust their supervisors' apparent attempts to comprehend their professional experiences in essentially the same terms as they do themselves.

In any case, one discovers that supervision conferences abound in problems of this genre:

Supervisor flatly asserts his or her own view of things without attempting to envisage the teacher's.

1. *SUPERVISOR:* I have noted several specific reward patterns that I think we should look at today.
   TEACHER: I've been terribly concerned about whether the children should be prepared in some special way for the achievement tests that are coming up.
   SUPERVISOR: Well, I think we really have plenty of time to talk about that, but this question of rewards pertains to the teaching you're doing right now, and I think it should come first.

2. *TEACHER:* I find Anthony's behavior very distressing. I want to be kind to him, but I'm afraid that if I give in, he will just continue to take advantage of me.
   SUPERVISOR: Oh, I don't know. I think maybe you just aggravate yourself too much. He's not such a bad kid. In fact, I admire his boyishness.

3. *SUPERVISOR:* So, really, we want the children to take much more initiative themselves for deciding what to do and for getting their jobs done.
   TEACHER: But they need to be disciplined, or else they just get wild and disorganized; and nothing gets done.
   SUPERVISOR: Yes, that's what I mean. They must exercise more initiative in disciplining themselves.

Supervisor "plays it from rank."

1. *SUPERVISOR:* I've decided that instead of my filling out this evaluation form for the county this time, it would be better if the two of us went over it together and then countersigned it.

2. *SUPERVISOR:* I thought you'd be pleased to hear that I've recommended you for a merit increase.

3. *SUPERVISOR:* Well, you certainly have my permission to try it if you'd like to.

Supervisor is overly committed to uniformity among various processes and classroom procedures.

1. *SUPERVISOR:* I can see why you feel that way; but, nevertheless, since all the other sixth-grade teachers assign homework on a regular basis, I think it's important that you do too; otherwise it will seem unfair to children in other classes.

2. *SUPERVISOR:* Yes, that would be nice for the children, very appropriate, except they're only supposed to take two field trips per year, and then, all the fourth-grade classes are supposed to arrange something together.

There are other important senses in which our (the supervisor's) frame of reference may obscure the supervisee's. We may, for example, be too distracted by our own anxieties to be able to sense the quality or intensity of Teacher's. We may react defensively to Teacher's behavior instead of taking some psychological distance on whatever Teacher happens to be doing in order to understand his or her meaning and, perhaps, feeling of urgency. We may be distracted by our own feelings of gratification, the flatteries that Teacher pays, the pleasures of being an object of Teacher's dependencies. We may even be distracted by problems of our own that have nothing to do with the supervisory relationship but, nevertheless, cause our mind to wander away from supervisory issues.

In both teaching and supervision, it is very common for one to misperceive another's experiences because of strong tendencies to generalize from our own and to assume, implicitly, that things seem to others as they do to us. If, for example, we have always felt, as teachers, that whispering among the pupils constituted a personal affront, we might invalidly assume that our supervisee's feelings about such behavior are essentially the same.

Especially as a beginning supervisor, our conscious preoccupation with our own professional history and technique may eclipse the ideas and feelings that Teacher is trying to communicate. Transference-like processes may, additionally, cloud each member's views of the other. Our *idealized* image(s) of teachers may partially blind us to Teacher's *actual* condition. And, perhaps, what is most common of all, when we as clinical supervisors fail to comprehend our supervisees' frames of reference, it may be because we do not understand strong reasons for doing so or because, even having reasons, we do not know how — that is, we lack practice in dealing with or assimilating others' experiences.

One common manifestation of incongruency between supervisor's and teacher's frameworks occurs when Teacher is principally concerned with the problem of what to do next, that is, in tomorrow's teaching, whereas Supervisor is caught up today in the mysteries of analysis. Sometimes this discrepancy works in reverse: Teacher is anxious to know, fully, what we thought of the lesson observed, whereas we may think it is better to get on with planning for the future and pay only cursory attention to the completed lesson. Closely related is the frequent discrepancy between our concern with relatively abstract issues, while Teacher hungers for concrete solutions. The opposite condition may also occur occasionally.

Depersonalization, at least to the extent that dialogue hinges on technical issues and disregards such things as what Teacher hopes for or what makes Teacher afraid, is another common phenomenon in supervision conferences. In this connection, besides simply failing to share Teacher's perceptions of and feelings toward the work performance, we also avoid sufficiently intensive human encounters with our supervisees to produce "therapeutic" and developmental benefits that require a high degree of emotional rapport. Unempathic supervision — that is, supervision that lacks sensitivity to Teacher's emotional vectors — frequently is coupled with overconcern with technical matters. Instead of functioning as a facilitator of Teacher's professional development and fulfillment in terms that we ourselves formulate, we sometimes set out to make Teacher into our own images — to create a protégé.

Judging from complaints by teachers some of their most common grievances relating to conferences are:

1. It's just a lot of talk; we never seem to get anything done.
2. I'd be much better off to have that time for planning and for reading pupils' papers.
3. No matter what I come up with, my supervisor always finds some way to make things more complicated by raising all sorts of questions.
4. If I didn't have so much teaching and preparing to do, then this kind of thing might be OK: but as it is, it just burns up time that I don't have, then, for doing other things that have to get done.
5. The supervisor seems to feel I have problems in my teaching and doesn't seem satisfied unless there are problems to discuss.
6. I'd appreciate more answers; we never seem to come to definite conclusions about anything.
7. Sometimes I can't really see what we're after.
8. We keep going over the same basic things, time after time.
9. I know why supervisors want me to take the lead in analyzing my own teaching; but they're better at it than I am, and it wastes an awful lot of time to do it this way.
10. When the supervisor tells me what effects some of my teaching patterns are having on the pupils, it seems like just guessing about that most of the time. I don't know where these ideas come from. It's like a contest of wills.
11. I'd feel a lot better if the supervisor would just come right out and say when things are good or bad.
12. We seem fixed on the things the supervisor wants to talk about but not very interested in things I feel are important sometimes.
13. The supervisor seems to be afraid to say anything, as if my feelings will be hurt or something.
14. I never feel that there's time to fully understand what the supervisor's trying to show me. And so I often don't have anything to say, and then I feel kind of stupid.
15. This kind of supervision makes me feel like a rat in a maze, like a guinea pig.
16. It's as if there's no connection between the analysis and the plans we make for the next lesson.
17. I don't think the supervisor had much teaching experience, doesn't really know what it's like to be in there with the kids, and does the very same things I'm being told not to do, like saying, "I" a lot when you teach.
18. Supervisors try to make believe that we're equals, you know? But that's foolish; there's nothing democratic about this. I mean, they're supervisors, so why don't they just say what's on their mind and get it over with?
19. She seems to ask a lot of questions to find out whether I think she's doing a good job as a supervisor.
20. I get suspicious when he makes such a point of analyzing his technique. I don't know what he's trying to prove.

21. This business about "it's OK to fail," you know, "to make mistakes" — that's all right for a supervisor to say.
22. No matter what I say, the supervisor finds some way to attack it.
23. We seem to spend a great deal of time just talking about what we're doing, you know? That is, besides just doing things, the supervisor keeps talking about doing things: why we should do them, and how we're doing them, and things like that.
24. Sometimes I get the feeling that the supervisor really feels that it (the teaching) stinks, but that he has to find something good to say about it anyhow.
25. He seems much too worried about me — like I'm about to fall apart any minute.
26. Sometimes I worry about her because she seems to worry so much.
27. I'm sure he really has ideas about how to do these things, I mean, after all, he is a supervisor; but he just won't tell me the ways he's used, and I can't understand why he's so resistant. I know it's better to do things for yourself, that you learn better that way, but, well, there must be some reasonable limits to that sort of thing. Is this how he would really want us to teach the kids (that is, by "never" telling them how to do things)?
28. Sometimes I get the feeling that she's treating me as if I were a mental patient.
29. I often get the feeling, and sometimes it makes me very uncomfortable, that I'm being put on — that the supervisor knows the answers she's after, but is just going through a lot of phony motions in this "inductive" business.

Comments such as these are representative of problems revealed in studies in various regions and states concerning supervision conference techniques. Complaints registered by teachers, as revealed by these studies, are clear and warranted. Such complaints seem to fall into a relatively few prominent categories. Partly because of conditions that often surround supervision and partly as a result of mistakes that we as supervisors make, teachers often seem to feel thwarted by:

the pressures of time;
absences of closure;
the unavailability of simple solutions to professional problems;
apparent "manipulations" to which they are subjected, but whose reasons and intentions they do not understand;
intellectualizations and analysis at a level of abstraction to which many teachers are unaccustomed in their work;
an absence of authoritarianism, whose motives are difficult to understand and to trust;
an equally unfamiliar unstigmatized conceptualization of "problems" and, even, of "failures";
the practice of unearthing implicit assumptions and playing devil's advocate, which sometimes seems more like personal attack than professional inquiry;
inquiries whose outcomes are not foregone;
a novel absence of value judgments, particularly of reasoned ones;
a seemingly unremitting insistence upon examining ideas, behaviors, and practices;

interpretive hypotheses concerning the effects of teaching upon pupils that often seem to be contrived;

"gentleness" that sometimes seems implicitly condescending and occasionally gives rise to fantasies that supervisors view teachers as being psychologically fragile (this effect seems to result, simply, from an absence of punitive supervision, which many teachers tend to expect and against which they sometimes seem perpetually girded);

a feeling of unproductive repetition — a returning, over and again, to issues that seem to be exhausted;

a seeming unconnectedness between abstract inquiries and activities aimed at developing concrete products, for example, teaching (sometimes) and planning;

a feeling that, from a safe vantage point, supervisors criticize but are, themselves, invulnerable to criticism;

inconsistencies between the supervisor's own technical behavior and technical prescriptions;

reflexive examination (that is, of the supervisor's own processes) that seems unauthentic or whose reasons are not clearly understood;

tempos of supervision that are too rapid for effective assimilation to occur or too slow for interest to be sustained.

When supervision generates perceptions and frustrations of this kind, especially when we as supervisors are not aware of their existence and consequently cannot rectify them, our professional relationship is in trouble — and its constructive potentialities may diminish rapidly. It seems, developmentally, that various problems of trusting and of understanding — problems, more generally, of operating by new conventions and often within essentially new conceptual frameworks and value systems — are inevitable. It is not so much their existence as it is the possibility of failing to recognize them that constitutes a hazard in clinical supervision. In this connection, one deficiency that commonly exists in our practice is that we often become so absorbed in issues of the moment that we may neglect to take longitudinal and developmental views on teachers' professional behavior and maturation.

Two errors tend to result from this omission: The first is that supervisors sometimes become unduly alarmed by the manifestation of certain problems that they fail to recognize as being fairly normal and basic; the second is that because it may require a developmental perspective to articulate existing difficulties, such difficulties remain undetected.

The following short compendium is of developmental and acute problems, most of which arise from conditions inhering in the supervisor's behavior, rather than from external factors:

1. Either Supervisor has squandered too much time on analyzing the observed teaching to enable planning to take place in the conference or assumes that the positive modification of faulty teaching patterns requires only an identification of those patterns rather than development of new teaching strategies and their rehearsal.

SUPERVISOR: So you see that to make use of the student's substantive responses, using their own terminology, is likely to provide much stronger rewards for them than to merely say "very good" or to paraphrase everything in your own terms, as you've tended to do. OK?

TEACHER: Yes, I understand what you're saying.

SUPERVISOR: Fine. Keep these things in mind, then; this is something for you to work on.

At least, in this example, Supervisor's injunction is relatively specific and might, therefore, be taken up by the teacher constructively — more likely than if Supervisor had said, more baldly, "Your rewards seem pretty ineffectual; that's something I would urge you to work on." In any event, Supervisor did not trouble, for example, to role-play a series of responses in order to give Teacher some opportunity to try using the technique.

2. Supervisor reverts to "social conventions" where professional ones are indicated.

TEACHER: I don't know. Sometimes I just feel like giving the whole thing up, quitting this work altogether. I get very depressed.

SUPERVISOR: Oh, things aren't really so bad, although I know they seem that way sometimes. Cheer up. Tomorrow's another day, and things are bound to get better. They always do, you know.

In this example, Supervisor's glib reassurance resembles the kind of social response one might typically expect from a friend or neighbor. Supervisor might have had a more supportive effect by reflecting the teacher's feelings in a more understanding manner; by attempting to encourage Teacher to explicate his or her feelings and to make them more articulate, especially in their connection to factors capable of being influenced by supervision; by providing some kind of concrete assistance to Teacher, for example, by helping to formulate plans for the next lesson or possibly by providing materials that would increase Teacher's chances of success; and, indeed, by doing any of a number of things that one would generally recognize as professional acts in favor of what was done. As it is, the teacher may have thought, perhaps without giving words to the idea, that in fact things do not always get better and that Supervisor, though a nice person who really wished to be helpful, was not very helpful at that moment.

3. Supervisor has begun to operate according to a new "contract" but has failed to define it explicitly.

SUPERVISOR: . . . And so those are the categories in which I think, particularly, the patterns in today's teaching were significant.

TEACHER: Umm. *(Pause.)* Uh, did you get much about Paul?

SUPERVISOR: Pardon?

TEACHER: Uh, I had asked if you'd keep an eye on Paul to get some idea of where it is that he begins to lose touch with things.

SUPERVISOR: Oh! Yes, uh, yes. Truthfully, I became interested in this whole business around problem solving, and, I guess, I lost touch, myself, with Paul. I don't really have any observations of him that I think you'd find useful. I'm sorry.

Two additional problems occurring occasionally in relationship to contract setting are, first, that we permit ourself to accept a contract, stipulated by Teacher, that centers around issues of processes of whose value we are skeptical and, second, that we stipulate a contract that is either unacceptable or in some measure is incomprehensible to Teacher, who accepts it nevertheless, often out of deference to our status. Teachers might actually accept odious supervisory contracts simply because they are afraid to resist. Supervisors err when they are not alert to such possibilities and fail to detect differences among agreements arising from genuine interest and optimism and those resulting from feelings of coercion.

4. In zealousness to engage Teacher in objective, systematic, self-evaluation Supervisor fails to function as a source of adult rewards whose effects upon Teacher could be highly reinforcing and gratifying.

TEACHER: . . . And so it suddenly seemed that after having struggled with it for so long, the questions were coming out just right today. I could just feel it, as my words were coming out, that the questions were being formulated in just the right terms — and their response! I've never seen them so active in a discussion before. And I could tell, uh, that is, I was aware, even while I was saying them, that the kinds of words I was using in the questions would have to stimulate discussion, you know? Instead of the short, flat, answers that they usually give.

SUPERVISOR: You felt more success in "questioning" today than you had before?

TEACHER: Yes.

SUPERVISOR: Umhm.

5. Supervisor, though espousing a priority on "self-supervision" (self-initiated inquiry and self-examination among teachers), does not allow Teacher that opportunity in the supervision process.

TEACHER: So it began to seem to me that it was mainly when the kids had nothing in particular to do — not just to keep busy with; I mean something to do in which they were really interested — that their behavior began to get disorderly. And from your notes, it seems that way too. When they were really doing things they cared about, there wasn't any discipline problem at all.

SUPERVISOR: Yes, that's how I feel about it too. Let me show you, here, exactly at which points they began to act up, and then I'll make some suggestions about how you could time tomorrow's lesson, uh, the sequence of activities in it, so that they don't run out of things to do.

In this example, Supervisor assumed a degree of responsibility for planning that, at face value, seems gratuitous. One might infer from the remarks that the teacher already possessed both the insights and the incentives to exercise self-control and the ingenuity to create appropriate modifications.

6. Supervisor does not have an adequate understanding of discrepancies between the professional values of the supervisor and those of the teacher and thus cannot effectively deal with them. This situation does not lead to successful collaboration in supervision, often because Supervisor underestimates their importance; sometimes because Supervisor aims directly at modifying values instead of dealing with the technical behaviors they generate, that is, at the behavioral level; or, in reverse, dealing with behaviors that are unlikely to change as long as their underlying values are not examined explicitly. In the following example, Teacher's vehemence might be taken as an indication that rather than to attack the value in question directly and to provoke sharp resistance in doing so, Supervisor might be better advised to work toward less central and conspicuous technical modifications, which, even if they initially did not have influential effects on Teacher's professional outlook, might at least result in immediate benefits for the pupils.

SUPERVISOR: . . . So, it seems inescapable to me that the kind of instruction that aims, simply, to teach the kids a lot of specific information is largely a waste of time. They have to be given enough freedom — to make decisions and to follow through on them — to really learn, from experience, to be intellectually sharp and creative.

TEACHER: I get what you're saying, but — I just know that, I mean, anyone who's constantly in the classroom with these children will tell you — you just have to show them who is boss in the beginning. You have to start tough and then, gradually, ease up and give them controlled freedom. If you don't, they'll figure you for a pushover and learn that they can get away with murder, right fom the beginning. These things you're talking about might be OK for very bright, gifted, suburban children, maybe, but they won't work here. You know, I sort of see this as frosting. And what these kids need is more basic. They need, most of all, to find out who's in charge, in no uncertain terms.

SUPERVISOR: Well, I don't see it that way. I think it's mistaken to assume that the way these kids learn is especially different from the ways in which any kids learn. And I think, to the contrary, that if what they learn from the beginning is that you're the boss, it will be exceedingly difficult later on for them to learn to behave more independently.

TEACHER: Well, I don't want to disagree with you, but all I can say is that if *you* spent some time teaching these kids, I'm positive you'd find out that I'm right. I mean, if you want to try this approach with them — I'd love to see it. If I could see it, then maybe I could believe it.

7. Supervisor permits global perceptions and interpretations to go unchallenged and, consequently, to remain undifferentiated.

> *TEACHER:* These children are just lazy and negative. I've never had a group like this before. They're all impossible.
> *SUPERVISOR:* You can't find any way to get them in line?
> *TEACHER:* No. They are all totally uncooperative.
> *SUPERVISOR:* Well, maybe, then, it's time to get tough with them and also to find special ways to motivate them better.

In this example, Supervisor has apparently accepted the teacher's characterization of the pupils, which, first of all, incorporates ambiguous images — namely, "lazy," "negative," and "uncooperative" — and, second, implies that in relation to these characteristics all of the children are the same.

8. Supervisors are sometimes trapped by some teachers' tendencies to externalize problems, mainly through attributing them to outside sources, by their use of external issues as substitutes (evasions) for genuine problems in their teaching, and their efforts to avoid confronting these problems.

> *SUPERVISOR:* . . . So I wonder about what price you pay for the efficiency you enjoy when all of the children make exactly the same kind of Christmas wreaths at the same time. I also wonder, more generally, how useful an experience it is, for them, to work on decorations for a teacher's dinner that they won't even attend.
> *TEACHER:* Yes, perhaps. But the other fourth grade prepared the Thanksgiving decorations and I guess, the way they feel about it, it's our turn now. Mrs. Johnson just told me that she thought it would be best for our group to do it; and since she's more experienced here than I am, I thought it best to follow her suggestion. The children seem to enjoy doing this very much. Yesterday we spent all afternoon on it, and you could have heard a pin drop. By the way, we're running short on red and green construction paper, and I'm not sure we'll be able to get the entire bulletin board covered. They have been very slow in filling requisitions for materials this month.
> *SUPERVISOR:* You need more art supplies immediately?
> *TEACHER:* Yes, if they want us to finish this job.
> *SUPERVISOR:* Have you tried to borrow . . .

9. Supervisors are sometimes too assertive in their references to incidental learnings. What ought to be hypothesis too often becomes reified and is proffered as an element of reality.

SUPERVISOR: So, when you constantly repeat what the children say, they'll learn, from that, that they never have to listen to anybody except you and they won't listen to each other.

TEACHER: You think they actually think of it that way, I mean, "We don't have to listen to anyone except Mrs. Hardesty?"

SUPERVISOR: Yes, of course.

10. Supervisors sometimes seem compelled to include some reference to both strengths and weaknesses of the observed teaching in supervision conferences. Several principal errors in the approach are: losing sight of the possibility that, in fact, we are never forced to render value judgments on any specific occasion; the idea that conferences may proceed without including specific value judgments at all; and the idea that when evaluation is appropriate, many processes can be employed that may enable Teacher to initiate self-examination and evaluation of the issues in question. Indeed, such errors generally reflect a less than sufficient role conceptualization by the clinical supervisor.

SUPERVISOR: I must say, though, that your personal warmth toward the children is most impressive to me.

SUPERVISOR: By the way, I know it's not terribly important, but, at one point, you did say, "preventative" rather than "preventive." That's the only thing I can find. Except for that, the lesson was very successful.

11. Supervisors may provide too little time for their supervisees to assimilate important questions or to engage in reflective thought pertaining to the salient issues with which the two are dealing. When time for assimilating questions is insufficient, such questions are likely to take on a ritualistic and rhetorical character. Certainly, any question to which one is unable to begin formulating a response is a gratuitous question.

SUPERVISOR: You don't mind, do you, if I tape-record these sessions for the seminar in supervision that I'm attending? *(No pause.)* The first thing we ought to do, I think, is begin talking about the "cycle of supervision" and how it generally operates.

SUPERVISOR: Do you think it would be better for the children to evaluate their own work in this unit? I think they could use some practice in objective self-evaluation and that in social studies you have an ideal opportunity to give them that. I think the way to handle this is to . . .

12. Supervisors' errors may be most disastrous when they parallel the very errors being addressed in the conference.

SUPERVISOR: What I'd really like you to do for me is to try not to teach the lesson in the first person. I mean, I think that when you use "I" so often, the kids are likely to learn that whatever they do in school is for your sake, that is, for Teacher's sake. I really wish you'd try to work on this pattern.

13. Supervisors sometimes have a tendency to operate by double standards, and thus, for example, values espoused in the supervision are not fulfilled in the supervision.

SUPERVISOR: I can tell you, from a great deal of professional experience, that it's bad to expect the pupils to take information mostly on faith. It just teaches them a slavish dependency upon authority and dulls their critical thinking. A fact should never be accepted just because you say so and because you use your authority to impose it on the students.
TEACHER: I think that a teacher should represent authority and authoritative information to the students. After all, I'm an adult, and I've been around; and they're still children.
SUPERVISOR: Well, studies show that that's poor teaching, in the long run, and I'm afraid I must insist that you try to improve in this respect, Jim.

14. Supervisors sometime alienate supervisees by hedging and pussyfooting.

TEACHER: So you think I was really sarcastic with them?
SUPERVISOR: Uh, no, I didn't really say that. You are generally sympathetic and friendly with the youngsters, but some of your remarks today, were, uh, less kindly than I've known them to be in the past.
TEACHER: Some of my behavior today was unkindly?
SUPERVISOR: Well, uh, no, not really, but, uh . . .

Many additional problems of the conference, a good number of which have already been cited at various points in this writing, are difficult to illustrate by short excerpts, but are nonetheless vivid and common in clinical supervision. We have brought them together in the following short inventory. Collectively, they project an image of conferences at their most troublesome complexity; conferences in which problems are generated sometimes because of supervisors' errors but, ironically, sometimes as a direct outcome of well-executed clinical supervision. Any professional discipline may be badly performed because of inadequate understanding or poor technique. But every such discipline also creates or embodies problems that result not so much from its practitioners' technical weaknesses as from the premises, values, and theoretical formulations that constitute its very fiber and generate certain difficulties even while they prevent or remedy others.

1. Supervisors' zeal to take active leads in analyzing teaching and in developing strategies for its modification may, self-defeatingly, serve to reinforce Teachers' dependencies upon them for such activity.

2. Supervisors sometimes misjudge the most productive process to employ at any given moment in supervision — whether, for example, to use the conference primarily for diagnosing professional problems, for dealing with emotional ramifications of the teacher's professional work, for addressing technical issues didactically, or for developing concrete aids such as teaching plans or instructional materials for the teacher's use. When timing is off, not only may the potential efficacy of any specific approach be lost, but the gains that might otherwise have been achieved by an alternative approach are lost as well.

3. Supervisors sometimes use their data ineffectually, either because their meaning is inherently obscure, because too few of them have been collected to document the issues in question, or because they are examined excessively and redundantly after their purpose has been satisfied.

4. Supervisors occasionally err by confusing literal patterns of teaching behavior with the effects upon the students that they are supposed to produce. If anything, besides the misdiagnosis that may result from this process, the tendency to identify effects with causes generally creates intellectual closure; that is, it stops inquiry from commencing at precisely the moment when its continuation might be most critical.

5. Supervisors sometimes confuse the goal of avoiding unexamined value judgments with a practice of withholding value judgments generally. In some instances we have even observed clinical supervisors enjoining teachers to defer their own reasoned evaluations as a result of this misconception. Such supervisors get the idea that it is bad to say "good" or "bad," but seem to miss the point that what is wrong with such judgments generally is that they are glib, global, dogmatic, and uninstructive. That they are indeed value judgments does not make them inherently undesirable. On the contrary, the principal purpose of analysis is to formulate such judgments in order to modify the teaching performance rationally and constructively on the basis of objective evaluations of the teacher's work.

6. Psychological defensiveness represents a category of behavior with which clinical supervisors are often least competent to deal. On the one hand, being untrained in such issues, they sometimes fail to recognize the defensive underpinnings of various behaviors in which teachers engage in conferences. On the other hand, they sometimes become angered by teachers' defensiveness by which they, in turn, feel threatened, and toward which they react subjectively rather than with appropriate clinical distance. Additionally, supervisors are often unaware of their own defensive responses and deceive themselves by not recognizing the sources of their ideas and strategies and their professional behaviors generally, that is, by not understanding the defensive origins of motives for the actions they take in supervision. Too often, it appears, supervisors feel required to attack teachers' defenses, to strip them away as quickly as they can. Unfortunately, their impatience to do so generally results in wasted motions, largely because it prevents them from dealing sympathetically and supportively with the teacher to alleviate the anxieties that give rise to such behavior in the first place.

7. Not only in relationship to anxiety and defenses, but in connection with feelings generally (with frustrations, disappointments, confusions, and needs for acceptance and support), supervisors often lack sensitive "pickup." The same deficiency pertains to their ability to interpret the meanings of interactional processes that occur during supervision conferences — the implicit meanings attached to explicit communications in which the teacher engages, meanings that frequently communicate affection or hostility or fatigue or distraction which require considerable clinical acuity to recognize.

8. Suggestion making and advice giving are problematical techniques for various reasons. Besides being generally inconsistent with process goals aimed at establishing self-supervision at progressively more autonomous levels, the two most common difficulties arising in this connection are, first, that supervisors withhold suggestions at moments when, still being relatively dependent on such things, teachers have little tolerance for anything but suggestions; and, second, even after teachers have demonstrated that they will subvert the supervisor's suggestions by following them literally and rigidly to outcomes in which failure is practically inevitable and can be blamed on the supervisor's poor advice, some supervisors persist in suggesting things, self-defeatingly.

9. A general problem, whose specific forms are countless, occurs when supervisors fail to be innovative and flexible during conferences, when they hold on tightly to prior strategies (largely as a result of their own anxieties), and when they fail to respond creatively and spontaneously to unpredicted events. The opposite problem — namely, being unprepared with supervisory strategies — is considerably less common among clinical supervisors.

10. Supervisors sometimes underestimate their supervisees' personal and professional resources and falsely assume their own indispensability in the teacher's development. More accurately, they misconstrue the sense in which supervision may be truly indispensable, namely, as a dialectical medium, and instead they think of themselves as having power to change, to cure, to reform — in effect, to create better teachers. The implicitly condescending assumptions of such a posture seem, from what teachers tell us, to be communicated so potently that nothing positive is likely to result from the supervision to which it gives rise. When teachers sense that somehow the supervisor thinks of them as needy patients or that supervisors' responses are censored instead of being authentic, their self-confidence and their confidence in supervision generally falter.

11. Until the stage of professional development has been reached in which the various performed functions and employed processes are integrated into a cohesive supervisory style, the supervisor's shifts from didactic to diagnostic to "therapeutic" roles are likely to seem awkward and inconsistent and to disorient the supervisee. By and large, it seems that such images of apparent instability operate against the establishment of relaxation and trust in supervisory relationships.

12. Because they sometimes rely upon rote formulas of "accepting" and "supportive" supervisory behavior, some supervisors invalidly assume that when they have "been supportive" with a particular teacher, that teacher has felt supported; in other words, they confuse their intentions with their effects.

13. Some supervisors err by refusing, out of hand, to deal explicitly with personal material that teachers sometimes introduce into supervision conferences. Others would like to respond to such material but feel very shaky about how to do so. Still others seem so set on ferreting out such issues that, in effect, they trespass unwarrantedly on teachers' privacy. Although teachers generally seem ready to forgive lack of technical sophistication in treating personal issues, often they also seem to feel rejected both by refusals to look at such things and by excessive interest in them. Even well-intentioned and relatively sophisticated clinical supervisors frequently find it difficult to sift spontaneously presented personal issues in order to maintain a supervisory relationship (rather than a treatment relationship) by enforcing a criterion of relevancy (namely, to a teacher's professional activity).

14. Particularly during their early period of work with teachers inexperienced in clinical supervision, various factors tend to produce a mystique around the supervisors' professional activity. For one thing, supervision in the schools has always been a fairly mysterious process, even to those who practice it. Additionally, clinical supervisors' unprecedentedly detailed analyses of the teacher's work, coupled with a tendency to play devil's advocate, create novelties in the teacher's experience that, not infrequently, they revert to "magic" to explain. "They can make things come out any way they please, good or bad" is not an uncommon allegation for teachers to level against their clinical supervisors early in the game. Partly because they have become so accustomed, one might suspect, to dichotomous criteria in professional evaluation (most things are either good or bad, right or wrong), such teachers often mistake their supervisors' complex evaluations of teaching patterns, especially of patterns that seem concurrently useful and hazardous, for cowardly equivocation.

15. Supervisors themselves sometimes revert to evaluational polarities, either for want of the energy required for complex analysis or because they have followed their supervisees' thinking in that direction and have become subtly trapped by it.

16. Supervisors' own anxieties generate a multitude of problems in supervision conferences. Most commonly, we suspect, anxious supervisors hold on too tightly to their prior strategies and lose spontaneity and flexibility when in a state of heightened anxiety. By contrast, other supervisors — our experience suggests a smaller proportion — lose sight of their strategies and become scattered and unfocused in their conferences. Often objectivity is diminished when self-anxiety sparks defensive behaviors. Under such conditions it sometimes appears to the outside observer as though supervisors' perceptions of responses to teachers arise principally from a transference-like relationship

instead of from the objective realities constituted by the teachers' actual behavior. Clearly, when the supervisor-supervisee relationship assumes the character of a parent-child or sibling relationship, particularly when the supervisor
is unaware of its paratactic character and consequently is unable to do anything
deliberate about it, the supervision ceases to produce the outcomes for which
it is generally intended.

17. Supervisors occasionally lose out by neglecting to say what they are doing
in addition to executing the act in question. Especially when the act represents
a novelty in the teacher's supervisory experience, its rationales and purposes
must sometimes be stated explicitly in order for its intended outcomes to be
realized. For example, if supervisors truly believe in making productive use
of failure and conceptualize failure in a dispassionate and constructive manner,
then ability to educate teachers' values in order for them to confront their own
failures without shame — an objective that sometimes seems impossible to
achieve — may be enhanced if they take the time to explain their own conceptual framework around failure or to lead the teacher through inductive
inquiry on the issue. When the supervisor simply proceeds, without warning
or explanation, to name failures and to deal with them, the teacher is likely
to feel beaten up by the process (if, while the supervisor moves blithely along,
the teacher remains encumbered by all of the old painful connotations of
accumulated past failures) simply for want of appropriate preparation. The
same difficulty attaches to process confrontations, which, if they are suddenly
made without warning, may simply seem argumentative or unduly aggressive
to the teacher. As one might ordinarily predict, few teachers are accustomed
to facing such questions as, "What, exactly, have you been doing in this conference for the last ten minutes?" And again this same problem arises in connection to supervisors' technique of employing examinations of their own
technical behavior of didactic purposes in the conference. Having probably
never witnessed such behavior by a supervisor before, the teacher is often
dismayed and distrustful and unable, without some prior explanation, to make
very good use of a supervisor's gambit. Without an understanding of the purpose of such public self-examination, the approach may easily seem overly
righteous or defensive.

18. Process confrontations are sometimes made so frequently that they dis-
tract supervision from the substantive issues being addressed. More often,
supervisors err by neglecting to make such confrontations at moments when
the dialectical process has bogged down, for one reason or another, and might
be freed again by refocused inquiry in its direction.

19. Depending on the stage of training, the supervisor may commit one of
two general errors related to the technique "hierarchical intervention." Early
in the training, if error occurs at all, the supervisor is most likely to move
precipitously to the terminal, highly directive steps in that process (sometimes
through impatience, but more often through not fully recognizing the tech-

nique's applicability to the issue in question). More highly trained clinical supervisors are more likely to be too scrupulous and to overextend the duration of early stages in this process, even after the teacher's manifest confusion and the ambiguity of the supervisor's own behavior should have been taken as indications to move on through the sequence.

20. Supervisors frequently misjudge the timing of conferences, more often by extending them too lengthily than by quitting prematurely.

21. In connection with special clinical techniques, we find innumerable errors, some of them relating to the question of when a technique should be applied, others relating to the technique's actual use — that is, "how to do it." Role-playing, playbacks, role reversals, and reflections are sometimes employed gratuitously, lost by missed opportunities, or implemented awkwardly. One must be able to judge, for example, at what moment a reflection of feeling or meaning is likely to lead toward heightened insight and to provide a point of departure for more efficient inquiry. Moreover, one must reflect accurately or at least reflect tentatively enough to permit corrections toward accuracy, lest the technique fail altogether. One must be able to distinguish between reflections rightfully rejected on the basis of inaccuracy and those rejected for precisely the opposite reason — namely, because they are too accurate, too anxiety-provoking, and, in short, too generally threatening to be accepted all at once. Such determinations require considerable clinical finesse and, unsurprisingly, are performed erroneously in many instances in clinical supervision.

As one might expect in relation to any professional relationship, we find, abundantly, in our observations of clinical supervision that faulty techniques, weak conceptualizations of the supervisory model, or intellectual or emotional deficits that interfere with Supervisor's performance all tend to leave the teacher somewhat resentful or frustrated or angry or vaguely dissatisfied and, almost always, with a feeling of having been manipulated. Although reactions to such a feeling may vary greatly from person to person, among the teachers with whom we have worked they seem, inevitably, to be negative in one form or another. Indeed, it is easy to feel empathically toward clients whose discomfort and anger are provoked by faulty professional processes. Commonly, in new clinical supervisory relationships, teachers are inclined to ask, "What does Supervisor get out of all this? Why does he or she bother?"

Summing up, problems of the conference are essentially problems of operating at many levels and performing many functions concurrently. Supervisor must hear what Teacher is saying and also must understand Teacher's intended meaning and other meanings, the implicit communications, that may underlie spoken words. At the same time, Supervisor must hear his or her own inner voices, motives, impulses, anxieties, and so on — and, especially, values and professional biases — as they rise up to influence his or her mental responses and outward behavior. Supervisor must maintain an awareness of prior strategies and engage in behavior that is consistent with intended outcomes and simultaneously must be sufficiently sensitive and flexible to move in Teacher's directions, often when such movement follows unanticipated itineraries. Supervisor must be able to transform ideas and intentions into action and must, thereupon, engage in technically adroit actions. Supervisor must, all at once, draw upon technical repertoire, instantaneously and without labored effort, function by the specialized conventions of supervision discipline, deal with substantive curricular issues, and with equal authenticity draw upon the mental resources he or she possesses as a human being.

Supervisor must generally be directed toward both long-term and immediate goals and should sense the developmental outcomes and developmental unfolding that constitute the overall framework in which supervision of a specific teacher is occurring and must understand how to treat issues of the moment in a manner that facilitates those outcomes as well as meeting Teacher's immediate requirements. Professional behavior of Supervisor should exemplify many of the same processes and values and technical standards that have been set as goals for Teacher's performance. Supervisor must be self-reflective, insightful, and controlling and devote equivalent energies to self-examination as to the examination and analysis of Teacher's work; perform counseling and didactic functions and know which compromises between diagnostic and "treatment" goals are optimal at any given juncture in the supervision; be committed to process goals as well as to substantive technical outcomes and possess such theoretical information concerning professional development, human actualization, and learning as clinical accomplishments require; and earnestly want to be a successful supervisor.

In the existence of these conditions and in their establishment, we have problems in a positive sense: disciplinary problems, in the sense that problems of theoretical physics are problems of the parent discipline. When these conditions do not become established or maintained, or when they are imperfectly established, then we have problems in the negative sense: we have supervision in which something is the matter. Problems of the conference are, in effect, a composite of all the problems of clinical supervision. Inadequate preobservation, faulty observation, erroneous analysis, mistaken strategies, and a failure to have examined one's own professional behavior objectively — all manifest themselves in the conference, in the central and critical transaction that exists between Supervisor and Teacher. No matter how eloquently we as supervisors have performed the surrounding functions, we may botch up the whole act in this moment of encounter if, despite our most elaborate precautions and preparations, we are generally or momentarily unfit for productive interpersonal transactions. In short, we must be both well trained in the ideas and methods of clinical supervision work and potent, stable, and well assembled as a person; moreover, we must have strong capacities for learning and for changing. We suspect that Supervisor's own continuing enhancement and development are necessary concomitants of successful clinical supervision and that when we as supervisors are unable to engage in relationships that are mutually facilitating for the teachers and for ourselves, then, as they say, "We've really got problems!"

Chapter 10

THE
POSTCONFERENCE
ANALYSIS

* Methods
* Problems

METHODS

Perhaps the most telling mark of any practitioner's commitment and fitness to perform professional work is the readiness to have such work examined and critiqued by other competent workers — that is, to include subordinates and peers, on appropriate occasions — for the purpose of self-improvement. We feel this way particularly about clinical supervision, for it is all but impossible to imagine a rational double standard that could free supervisors from the necessity of being supervised themselves. Teachers should retain the love of learning; in so doing they willingly engage in self-improvement activities. And by retaining the role of learner, they become even better teachers. Supervisors in turn should retain the roles of teacher and learner, for by accepting both they exhibit their willingness to improve their supervisory concepts and techniques while keeping in mind the teacher's perspective of the whole supervision process.

Supervisory critiques originally arose in training situations where group supervision was being practiced and where, consequently, it was easy for a supervisor's work to be observed and analyzed by other supervisors reciprocally. Under such conditions the models of supervision that we have been examining in relation to instruction could be applied to supervision, with little need for alternation. However, in most scholastic settings today, supervision is not conducted in groups, although the current continued expansion of team teaching, both on the elementary and secondary school levels, creates possibilities for multiple supervision that should be considered carefully by modern school administrators.

For the present, however, we must conceptualize possibilities for reflexive supervision designed to fit existing situations in which supervision generally is conducted by one supervisor with one teacher at a time. Although we can imagine various arrangements in which teachers, and even pupils, participate in supervising Supervisor (we think that supervision's future urgently requires these innovations), our immediate and practical question might be simply how supervisors might supervise themselves on a regular and systematic basis.

Procedurally, the most useful device we have found for self-supervision is to tape (either audio or video) supervision conferences and use such tapes as the objects of analysis, along with whatever notes (for example, on observation, analysis, and strategy) are taken in the process. Once these data have been collected, Supervisor uses them in essentially the same way as he or she uses classroom data. Because there is no necessity to plan a conference, the post-conference analysis can represent a highly abridged process, involving only an analysis of the supervision that has taken place and the subsequent planning based upon such analysis. We do recommend, however, that in many cases, a postconference analysis session be conducted with Teacher or significant others present as active participants in the process.

The postconference analysis is, in effect, a self-improvement mechanism whose purposes include:

1. Assessment of the conference, in terms of
   (a) the teacher's criteria, as determined in the preobservation conference,
   (b) the supervisory criteria, and
   (c) the apparent value of the conference to the teacher.
2. Evaluation of the supervisor's skill in handling the several phases of the cycle.

In a sense, this analysis represents supervision's "superego" — its conscience. It provides, then, a basis for assessing whether supervision is working productively. Ideally the postconference analysis should comprise both a tête-à-tête session and Supervisor's self-reflective session. The tête-à-tête session is a postconference analysis with Teacher or, in some cases, with colleagues or significant others. In this joint session are examined the pluses and minuses of supervision techniques used, the implicit and explicit assumptions made, the values and emotional variables considered, and the technical and process goals effected. Data obtained from this examination assist Supervisor in making decisions to modify practices to better meet both Teacher's and Supervisor's needs. Participation in this part of the observation cycle enhances Supervisor's efforts to understand the intellectual and emotional dimensions of Teacher's work. The self-reflective session is a singularly planned and attended analysis by Supervisor, with the aid of notes, tapes, and any observational analysis gathered during the process of the cycle, together with other prior information relating to the supervisor-teacher relationship and interaction. This session need not necessarily be formal; rather, it can be an ongoing process. Perhaps it ought to happen throughout the cycle.

Once again, we as supervisors work from the assumption that the repetitive patterns in our professional behavior constitute its most potent features; they are those components that are most likely to lead us toward successes or failures. But intuitively, it seems clear from the very beginning that the analysis of our work will not feel or proceed as though we were examining just work — that is, just anybody's work — for once we begin to employ our skills reflexively, we must face the problem of distance more energetically than we would ever be likely to in relation to Teachers' work. The principal problem of self-supervision is objectivity: the problem of looking at our work from a proper distance, the problem of maintaining sufficient objectivity to perform an analysis that is likely to be worth something. As participant-observer, the clinical supervisor's role in the postconference analysis is difficult indeed since the observer (supervisor) is of necessity, both detached and affectively, participating and sharing in face-to-face relationships with a teacher, peer, and/or significant others. Self-supervision's task is thus doubly difficult because at the same time that we must strive to be objective, we are also turning our attention toward our own behavior and looking at our products in very fine detail. What could be more difficult than to maintain distance in an activity that requires intense concentration upon one's own behavior?

We know of few methods per se, that is, of "methods" in the ordinary sense, that can be described for use in the postconference analysis. Those few methods are borrowed, mostly, from the field of anthropology of education. The immediate problem is to capture the sense of Supervisor's difficulties in this stage of the sequence and to find some rules of thumb that might help to keep those efforts productive. If both the supervision conference and tête-à-tête session are taped, the postconference analysis becomes potentially more powerful for effecting improvement for future cycles. Suggestive procedures for viewing and analyzing those tapes might include the following: (1) Try to establish a condition of unself-consciousness by listening to or watching casually enough tape to become accustomed to your voice and mannerisms so that you can listen to and/or view it with a degree of objectivity. (2) Try to be aware, particularly, of episodes in the supervision about which you feel very positively or very negatively. Working from the assumption that strong evaluative feelings tend to be global and to incorporate halo effects, you can try to pay particular attention to those episodes about which your feelings seem least equivocal. As you listen the second time (or third), pay special attention to Teacher's words and inflections and try very hard to discipline yourself against projecting your feelings upon Teacher. Try, in other words, to break free from your own feelings — for example, that at some particular moment you had been particularly supportive or accepting or instructive or punitive — and listen to the *teacher's* responses to see what clues they provide about how Teacher was actually responding to your behavior, or feeling about things generally. Even after this kind of effort, possibilities of self-deception remain, but at least you have tried to see things as realistically as possible. (3) Seek opinions for collaborative analysis of critical episodes; ask others to listen cold, and to tell you what they hear. (4) It may even be beneficial to go *directly* to the source if you feel that it is important enough to matter (and if it does not interfere with what you are after in the supervision) and replay problematic episodes *for the teacher* to learn better about the significance they may have carried for him or her. Although no such method is foolproof, it is sometimes very useful to take such pains, especially when they protect you from proceeding on false assumptions concerning Teacher's experiences in supervision. (5) Besides listening with special acuity to hot spots and cold ones, try to stay alert to long passages of tape that feel flat and featureless. More often than not, flatness is in the ear or eye of the listener and what has actually been flattened by anxiety or defensive blocking of one sort or another is Supervisor's perceptual apparatus or own level of intellectual energy available for finding the significant meanings in Teacher's behavior. Try to overcome that by forcing attention to gray episodes. When you find your mind wandering, try to set it straight again by listening and relistening to the episodes it has wandered from until you feel relatively certain that you have heard whatever there is to hear and that you have found whatever you are likely to find in them.

Just as our analyses of teaching behavior generally require us to search for likely incidental learnings by trying to assume the pupils' frames of reference as they experienced the lesson, in the postconference we should try to use the same techniques for calculating our effects upon Teacher. A constant question should be, "What might Teacher have been learning at any given moment in the conference as a result of my supervisory behavior?" And again, the unremitting problem is to keep as distinct as possible a difference between what I as Supervisor would have learned, had I been Teacher, and what, indeed, Teacher might have actually experienced.

In connection with incidental learnings, we should try, especially, to stay alert to certain questions that have proved critical in many postconference analyses:

Where does the locus of initiative for supervisory inquiry tend to be? When either the teacher or the supervisor consistently initiates supervisory issues and the other member does not, the imbalance of initiative may signify unproductive processes that tend, for example, to reinforce resistance to inquiry or excessive dependency upon the supervisor for structure and direction.

What kinds of rewards tend to be provided? Supervisory behavior may be modified appropriately if it should appear, for example, that our intended rewards are not experienced rewardingly by the teacher; that rewards tend to be more social than substantive; that an implicit expectation of negativeness (or some sort of implied punishment) has become established as a motivational element in the teacher's work; that initially potent rewards have become ir

effectual as a result of excessive use; or that, except in the supervisory interaction, the teacher experiences a paucity of rewards in his or her professional
work and is at some loss to conceptualize activities from which they will be
generated.

*What is the proportion of questions in each member's dialogue (and what
are the questions' formal characteristics)?* A preponderance of questions may
reflect avoidance of problem-solving activity. Excessive questioning by the supervisor may create a feeling of "interrogation." Excessive questioning by the
teacher may reflect an inordinate dependency upon the supervisor for answers.
Questions' formal structure may be identified as a source of frustration, inef-
ficiency, or, on the other hand, of positive achievements in supervision.

*Whose products are most abundant in the conference (for example, who
authors whatever plans are laid for future teaching)?* Especially when the
supervisor is the actual inventor of teaching plans, evaluation strategies, and
disciplinary techniques that the teacher subsequently employs, the supervisor
may, as it frequently happens, begin to confuse enthuiasm for his or her own
products with objective appraisal of the teacher's performance and fail to
perceive deficits in the sufficiency of the teacher's technical behavior.

Does either member's behavior become stereotyped? In addition to reward
patterns, other elements of supervision may become stereotyped. When supervisory procedures become ritualistic, or established as "traditions," their
utility is almost bound to decline. We have generally found it useful in postconference analysis to examine the question of whether any activity, in either
the teaching or the conference, has seemingly taken place "as a matter of
course."

*How abundant are explicit rationales and reasons for value judgments and
for decisions affecting future work?* The teacher's or supervisor's proceeding,
regularly, on the basis of unexamined value judgments and decisions would
oppose the rational analysis that clinical supervision has been invented to
establish more securely in the teaching profession. The supervisor should never
teach, incidentally, that the goodness or badness of specific techniques is sufficient to be determined on wholly subjective bases — for example, in reference
to the simple fact that either the supervisor or teacher likes them or dislikes
them.

*How likely is it that semantic confusion or the ambiguity of language gen-
erally has created illusions of agreement or disagreement?* Reference to this
question has frequently led to the decision to employ playback techniques more
extensively in future supervision conferences.

When we have done the job fully and have prepared our supervision (of
Teacher) by planning explicit substantive and process goals and have, additionally, specified our goals in behavioral terms as well as in the form of
cognitive outcomes, then we should be in the best possible position to undertake
a productive postconference analysis unless, of course, it became necessary to
quit our plans during the supervision conference. But even in the latter case,

our goals are likely to have been superseded by other goals rather than to have been forfeited to aimless wandering. In any event, the existence of specified outcomes is very handy for evaluating actual outcomes. At least such prior goals generate a structure within which it is relatively efficient to evaluate what took place; a set of more or less delimiting categories in which to focus examination. Even when it is possible to refer to a priori goals for analyzing the supervision, and to employ them essentially as evaluation criteria, and this can be done most efficiently if *criterion behaviors* have also been stipulated in advance, it behooves us to follow the question of what outcomes occurred, irrespective of goals. Sometimes unexpected outcomes are more useful and productive than planned ones. It sometimes appears, however, that even if planned outcomes have been achieved, other elements of the supervision have produced cancellation effects or interference or, in some manner, have operated at cross purposes to our explicit intent. Most commonly, such static takes the form of negative process learnings incited concomitantly with intended substantive learnings.

Although it is possible to perform a postconference analysis without having video taped the supervision, it is generally clear that to do so is more difficult, less efficient, and less trustworthy than with analysis of tapes. The more memory work required, the more distortion occurs, and the less valid are the processes and outcomes of our self-analysis. We do not mean to suggest that in the absence of recorded data Supervisor should give no afterthoughts to what he or she has done, but there is little room to doubt that the more actual data are available, the better the chances are to achieve something useful from expended efforts. Besides, planning for the next sequence of supervision often begins in the postconference analysis, inescapably so when Supervisor unearths puzzles whose solution requires Teacher's participation.

In actual practice, not even the most committed supervisors are likely to have enough time or psychic endurance to postanalyze every sequence of supervision in which they function, nor, one suspects, would it be necessary or useful for us to do so any more than it would be desirable to apply our complete model of clinical supervision, in all of its procedural detail, in every instance of supervision. Such scruples would quickly produce diminishing returns. As in most other human and professional endeavors, the question becomes one of determining how often and how much and at what moments a potentially useful activity should be undertaken. We have not found any certain answers, but we do think there are guidelines that can be followed.

We think, for example, that to build some protection against avoiding self-analysis regularly in just those relationships or at just those moments at which it might be most critical to undertake it, the clinical supervisor should generate enough self-discipline to perform the postconference analysis at some arbitrarily decided interval — for example, in conjunction with every fourth or fifth sequence of supervision performed. More rationally, depending upon Supervisor's purposes, Supervisor may decide to employ a conference analysis at the conclusion of a supervisory cycle (if there is interest, generally, in keeping watch over professional self-development) or, depending on the difficulty and complexity of the supervision in question, to do so with special rigor during the initial sequences in a cycle. Whatever the decision, the postconference analysis is most likely to succeed when it involves the participation of a second supervisor, if only because under such conditions Supervisor is relieved of some of the terrible burden of keeping oneself realistically objective.

Unless there are important contraindications, we are especially enthusiastic about the idea of having the teacher who is being supervised fill the role of the supervisor's supervisor at propitious moments. First of all, no one is more likely to have pertinent information about the supervisor's effects than the teacher who has been affected. Second, and we see this as a pregnant proposition for research, this technique provides desirable role reversals on a regular and dependable basis. We are becoming progressively more convinced that this is an excellent measure in that it relieves some of the old status anxieties of supervision, cuts across its real and imaginary hierarchies, enhances Teacher's feeling of dignity in the supervisory relationship, enables Teacher to gain higher degrees of objective distance on his or her own work, and keeps Supervisor fully aware of the effects of supervisory techniques and strategies. Another bonus we see in this approach is that, among other things, Teacher stands to gain some supervisory competency and consequently stands to become a more potent and valuable member of the school faculty.

Although there is no clear-cut methodology for self-supervision, the postconference analysis should not be considered simply a collection of good intentions and ritualistic motions. It is not a ceremony or a penance or an absolution or a nicety. The postconference analysis should afford a time for professional self-examination and management that exists for the profession's good, for Supervisor's own growth and development, and for Teacher's protection and advantage. It is probably true that all persons must work out the incentives and tools of self-examination for themselves, and that no one can chart the engagement that should occur for all persons as they search to improve. Although these limitations may be inevitable, it is nonetheless frustrating to be unable to do much more than to express these wishes and simple injunctions to clinical supervisors.

PROBLEMS

Two tendencies lie at the source of problems in this context of clinical supervision: (1) to feel as though one knows, generally, what one is doing and (2) when the opposite feeling exists, to shrug one's shoulders and to avoid examining one's own behavior closely in order to understand more clearly what the trouble is. There are various ways to express the basic difficulties of this stage. There is always the problem of engaging an objective distance with one's own work and one's own behavior. In this connection, many specific problems may be pinned to the various defenses that operate in human personalities to obscure, to deny, to rationalize, to avoid reality, often in the same manner for all of us but always differing in detail from one individual to another.

In our own experience and in those of colleagues with whom we have been closely associated, we often find that supervisors feel consciously afraid to look inward. When "being scared" does not exist explicitly, the underlying anxiety is variously experienced, either as fatigue ("I really believe in the postconference analysis but, generally, by the time I've finished going through a whole sequence of supervision, I'm just too pooped to get involved in one") or as an absence of motivation ("There really didn't seem to be any need for self-analysis; I mean, it wasn't as if it had been a particularly complex sequence up until then").

Occasionally Supervisor's mechanism for protecting the self from threatening potentialities of self-examination is not conscious fatigue or fear but superficial ritual — that is, performing postconference analysis sessions as if they were ceremonies to be endured. Going through the motions tends to satisfy both of these purposes: Supervisor has done what ought to be done — without pain, but unfortunately with self-deception. In our work with supervisors it has frequently seemed that although their performance of supervision sometimes became jaded and automatic and rote, these characteristics surfaced much earlier in the self-supervisory activity. Thus postconference analysis is generally the first stage of the cycle toward atrophy in practice.

Problems of the postconference analysis, especially among beginning supervisors, are occasionally associated with inadequacy of analytical skills across the board. When supervisors are not competent to interpret behavioral data generally, there is no reason to expect them to be particularly competent in analyzing their own behavior. From time to time, incidentally, we have observed an interesting related phenomenon: that some supervisors were, in fact, highly capable of performing insightful analyses of their own work but were less capable of analyzing teachers' work and of conducting conferences based upon such analyses. In such cases it has usually appeared that supervisors' problems, even in Stage 3 (analysis and strategy), derived from anxieties around confrontation. This says that besides lacking the fortitude for confrontations in the conference, supervisors could not even design strategies for themselves adequately for prospective confrontations during the strategy stage. In one case that left us with particularly vivid impressions, Supervisor was so inhibited in this respect that although the self-analyses were quite sophisticated, the analyses of other people's teaching, *even when performed upon case materials*, were generally puerile.

In yet another sense, failure to achieve successful postconference analysis frequently seems associated with a simple lack of self-discipline that is expressed in other manifestations of sloppiness throughout Supervisor's work. The very same supervisor whose observation notes are slipshod is likely to be the person who forgets to employ a tape recorder during the conference. Inadequate self-discipline is, however, more likely to be expressed by the habit of promising oneself that although there really is insufficient time or energy to perform a postconference analysis today, one will definitely do so tomorrow — or the next day, or the next. Lazily, some supervisors also do not bother to specify behavioral outcomes and behavioral criteria for successful conferences beforehand and, consequently, reduce the certainty and efficiency with which they might otherwise evaluate conferences retroactively.

Sometimes supervisors repress data about their own performance. Sometimes, although the data are admitted to consciousness, they are processed through defensive filters. Sometimes supervisors' findings are influenced by temperamental factors, for example, when a self-deprecatory analysis emanates from a spell of gloomy despondence.

Even when supervisors are able to perform an adequate evaluation of their work, unless they are blessed by the existence of colleagues whom they may employ as professional foils, they are often frustrated, if not hamstrung, by the difficulties involved in progressing from psychic realizations to behavioral modifications. As a rule, their opportunities for rehearsal are not nearly so abundant as those they may provide for their supervisees. While self-supervision represents a highly valued practice to us, ironically, perhaps, once such activity has been established on a systematic basis, it generally seems that the requirement for *other* people to participate in the process becomes more pressing. This is the principal sense in which we believe that Supervisors never become obsolete: The more autonomously Teacher engages in self-supervision, the more productively he or she can employ Supervisor's services, and the same holds true for supervision of supervision.

Although such phenomena have not appeared with great frequency in our work (perhaps this says, simply, that we did not sense their existence as often as we might have), certain other peculiarities arise from time to time in relation to postconference analysis. Some supervisors employ the idea that, ultimately postconference analyses are performed for the supervisees' sake and manage, by that rationale, to escape genuinely productive involvement in a process also intended to be for their own benefit. One thinks, analogously, of parents, in child guidance clinics, who agree to enter psychotherapeutic treatment of their own but who do so primarily because such treatment represents a condition set by the clinic for accepting their children. They say something like, "If we enter treatment grudgingly in order for our children or our spouse to be offered the treatment we believe them to need, then the therapeutic effects of our own treatment experience are likely not to materialize very substantially."

We have also occasionally observed some supervisors who become so hooked by the postconference analysis — that is, their self-directed inquiries and their fascination with their own behavior become so ascendant — that their interests in the supervisees and the energies they develop in supervision are depleted. In such cases it has generally seemed to us that the supervisors in question made early use of their own supervision and, particularly of the postconference analysis, as a surrogate for more personally oriented counseling, which in fact was the service they required. Even under the most favorable conditions, it is not always easy to maintain a productive balance between Teacher's interests and one's own, in the activities of this stage. Being neither for Supervisor's own technical development nor for the individual supervisees' welfare, the postconference analysis must serve both purposes adequately to be consistent with our conceptualizations of its ideal effects.

Just as it is with many analogous processes, the postconference analysis may come to symbolize many of the wrong things and, even for an individual supervisor, its purposes may fluctuate among appropriate and inappropriate rationales and objectives. It may, as we have noted, become a penance. It may become a source of invidious comparisons between Teacher's willingness and competency to have his or her work analyzed and Supervisor's own readiness for such activity. It may become a time-waster: One supervisor-in-training insisted that his repeated failure to prepare certain materials for a teacher, which he had voluntarily promised her, resulted from engaging in lengthy conference analysis that consumed all of the time in which he might otherwise have followed through. Implicitly, the supervisor assumed that postconference analysis was a more noble and more-likely-to-be rewarded activity than assembling the instructional materials in question. It's a matter of balance, then.

One cannot escape the conviction that postconference analyses are most likely to succeed in a context of group supervision or in a training program in which other supervisory personnel are available to participate, on a regular basis, in supervising the supervisor. For individual supervisors working alone,the problem of engaging in systematic self-examination will never be an easy one to resolve. Nonetheless, we cannot overstate the urgency of such activity if clinical supervision is truly to emerge as a potent and useful professional practice.

Chapter 11

CLINICAL SUPERVISION TODAY

* Texts and Special Issue Periodicals
* Periodicals
* Dissertation Studies
* Summary

Conceived at Harvard University more than fifteen years ago "clinical supervision," as it is commonly called, still remains primarily a latent force for the improvement of instruction. Written about, discussed, taught and sometimes attempted, clinical supervision has yet to be fully born to the world of public education, K-12. Scholars and practitioners alike have made valiant efforts to stimulate its birth, yet clinical supervision remains largely in the womb. Perhaps though, and hopefully so, its promised emergence is near.[1]

This, Krajewski's opening paragraph in the preface of the Winter 1976 *Journal of Research and Development in Education,* depicts the present status of clinical supervision in schools. Yet the valiant efforts toward which it speaks continue, with increasing fervor, in the hope that to include clinical supervision more securely in the instructional improvement repertoire will indeed become a workable reality. However, at present it remains for the most part only a hope.

In this volume we express the strong conviction, which we share with Cogan (in particular) and others, that many of the weaknesses in American schools today stem in large part from the near-universal neglect of supervision, through which teachers could be assisted toward better performance and a clearer vision of what improvements are possible. We are convinced that with such assistance, teachers could cope much more effectively with the difficult problems

[1]Robert J. Krajewski, Editorial, *Contemporary Education* 49 (Fall 1977), 4.

they face, and in turn we might well see a reversal of some of the gloomy statistics about the schools and their impact.

There are many indicators of present practice that show how difficult and yet how urgent it is for American schools to improve their instructional/clinical supervision programs. For instance, only a paltry 3 percent of the entire school budget in Toledo, Ohio, is allocated for administration. As a result, in-service training for teachers has been abandoned. Curriculum development and supervision has suffered tremendously in the absence of adequate personnel to carry on school program needs.[2] Front-page headlines frequently declare "City's School Budget in the Red." Predictions are that many teaching and administrative jobs will be lost in the next decade. As more and more school referenda are voted down, school systems will be harder and harder pressed to establish adequate programs to fit the needs of their clientele and to offer the best teaching staff possible. We are persuaded that such efforts must include clinical supervisors who can work with teachers and curriculum so that students can be the recipients of an education of the highest quality possible.

The purported objectives of instructional/clinical supervision programs in the schools — to oversee the design of the instructional program and to work with teachers for instructional improvement efforts — are not presently being met. Instructional supervisors labor under a great many pressures. Job descriptions of instructional/clinical supervisors include so many nonrelated tasks that in some cases they border on the absurd. The added problem of whether instructional supervisors should be line or staff personnel has added to the confusion and widespread lack of progress. Presently line personnel dominate supervisors and expect them to become administrative supervisors rather than instructional/clinical supervisors. Worse, they then discharge supervisors from the duties for which they have been in part trained. This contradiction may result partially from administrators' feeling uncertain about the role of supervisors and the supervisory program itself. But unless supervisors are present to assist teachers in instructional improvement efforts, the inevitable decline in teaching efficiency will take effect. Instructional/clinical supervision programs should receive strong support from the administration of the school district, and they should be considered one of the most important of all funded efforts in the district. But instructional/clinical supervision has not yet been appropriated a major slot in the organization of schools, and the question of whether it belongs in administration or curriculum has not been answered adequately enough to get instructional improvement progressing as it should.

One of the first stumbling blocks to effective instructional supervision is the lack of consensus about its purpose. Another is that there has been no uniformity of instructional thrust; rather, supervision is conducted on a piecemeal or crisis basis. Yet another obstacle is that supervision decisions are either

[2]Gene I. Maeroff, "The Cupboard Is Still Bare in Toledo," *Phi Delta Kappan* 59 (February 1978), 379–382.

made by or influenced by administrators. And therein lies much of the problem, because it follows that most instructional decisions are made by administrators. There is a need to approach instructional decisions in a more balanced way.

Supervisors rarely have opportunity for hands-on experiences with teachers. Overall, the present structure of instructional supervision is too unrealistic to be effective — unrealistic in terms of the numbers of people being supervised and unrealistic in terms of those doing the supervising. Bruce Joyce recently estimated that about 150,000 public school personnel are directly or indirectly involved in instructional improvement activities, approximately 40,000 of whom are supervisors. Principals and assistant principals, he feels, provide the bulk of instructional improvement efforts in the schools.[3] The latter statement, though true, presents an engima. Most principals and assistant principals are not trained to provide instructional improvement services — especially those under the purview of clinical supervision. Granted that the job description of a principal asserts that the principal should foremost be an instructional leader, his or her actual performance on the job does not reflect such leadership. Most research, including our own, supports this statement.[4] Yet, although they are not trained in clinical/instructional supervision procedures, principals are expected to perform that task and actually, as Joyce claims, they perform the supervisory function more often than do supervisors themselves. This statement supports previous descriptions of the instructional/clinical supervisor: The role is ambiguous, has various constraints placed upon it by administration, and thus has limited opportunity.

The initial portion of Joyce's statement may not necessarily be accurate; at least we do not believe it to be. NEA figures indicate that the number of classroom teachers in the 1976 school year totaled 2.46 million.[5] That there are supposedly 150,000 personnel involved in instructional improvement activities may be misleading. Moreover, the statement that there are 40,000 supervisors involved in instructional supervision may be a factual mistruth. Far fewer than 40,000 supervisors are performing only instructional supervision duties. If we were to figure the ratio, supervisor to teacher, considering only those supervisors who actually worked with teachers on a full-time basis in instructional/clinical procedures, the actual ratio would be staggering and would reflect an overall problem completely out of range for supervisors to effectively deal with. Given that kind of ratio, clinical supervision simply cannot work.

[3]Bruce R. Joyce et al., *ISTE Report II: Interviews. Perceptions of Professionals and Policy Makers* (Palo Alto, Calif.: Stanford Center for Research and Development in Teaching, June 1976), monograph. Data taken from the preliminary draft, pp. 1–2.

[4]Robert J. Krajewski, "Secondary Principals Want to Be Instructional Leaders," *Phi Delta Kappan* 60 (September 1978), 65; Robert J. Krajewski, "A Study of Texas Elementary School Principals' Role Perceptions," *Texas School Business* 23 (January 1977), 6, 27.

[5]NEA, *Estimates of School Statistics*, 1976–77, p. 30.

In some school systems, teachers' unions are determining what the supervision function should be and how supervision should be carried out. By negotiated agreement, the instructional supervisor visits nontenured teachers a minimum number of times during the year. Specific rules for each visit are determined by the agreement between the union and the school board, as well as the disposition of the written statements of the teaching episode observed and the conference between the supervisor and teacher (perhaps witnessed by a union representative, if so stipulated in the contract). Supervisors visit and observe not only new teachers but tenured teachers as well under the union contracts, although the number of visits made with the tenured teachers may be fewer and the manner in which the observation is conducted and the disposition of the materials used in conjunction with the visit may not be the same as in the case of the beginning teacher. On the one hand, the unions have been a proponent of the types of clinical supervision practices we advocate; on the other, their use of the clinical supervision method is primarily for evaluation — at least that seems to be the bottom line.

In any clinical supervision effort, unions nonwithstanding, staff development must be the key. Observation and analysis of teaching by supervisors must exist for the purpose of instructional improvement, not evaluation. At present, however, evaluation seems the dominant feature of the program — even if it is not meant to be. This error in emphasis can (and must) be overcome. Suffice it to say that one of the prime reasons for the problems we face today in the nonimplementation of clinical/instructional supervision is that the top-level school administrators are not instructionally oriented. This situation is unfortunately typical.

The American Association of School Administrators estimates that approximately five of every eight superintendents come from secondary school backgrounds. Of these, 80 percent began their school careers as coaches.[6] Now this bit of information does not mean to imply that ex-coaches do not make good administrators but rather to illustrate the noninstructional orientation of the administration. Since administration is as it is, there is little difficulty in seeing why schools are caught up in the problems of instructional bureaucracy. Thus the problems of change are monumental, and clinical supervision, being what it is and doing what it does, faces an uphill battle all the way.

Many school personnel are maintenance-oriented. That orientation, together with role discrepancies, creates problems for instructional supervisors and instructional supervision programs. Too many things are now being done superficially that could be done better if the supervisor would and could organize allotted time more effectively to meet the needs of the situation.

Overall, the instructional supervision program seems to lack any significant

[6]Stephen J. Knezevich (ed.), *The American School Superintendent: An AASA Research Study* (Washington: American Association of School Administrators, 1971).

leadership or direction. Leadership from the national associations is not particularly strong, nor well defined. Only within the past several years has the Association for Supervision and Curriculum Development begun to emphasize supervision of instruction. ASCD seems to support the idea in theory[7] but offers a few or no guidelines or avenues of actual support save the occasional working group within its organization, which purports to study the supervision scene and invariably comes up with the suggestion that ASCD should be more active in determining supervisor roles and preparation standards.

Perhaps the reasons listed above may give an indication of why clinical supervision has not yet been the force in education that it should and could be. There are other reasons, too, mainly related to the dearth of both literature and studies in clinical supervision.

TEXTS AND SPECIAL ISSUE PERIODICALS

Robert Goldhammer's text, *Clinical Supervision: Special Methods for the Supervision of Teachers*, 1969,[8] of which this book is a second edition, was the first major text on the subject of clinical supervision. Two other major texts were completed within the next few years, both of which (like Goldhammer's) grew out of experiences in Harvard–Newton and Harvard–Lexington programs. In 1971, Richard Weller wrote *Verbal Communication in Instructional Supervision*,[9] a text that grew out of his Harvard doctoral dissertation and examined the definition and practice of clinical supervision. In it, Weller developed an observational category system for analysis of teaching, Multidimensional Observational System for the Analysis of Interactions in Clinical Supervision (MOSAICS). In 1973, Cogan's *Clinical Supervision*[10] provided a rationale for the use of clinical supervision as well as a full description of the process. His text is concerned with both the setting and practice of clinical supervision. Of the three texts that grew out of the work at Harvard, both Cogan's book and Goldhammer's book are considered milestones — each in its own distinctive style and content. Cogan, the mentor, delivered a precise, well-documented text on clinical supervision. Goldhammer, the student, offered a free-wheeling, yet deep-thinking, personal analysis and description of the clinical supervision

[7]As evidenced by the number of articles recently afforded supervision in *Educational Leadership*, the number of sessions at the national conference dealing with supervision, and the recent designation of working groups in ASCD for supervision of instruction.

[8]Robert Goldhammer, *Clinical Supervision: Special Methods for the Supervision of Teachers* (New York: Holt, Rinehart and Winston, 1969).

[9]Richard H. Weller, *Verbal Communication in Instructional Supervision: An Observational System for and Research Study of Clinical Supervision in Groups* (New York: Teachers College Press, 1971).

[10]Morris L. Cogan, *Clinical Supervision* (Boston: Houghton Mifflin, 1973).

method, with an impassioned plea for its use in the schools. Both served their purposes well.

No other major works in clinical supervision appeared in texts or as issue themes of journals until 1976. Bellon et al. produced a version of clinical supervision in the text *Classroom Supervision and Instructional Improvement.*[11] In that same year, the winter issue of *Journal of Research and Development in Education,*[12] featured the theme "clinical supervision." Also in 1976, Abraham Fischler (another former Harvard faculty member) wrote a chapter in Louis Rubin's text, *Improving In-Service Education: Proposals and Procedures for Change,*[13] entitled "Confrontation: Changing Teacher Behavior Through Clinical Supervision." In the article he emphasized data acquisition for the teacher via videotape and audiotape to enable the teacher to become a partner in the improvement process. The Fall 1977 issue of *Contemporary Education*[14] also featured clinical supervision as the theme. More recently, a Phi Delta Kappa "fastback" on clinical supervision was written by Reavis (1978).[15]

The aforementioned works rank as the most scholarly and comprehensive on clinical supervision — in text and journal issue theme format. Still other texts mention clinical supervision and afford some ideas on the topic. Both Mosher and Purpel, in their text, *Supervision: The Reluctant Profession,*[16] and Sergiovanni and Starratt, in *Supervision: Human Perspectives*, second edition,[17] devote a chapter to a realistic appraisal (description) of clinical supervision. Fred Wilhelms, in an ASCD publication, *Supervision in a New Key,*[18] also provides information about clinical supervision in a separate chapter of his monograph. He declares that clinical supervison "is not so much supervision in a new key as it is traditional supervision with full orchestration and with every instrument finely tuned." Too, Blumberg[19] points to the clinical supervision method in his texts.

[11]Jerry Bellon et al. *Classroom Supervision and Instructional Improvement* (Dubuque: Kendall/Hunt, 1976).

[12]*Journal of Research and Development in Education* 9 (Winter 1976), Robert Krajewski (ed.), University of Georgia.

[13]Abraham S. Fischler, "Confrontation: Changing Teacher Behavior Through Clinical Supervision," in Louis J. Rubin (ed.), *Improving In-Service Education: Proposals and Procedures for Change* (Boston: Allyn and Bacon, 1971).

[14]*Contemporary Education* 49 (Fall 1977), Robert Krajewski (ed.), Indiana State University.

[15]Charles A. Reavis, *Teacher Improvement through Clinical Supervision* (Bloomington, Ind.: Phi Delta Kappa, 1978).

[16]Ralph L. Mosher and David E. Purpel, *Supervision: The Reluctant Profession* (Boston: Houghton Mifflin, 1972).

[17]Thomas J. Sergiovanni and Robert J. Starratt, *Supervision: Human Perspectives*, 2nd ed. (New York: McGraw-Hill, 1979).

[18]Fred T. Wilhelms, *Supervision in a New Key* (Washington: ASCD, 1973).

[19]Arthur Blumberg, *Supervisors and Teachers: A Private Cold War* (Berkeley: McCutchan, 1974).

As can be observed, the text literature is beginning to support the idea of clinical supervision. Perhaps, as Wilhelms suggests, it is time to listen to the music.

PERIODICALS

Most of the pre-1976 periodical literature on clinical supervision was not classified under the terminology *clinical supervision*, and so few, if any, articles can be found with *clinical supervision* in their titles. They may be listed under *supervision, instructional supervision, teaching analysis, teacher improvement, teacher supervision, teaching skills, instructional improvement, classroom observation techniques*, or some combinations of the above. Many articles deal with aspects of clinical supervision; they include such elements as observation, analysis, and conference with the teacher.

Since 1976 the periodical literature has witnessed an increased emphasis on clinical supervision. We do not intend to list the various pre-1976 articles on aspects of clinical supervision; rather, we refer the reader to the descriptors listed above and to the bibliographic references listed in the supervision texts mentioned earlier in this chapter. In particular, the reader should refer to Weller, pages 20–30, in which he examines representative clinical supervision research in three categories: (1) status studies of specific supervisory activities, (2) experimental studies of specific supervisory techniques, and (3) theoretically based studies of total supervisory methodology.[20]

In this section we shall present bibliographic information for various categories of clinical supervision study articles recently published. We have arbitrarily chosen five categories: rationale and assumptions, specific techniques, methodology, appraisal, and field research.

RATIONALES AND ASSUMPTIONS

Cogan, Morris L. "Rationale for Clinical Supervision," *Journal of Research and Development in Education* 9 (Winter 1976), 3–19.

Eye, Glen G., Krey, Robert D., and Netzer, Lanore A. "Assumptions Supporting Structure in Clinical Supervision," *Contemporary Education* 49 (Fall 1977), 16–23.

Krajewski, Robert J. "Some Thoughts on Clinical Supervision," *Professional Educator* 1 (Fall 1978).

---

[20]Richard H. Weller, *Verbal Communication in Instructional Supervision: An Observational System for and Research Study of Clinical Supervision in Groups* (New York: Teachers College Press, 1971).

Riechard, Donald E. "Needed: Resident Clinical Supervisors," *Educational Leadership* 33 (February 1976), 364–366.
Sergiovanni, Thomas J. "Toward a Theory of Clinical Supervision," *Journal of Research and Development in Education* 9 (Winter 1976), 20–29.
Sergiovanni, Thomas J. "Reforming Teacher Evaluation: Naturalistic Alternatives," *Educational Leadership* 34 (May 1977), 602–607.
Shane, Harold G., and Weaver, Roy A. "Educational Development Anticipating the 21st Century and the Future of Clinical Supervision," *Journal of Research and Development in Education* 9 (Winter 1976), 90–98.

SPECIFIC TECHNIQUES

Burke, Robert L. "Improving Instruction with Management by Objectives and Clinical Supervision," *Contemporary Education* 49 (Fall 1977), 29–32.
Flanders, Ned A. "Interaction Analysis and Clinical Supervision," *Journal of Research and Development in Education* 9 (Winter 1976), 48–57.
Zahorik, John A. "Supervision as Value Development," *Educational Leadership* 35 (May 1978), 667–669.

METHODOLOGY

Abrell, Ronald L. "The Humanistic Supervisor Enhances Growth and Improves Instruction," *Educational Leadership* 32 (1974), 212–216.
Anderson, Robert H. "The O Cycle: A Versatile Tool for Principals," *The National Elementary Principal* (June 1979).
Graves, Audrey S., and Croft, John C. "ERA (Empathic Rational Action): Refinement and Specification of Process Model and Development of Introductory Training Model for Clinical Supervision," *Journal of Research and Development in Education* 9 (Winter 1976), 77–84.
Marsh, Colin J. "The Clinical Supervision of Student Teachers," *Teacher Educator* 11 (Winter 1975), 9–14.
McGee, Jerry C., and Eaker, Robert. "Clinical Supervision and Teacher Anxiety: A Collegial Approach to the Problem," *Contemporary Education* 49 (Fall 1977), 24–28.
Melnik, Michael A., and Sheehan, Daniel S. "Clinical Supervision Elements: The Clinic to Improve University Teaching," *Journal of Research and Development in Education* 9 (Winter 1976), 67–76.
Reavis, Charles A. "Clinical Supervision: A Timely Approach," *Educational Leadership* 33 (February 1976), 360–363.
Simon, Alan E. "Analyzing Educational Platforms: A Supervisory Strategy," *Educational Leadership* 33 (May 1977), 580–584.

APPRAISAL

Denham, Alice. "Clinical Supervision: What We Need to Know About Its Potential for Improving Instruction," *Contemporary Education* 49 (Fall 1977), 33–37.

Harris, Ben M. "Limits and Supplements to Formal Clinical Procedures," *Journal of Research and Development in Education* 9 (Winter 1976), 85–89.

Reavis, Charles A. "Research in Review Clinical Supervision: A Review of the Research," *Educational Leadership* 35 (April 1978), 580–584.

FIELD RESEARCH

Buttery, Thomas J., and Michalak, Daniel A. "The Teaching Clinic: A Peer Supervision Process," *Education* 95 (Spring 1975), 263–269.

Gallo, Vincent A. "Should We Abolish or Retain the Principalship?" *Oregon School Study Council* (April 1970), 14 pp.

Huffman, James O. "Clinical Supervision: A Supervisory Process to Facilitate Instructional Improvement," *Tennessee Education* 3 (Summer 1973), 11–15.

Krajewski, Robert J. "Clinical Supervision: To Facilitate Teacher Self-Improvement," *Journal of Research and Development in Education* 9 (Winter 1976), 58–66.

McCleary, Lloyd E. "Competencies in Clinical Supervision." *Journal of Research and Development in Education* 9 (Winter 1976), 30–35.

Reavis, Charles A. "A Test of the Clinical Supervision Model," *The Journal of Educational Research* 70 (July/August 1977), 311–315.

DISSERTATION STUDIES

A search of doctoral dissertations reveals that during the 1960s and 1970s there were more studies dealing with clinical supervision than there were journal articles on the subject, although the number is not disproportionate. The dissertations report on teacher performance improvement, teacher attitudes and perceptions toward supervision, status and evaluation of student teachers, specific supervisory techniques (e.g., Flanders Interaction Analysis), supervisory conferences, and change in actual teaching behavior (to include both nonverbal and verbal behavior), and studies of the supervisory methodology. We also refer the readers to those sources that offer the information and listing of such studies, as *Educational Administration Abstracts, Research in Education,* and *Dissertation Abstracts International,* as well as some of the clinical supervision texts mentioned, such as Cogan and Weller.

In the previous section we delineated five categorizations of clinical supervision research and listed the entries for each in bibliographic format. Here
we present three categorizations of representative studies to date and provide
a short review of each study. The three categorizations will be: rationales and
assumptions, specific techniques/technology, and appraisal.

RATIONALES AND ASSUMPTIONS

Robert Eaker, "An Analysis of the Clinical Supervision Process as Perceived by Selected Teachers and Administrators," Doctoral Dissertation,
University of Tennessee, 1972. Teachers' and administrators' acceptance
of basic assumptions and procedures associated with clinical supervision
were studied. Teachers agreed with the assumptions, as did the administrators, but tended to agree less strongly than administrators on the procedures of clinical supervision.

SPECIFIC TECHNIQUES/TECHNOLOGY

Elizabeth Armstrong and George Ladd, "Rotating Peer Supervision: Implementation and Evaluation of Its Effect on the Inner-Direction and
Internal Control Constructs of Teacher Trainees," paper presented at a
meeting of the National Association for Research in Science Teaching, Los
Angeles, March 1975. Seventy-four college juniors in elementary education
taught each other and themselves in a science methods course. Experimental groups implemented the clinical supervision process with each
other. Personality traits pretests and posttests indicated that students
involved in the peer supervision group became more internally controlled.

Judith Aubrecht, "Teachers Do Change. How Much? An Empirical Study;
How and Why? A Clinical Study," Doctoral Dissertation, University of
Oregon, 1976. Factual information based on observation systems presented
a conflicting picture with what teachers perceived was happening in the
classroom or what they wished would be happening in the classroom.
Changes were made to reduce the conflict.

Warren Coffey, "Changes in Teacher's Verbal Classroom Behavior Resulting from an In-Service Program in Science Education," Doctoral Dissertation, University of California, Berkeley, 1976. Seventeen of 36
elementary school science teachers received in-service clinical supervision,
which included Flanders Interaction Analysis. No differences were perceived in teacher knowledge of science from posttests. The feasibility of
in-service programs to change teachers'verbal classroom behaviors was
substantiated.

G. E. Cook, "Supervisors for the Classroom: A Study of the Professional Growth of Educational supervisors in a Program of Clinical Training," Doctoral Dissertation, Harvard University, 1976. Graduate students in clinical supervision training were observed over a period of time for interpersonal relationships: teacher to supervisor. Supervisor assumptions were found to become less egocentric and more accurate, and their self-concept was enhanced as they better accepted their role.

Noreen B. Garman, "A Study of Clinical Supervision as a Resource for College Teachers of English," Doctoral Dissertation, University of Pittsburgh, 1971. Graduate teaching assistants in English were given a 12-week teaching seminar (the experimental group's training included clinical supervision) for a trimester. Most of those in the experimental group were able to design instructional changes and implement them given the clinical supervision training; almost none of those in the control group were able to do so.

Philip Hall et al. "A Teacher Evaluation-Supervision Model for a Small School District," Doctoral Dissertation, Nova University, 1974. Clinical supervision was used independently of evaluation with 30 Connecticut teachers to improve instructional practices. Attitude changes toward supervision were measured.

Betty Jane Kerr, "An Investigation of the Process of Using Feedback Data within the Clinical Supervision Cycle to Facilitate Teacher's Individualization of Instruction," Doctoral Dissertation, University of Pittsburgh, 1976. In a 15-week period, elementary school teachers, given clinical supervision, were able to increase individualization in their reading programs. Feedback data within the clinical supervision model facilitated teachers' selection, implementation, and evaluation of individualized instruction.

Thomas Kerr, "The Relationship among Attitude Scores, Dogmatism Scores, and Change in a Classroom Teaching Pattern of Teachers Who Have Experienced Clinical Supervision," Doctoral Dissertation, Temple University, 1976. Clinical supervision with Flanders Interaction Analysis was used with 20 teachers in determining whether they could, with proper training, move from direct teaching patterns to indirect patterns. Teachers, regardless of high or low dogmatism scores, were able to adapt more indirect patterns; the more open-minded teachers showed greater willingness to communicate with the supervisor.

O. W. Myers, "The Effects of Two Supervisory Approaches on Teacher Attitude toward Supervision, Evaluation, and Self," Doctoral Dissertation, University of Tennessee, 1975. Thirty-two respondents answered questions about teacher self-image and their attitudes toward supervision. Prior to administration of the questionnaire, experimental group participants were given a two-day training session in clinical supervision. More positive attitudes from the experimental group toward supervision were measured at the end of the experiment than from the control group.

Leon Pierce, "Supervisors' Managerial Talent and Their Verbal Behavior with Teachers During the Supervisory Conference in Clinical Supervision: An Exploratory Analysis," Doctoral Dissertation, University of Connecticut, 1975. Supervisors' verbal behavior during conferencing was measured with specific reference to managerial abilities, personality traits, and motivational needs. Structuring and reacting (the two moves consistent with concepts of clinical supervision) were found to be significantly related to personality traits, as indicated by Ghiselli's managerial inventory.

Karen Shuma, "Changes Effectuated by a Clinical Supervisory Relationship Which Emphasizes a Helping Relationship and a Conference Format Made Congruent with the Establishment and Maintenance of This Helping Relationship," Doctoral Dissertation, University of Pittsburgh, 1973. Pupil perception of teachers' behaviors in pupil response and the task organization and objectives match of teachers and pupils were measured. Those teachers given clinical supervision had a more positive attitude toward self and their profession and were more open to their own experiences than those teachers not experiencing clinical supervision.

N. D. Skarak, "The Application of Immediate Secondary Reinforcement to Classroom Teaching Observations in Clinical Supervision," Doctoral Dissertation, University of Pittsburgh, 1973. Clinical supervision used alone compared to clinical supervision used with immediate reinforcement resulted, in this study, with no difference in the amount of teacher behavior change. Visual and oral reinforcements used along with clinical supervision seemed not to have any effect.

Helen M. Turner, "The Implementation and Critical Documentation of a Model of Clinical Supervision: A Case Study," Doctoral Dissertation, University of California, Los Angeles, 1976. Questionnaires, tapes, notes, and journals were used to implement and document Goldhammer's model. Existence of the five stages was confirmed, as was the necessity for rapport in the clinical supervision relationship. Data recording during the observation posed problems.

Gail Witt, "Relationship between the Leadership Behavior of Supervisory Conference Cycle of Clinical Supervision as Perceived by Teachers," Doctoral Dissertation, University of Connecticut, 1977. Using supervisors similar in leadership styles, teacher perceptions showed no relationship between supervisory behavior and leadership styles as exhibited in the conference phase of clinical supervision. The LBDQ was used to obtain data for style, and the Blumberg/Amidon instrument was used for the behavioral aspect.

APPRAISAL

Anthony Mattalino, "Clinical Supervision: The Key Competencies Required for Effective Practice," Doctoral Dissertation, University of Massachusetts, 1977. The author found that the theoretical framework of clinical supervision provides a beginning point for listing competencies for the clinical supervision process. The author offers a list of competencies required for clinical supervision. Also the paucity of literature, unclear competencies, and the need for delicate and complicated procedures combine to make clinical supervision less accepted than it should be.

SUMMARY

The substance of this chapter is that clinical supervision is neither passé nor dormant. Clinical supervision contains key components for improving teaching techniques, approaches, and the classroom behavior of teachers. In turn, these components can provide a better learning atmosphere for students. But clinical supervision at present remains like music heard from a room far away. The interest it seems to be garnering indicates the potential it has to reach out for instructional improvement. Its potentially strong points are, however, sometimes in a floundering state. Both literature and present practices in the schools indicate that too many directions are being taken without looking at the common goals of understanding and utilization processes that lend themselves to advantageous results for teachers and students.

Clinical supervision lacks an air of continuity that could be provided by a stronger and more easily clarified and understood foundation from theory. This is clearly visible from the search of dissertation literature. Clinical supervision theory, as it applies to details such as personnel qualified to conduct such programs, methods of utilization, and positions on or within the staff, is almost nonexistent. Most studies are on method, but hardly any examine the assumptions/theory aspect of clinical supervision. The lone study on appraisal strongly suggests that the assumptions and theory upon which clinical supervision rests are unclear and unsupported by those who should provide the required support for acceptance and implementation.

These factors prevent clinical supervision from being the potent force in helping to create better teaching and learning situations in classrooms today. The productive direction in the clinical supervision effort is missing. Instead what we now find is that objectives are implemented without attention to the overall goals and philosophy within those goals.

Chapter 12

THE FUTURE

Jack Frymier recently noted that we create our future by what we do today, by the things we choose to include or exclude from our repertoire portfolio.[1] This has been most true of clinical supervision. During the early 1960s, those persons engaged in the development and application of clinical supervision were excited about the possibilities of clinical supervision helping to improve both instruction and curriculum in the public schools. Yet not enough has occurred to actuate those possibilities. By 1969 there still was great enthusiasm for the future of clinical supervision, yet by the mid-seventies it seemed less likely that clinical supervision would ever begin to realize its potential. Although it was still being supported by isolated bands of advocates and enthusiasts, it was being used in few, if any, public schools and was practically nonexistent in the literature.

But just as it seemed that clinical supervision was at a low ebb and perhaps destined to a "nonplace" in education, it suddenly experienced an awakening — a rediscovery. But why? We might conjecture that several factors played a key role in that apparent rediscovery, including accountability, the competency movement, public disaffection with school practices, and at last a genuine growing desire on the part of some public school personnel to improve instruction in fundamental ways.

Another contributing factor was that beginning in 1976, clinical supervision reappeared in the literature. The *Journal of Research and Development in Education* featured clinical supervision as a theme issue topic; in 1977, *Contemporary Education* did the same. Concomitantly, the Association for Supervision and Curriculum Development, through the efforts of some of its members, began putting more emphasis on supervision. Ben Harris, together with a group of university professors teaching supervision, formed the Council of Professors of Instructional Supervision (COPIS) and they too encouraged ASCD to emphasize supervision. Through COPIS, teachers of instructional supervision now had a vehicle by which they could more uniformly promote instructional supervision in the universities (the preparing end) and in the schools (the receiving end). COPIS members have in recent years shared ideas at their annual meeting held in conjunction wth the national ASCD convention.

[1]Jack Frymier, "Forecasting Future Trends in Supervision." Alabama Department of Supervisors and Directors of Instruction Fall Conference, Huntsville, Alabama, October 12, 1977.

They have had input into planning the ASCD convention, emphasized supervision within ASCD, and promoted supervision principles through sponsored publications within the COPIS organization. They have also recently instituted a yearly seminar meeting during which clinical supervision research is planned and research results disseminated to the members.

School personnel are demanding more emphasis on clinical supervision from the ASCD organization. ASCD is responding to these demands by including clinical supervision in its curriculum study institutes, several day in-service programs devoted to a single topic — such as clinical supervision. The institute participants are becoming more knowledgeable about clinical supervision and are requesting more advanced training than they have been receiving.

In a recent (1978) ASCD working group study, respondents were asked "What are the activities of instructional supervision?" Some 78 percent of the responses involved the techniques and practices of clinical supervision. When asked what should be included in the preparation program of instructional supervisors, more than 80 percent of the respondents addressed themselves to some aspect of clinical supervision, either to the analysis of the classroom interaction itself or to the provision of assistance in self-improvement to the teacher as the person directly responsible for that interaction.

In reality, however, clinical supervision does not enjoy a sufficiently wide following today. To what may we attribute such a phenomenon? We believe that the answers are found in problems of time, fiscal constraints, organizational constraints, psychological constraints, personnel constraints (in terms of inadequate training or inadequate knowledge base), constraints peripherally imposed by elements of the system (the unions or teacher bargaining agents), and also the great shortage of supervisors. If some of these constraints are indeed operating, what may be done in the future to circumvent them and allow clinical supervision to reach its potential? What plans may we envision that will promote our ideas about clinical supervision? And, indeed, what ideas about clinical supervision do we have, and which of these will be capable of functioning within the system as it now is and as we might envision it in both the near future and many years from now?

To be sure, any considerations must be based on what pressures may come to bear on the schools — financial and interest groups being probably the most influential sources — and how such pressures may lead to even further decline in the available resources for school improvement. We dare to hope that the recent trend will be reversed and that society will become more, rather than less, supportive of quality education. In addition, several assumptions must be made concerning the operation of the schools themselves: first, that the teaching of students will not be radically altered with regard to time requirements and second, that schools will continue in patterns of the present as regards staffing and the like.

When we speak of the future of clinical supervision, we have to deal not only with certain realities, including the aforementioned impact of negotiations and the tightening of budgets but also with the fact that more and more teachers are staying in their positions longer and have a greater need for improvement and that more and more teachers are tenured — with the average age of teachers increasing. These realities might portend a grim future for supervision. But on the other hand, we need a future about which to dream.

In more favorable times for education, which perhaps will arrive before long, resources would become more available; school systems would be able to restore some of the personnel services, including supervisory positions that were lost in budget cuts; universities, schools, teacher centers, and other agencies might combine their resources to offer better training (with a strong clinical flavor) to veteran as well as neophyte supervisors; team teaching, with its built-in potential for peer supervision and related teacher growth mechanisms, might become a more popular arrangement; and more and more instances of bona fide clinical supervision might become visible. Such events would, we are persuaded, have a remarkably invigorating effect upon learning environments in schools, even to the point where at long last the public would conclude that educators are in firm and confident charge of their societal role.

All of this is rather starry-eyed; but even in our sober moments we have the obligation to promote our vocation and to believe that it is possible to perfect the skills that we value. Supervisors are only a part of the large picture that is Education, and it would be naive to claim that supervision can be *the* major force in the achievement of excellent schools. However, there are among us enough skilled supervisors, and the schools in which they work are sufficiently different from most others, that we have more than assumptive reasons for proclaiming our faith and urging that our opportunities be expanded. In a better world resources would become more available and through clinical approaches we might turn some teachers on, to a point that they might say, "Supervision is rescuing me from the rut I'm in." Then we might hope to see supervision in the ascendance at last. But this will have to depend on the competence of supervisors to do a good job and their motivation as it is seen by the teachers they are trying to serve — as helpers and as persons who want to be useful and not evaluative, judgmental, or hostile. We have to be ultimately pleading for pure science, point out the things in which we need more research, more skill — such as data gathering, how to conduct conferences, how to deliver negative messages, and all the things that relate to skillful performance in this very delicate and demanding world. And we are only at the beginning of developing those skills. The state of supervision is now just about parallel to the state of teaching in that we know a lot more than we ever knew about teaching but at the same time we know more about intriguing problems that need to be examined and that we have not examined before. By the time the third edition of this book comes out, we hope to be able to celebrate the increasing impact of scientific information/technology upon the work the supervisor does relating to skillful performance of duties.

But at this moment it remains for us to consider that positive potentialities are embodied in the models of clinical supervision we have examined in the previous chapters for now and for the future. Those of us involved in the development of clinical supervision, having sensed varied problems and having encountered their manifestations in our daily work over long periods of time, hold the strong opinion that curricular deficiencies and faulty student evaluation strategies cannot be remedied, satisfactorily, from a distance. We do not have confidence, in other words, in the utility of mounting an assault on curriculum by attempting to create better curriculum at some remote drawing board. Similary, we have little faith that educational evaluation will be significantly strengthened, at least at present, by the invention of better standardized tests. Whereas this is not meant to suggest that better curriculums and better tests cannot be formulated, or even that professional activity should not proceed in such directions, it does express our examined conviction that regular, intense clinical supervision of teaching incorporates more abundant possibilities for establishing pertinent reforms in curriculum and in evaluation in today's and tomorrow's classrooms. It additionally implies an assertion that such supervision, in many instances, represents an ideal mode of improvement rather than simply an alternative one.

Educational offerings, unlike mass-produced consumer goods, cannot effectively be distributed in wholesale quantities. In the first place, when teaching properly incorporates process goals, the "goods" as such assume secondary importance. In connection with process goals, teaching aims to create, to strengthen, and to proliferate useful patterns of mental functioning — to expand the learner's cognitive capabilities. In effect, such teaching is aimed at the education of intelligence: at shaping, focusing, integrating, and broadening the human mind.

Because the systematic training of intelligence is such a complex undertaking, simple teaching devices such as textbooks are methodologically insufficient. To affect the learner's use of his mental apparatus requires intensely personal and idiosyncratic processes. If, as Carl Rogers has maintained, learning cannot be taught directly, but can at best be facilitated only by another's efforts, then deliberate education should occur in a context of regular and intimate encounters, in close relationships among people.

Clinical supervision is intended to provide such relationships for the sake of teachers' learning and to facilitate the teachers' establishment of such relationships with their pupils and among their pupils. Its observational and dialectical priorities reflect an underlying value on closeness: between supervisors and teachers, and between teachers and students. Our commitment to this value is essentially pragmatic.

By the same reasoning, if the teacher's commitment to testing and evaluating a student is to count for anything worthwhile, such evaluation must occur in a context of intimate communication and understanding between the two. Intelligence and achievement tests, by themselves, tell virtually nothing. Certainly, by themselves, they do not tell the teacher what to do next.

We see no reason to suppose that, in their relationships to teachers, supervisors should be guided by understandings and values and professional principles that are different from those pertaining to the instruction of pupils. As human beings, teachers and pupils are both involved in personal development. Their developmental requirements for interpersonal aliment and interactional stimulation are the same (although, as in regard to all such specific elements, they are individual and unique). Therefore we believe that an analogy with teaching is, and will continue to be, a sensible one.

Supervision from a distance is not likely to be any more useful, developmentally to teachers, than canned teaching is likely to be for the pupils. In this context, too, clinical intimacy is more helpful and constructive than nonintimacy. Although bureaucratic supervision (by directive, by fiat, by form, and by rote) may satisfy administrative priorities on efficiency, it simply does not speak to the critical questions of professional existence that determine each teacher's individual functioning.

Clinical supervision is intended to be both method and model. By exemplifying the very conditions of intimacy and encounter that it aims to establish in teaching behavior, it should both do and show. By its own intimacy, it should establish a mutual trust and openness in which the supervisor and teacher may build, together, toward satisfying outcomes. Perhaps the most important and distinguishing characteristic is that the supervisor's own behavior and the supervisory relationship itself are as vulnerable and as open to examination as the teacher's behavior, both in the classroom and in the supervision. Only in a clinical supervisory relationship is it possible for a supervisor to get close enough to sense the frame of reference in which the teacher exists: the teacher's values, ideals, concepts, feelings, and anxieties. By providing opportunities for constructive intimacy, such supervision not only can facilitate a teacher's individual actualization but also may demonstrate processes for creating intimacy in the teacher's relationships to pupils as well.

While intimacy alone may be a necessary condition for effective clinical supervision (and for teaching), it is not sufficient. That is why we refer to "constructive" intimacy. Although we are unable to specify completely the characteristics of such relationships — partly because, to be constructive, intimacy should assume different qualities in different partnerships — we can, nevertheless, describe certain elements that must generally be present, in this connection, in clinical supervision.

Experience and research both suggest that positive supervision will not develop unless both the supervisor and the supervisee feel authentic affection for each other. Sometimes, in our supervision, we have found that instead of being present from the outset, some sense of affection arose only after a number of collaborative encounters had occurred. Sometimes inauspicious beginnings developed into professionally strong relationships. More often, however, the counseling, teaching, and supervision in which we have engaged, when it seemed to produce useful results, generally began with an initial, intuitive liking and with a common, implicit expectation that affection would continue and deepen. In the other direction, it has been invariably true that neither in our own judgment nor in our supervisees' has supervison ever been very productive in relationships in which such feeling was absent.

Another element of constructive intimacy is its dyadic vector: that is, its thrusts in each participant's direction at compatible rates and intensities. Finally, for maintaining constructive intimacy, the focus of the member's inquiries should be oriented primarily toward the teacher's issues, and supervisory goal setting should occur primarily within the supervisee's frame of reference.

One set of serious questions raised by the critics of clinical approaches is of whether supervision *should* deal, so much, with "personal material"; whether at certain times it *should* become embroiled in teachers' emotional lives; whether we tend to overemphasize personality characteristics of teachers and variables in instructional effectiveness; and whether, particularly in light of the absence of psychological training in most supervisors' backgrounds, it makes very much sense to rely so heavily upon counseling models for supervisory practice.

Another fundamentally important question, which arises from essentially the same impression of clinical supervision, is whether "teacher development" is treated too much as an end and whether, indeed, it should be regarded more as an intervening variable, that is, as a collection of means directed toward the establishment of valued pupil behaviors.

We acknowledge the importance of confronting such issues. Innovations in supervision and instruction must, we agree, ultimately be expressed as beneficial changes in the pupils' experiences and behavior. But those changes depend in large measure upon the emotional capacities, the cognitive styling, the values, the role adjustment skills, and the self-concepts of the teachers, and we cannot for a moment ignore that fact.

The teacher, therefore, is no less valuable — no less an "end" — than the pupil, no less alive and, in many respects, no less needy. If clinical supervision seems to pause too long with the teacher, perhaps such an exaggeration is necessary in order to compensate for the oppressive abundance of supervisory systems that, if they do not devalue teachers, do not especially value them either. Clinical supervision seeks to replace such systems with ones that value and consider human beings in human relationships.

In summary of much that has motivated this writing, teachers in America have an almost desperate need to understand better the unintended as well as the intended effects of their behavior. In many categories of their work — for example, in "disciplining" children or in "motivating" a class — the teachers' actions are often naively self-defeating. We tend, it would seem, to reify various psychological constructs when, in fact, they are invalid, and to employ them often as fundamental truths in our professional work. We have attempted to demonstrate that teachers tend to lack awareness of incidental learnings likely to result from their teaching behavior; that most often they do not plan explicitly for measurable process outcomes; and that as a typical result it can easily arise thaᵗ besides teaching chemistry to a student, the teacher may also be teaching that student to loathe learning, to distrust the teacher, and to acquire a poor self-image.

Most significantly of all, we have been struck time and again by one particular form of perceptual and intellectual distortion that seems more salient than any other among educators — namely, their tendencies to see and to conceptualize phenomena in global and undifferentiated terms. We are aware that the human tendency to form such "gestalts" is compelling; and we see this condition, as constituting the principal need for clinical supervision to exist, in essentially the forms we have examined above. We require teacher training methods that help to facilitate strong capacities for differentiated thinking and observing, and our experiences suggest that the ideal arena for such training is in the school, and that the most advantageous medium for such training is supervision of this type.

We require a supervision that is basically analytical and whose principal mode of analysis comprises highly detailed examination of teaching behavior. We require a supervision whose precepts and methods are basically rational and unmysterious and in which teachers may participate with all of their intellectual faculties intact and without intellectual offense. We need a supervision whose effect is to enhance and to actualize and to fulfill, in degrees that are appreciable and sensible in the teacher's own experiential frameworks. Teachers (like anyone) must be able to understand what they are doing and the goals and process that govern their behavior, and supervision must provide adequate illumination for such understanding. We require a supervision that is basically teacher-initiated and consistent with independent, self-sufficient action. Our supervision must result, regularly and systematically, in palpable technical advancement; it must have methodological and conceptual rigor and it must produce real and measurable accomplishments.

Because of the ambiguity surrounding most educational issues, such a supervision must be open instead of closed; it must result in discoveries and must name its own directions, rather than to be committed to false, archaic, or otherwise invalid goals. Both the supervision itself and the teaching behaviors in which it culminates must, in other words, be basically creative and should not strive, as supervision has striven historically, to achieve greater degrees of conformity and uniformity in instructional practices. Of crucial importance is to have a supervision that is fundamentally humane, one that is emancipated from the dogma and authoritarianism and vested interests of administration and just plain troublemaking that have typified much of the supervision we have known before.

We do not see clinical supervision as an educational panacea; yet we are greatly optimistic that its general approach and specific habits of method are appropriate, consistent with an orientation that should characterize positive contemporary educational reform, and realistically feasible to establish and to disseminate in the school. There is nothing spectacularly new in the model; we do not offer it as a wonder drug.

Yet we have found more strength than weakness in a supervision that incorporates all the five stages about which we have written, and we are personally convinced that there are strong reasons to trust what we have been doing in the development of clinical approach and to hunger for continued experimentation in these directions.

It seems, at the same time, that our practices are ripe for more and better evaluative research *and* that such research, analogously to most of the research performed in counseling and psychotherapy, will itself have to be basically clinical and ideographic, at least for the immediate future. Our idealizations of teaching and of supervision must be modified constantly as more is learned about human behavior and professional development. Even now there are serious questions before us, such as how to train people to be clinical supervisors of the most ideal sort and how to administer such supervision and training in the typical school setting. Solid curriculums in teacher education and supervisor education are yet in the infancy stages of development, and too few school systems serve as the field bases for the necessary research and development work. Our notions of how to train and to administer in the field are, however, becoming more definitive. We cherish the hope that volumes such as this will be sufficiently provocative, in one manner or another, to stimulate a broader participation by workers in the educational field, both in the refinement and in the invention of training and administrative models for the future.

Appendix

THE CLINICAL SUPERVISION CYCLE: An Overview

Stage 1: Preobservation Conference
Stage 2: Observation
Stage 3: Analysis and Strategy
Stage 4: Supervision Conference
Stage 5: Postconference Analysis

I. The Preobservation Conference
  A. Purposes
     1. To obtain information as to the teacher's intentions (objectives of the lesson; planned procedures; criteria of evaluation).
     2. To establish a "contract" or agreement between the supervisor and the teacher (items or problems on which the teacher wants feedback).
     3. To establish specific plans for carrying out the observation (how supervisor should deploy; use of tape recorders or not; time limits).
  B. Possibilities
     1. The conference can serve to relax both parties, by allowing for frank discussion of any uneasiness or concern.
     2. Especially during a second or third observation cycle, the conference serves as a communication link with the past and provides for redirecting attention to leftover agenda, changes recently made.
     3. In some cases, the conference can be devoted to a rehearsal (or practice) of devices and techniques to be used.
     4. The "contract" is not necessarily restrictive. It is primarily to assure that the teacher's specific interests will be met.
     5. Last-minute revision or modifications of plans, as a result of ques-

tions raised in this conference, are not only possible but desirable; the supervisor then shares with the teacher a keen interest in assessing the effectiveness of the plan.

II. The Observation
    A. Purpose
        1. To view the lesson as planned in the preobservation conference.
    B. Commentary
        1. Logistics should be carried out as planned:
            a. observing (and recording) *what*.
            b. whether or not to be "essentially invisible" and detached from the observed events.
            c. when, or in what manner, the observation will be terminated.
        2. Use of interaction analysis; videotape or audiotape is highly recommended wherever feasible.

III. The Analysis and Strategy
    A. Purposes
        1. To "reconstruct" the observed events (essentially as historians attempting to agree on what actually happened).
        2. To assess the observed lesson, in terms of:
            a. the teacher's own intentions.
            b. pedagogical criteria (especially those which have been generated within the total team).
            c. the teacher's own "pattern" and history (as it becomes known).
        3. To consider supervisory implications.
        4. To develop a plan (strategy) for helping this teacher:
            a. points, questions, ideas, problems to be raised or elicited during the conference.
            b. role to be played by supervisor during the conference.
    B. Commentary
        1. Many lessons usually last longer than was predicted: it therefore makes sense to have an open-ended understanding with the teacher as to starting time of the supervisory conference.
        2. The strategy must include determination of priorities, since probably not all items can or should be brought up in the supervisory conference.
        3. The supervisor must aim to establish a climate within which supervision may take place. People have to be ready to hear what you are ready to say, or to voice the ideas you are attempting to steer them toward. There are many perceived threats to the individual and his or her perception of self, and the supervisor must create an atmosphere of *credibility* (for example, analysis supported by concrete evidence) and of *trust* (with reference to the supervisor's competence, motives, and essential "optimism" vis-à-vis this teacher's future). Such a climate is established by:

      a. using the ground rules of "inquiry" teaching: examine ideas, without intent of hurting people; open all ideas to examination; be flexible and objective.

      b. assigning priority to those items of teaching behavior that are amenable to change in the time (and under the conditions) available. The deeper, underlying patterns of a teacher's behavior are *less* amenable to change in a short program than are the relatively more superficial things (such as technical behavior).

      c. dealing with behavior, not with the person. Avoid psychologizing or analyzing people, and steer clear of ethical and other more dangerous problems.

      d. selecting only a few of the amenable behaviors on which to work, keeping the task manageable, and insuring that reward-for-change will be within each teacher's immediate grasp.

      e. working with *strengths*, if possible, rather than with weaknesses. It is easier to recognize and to talk about the failures, but do not fall into that trap.

4. The strategy session should continue until the supervisor has reached closure on some specific, achievable approaches that can be presented to, or elicited from, the teacher. It should also strive to identify behavioral criteria that will help the supervisor to know that the message has actually "gotten across."

5. Be sure to settle on a strategy for opening the supervisory conference (the opening ploy), including what will be said and in what tone of voice.

IV. The Supervision Conference

  A. Purpose

    1. To provide feedback and to provide a basis for the improvement of future teaching. It may be appropriate (at the outset or later as needed) to redefine the supervisory contract. Among other features or purposes are:

      a. to provide adult rewards and satisfactions.

      b. to define and authenticate issues in teaching.

      c. to offer didactic help (if appropriate).

      d. to train the teacher in techniques for self-supervision.

      e. to develop incentives for professional self-analysis.

  B. Commentary

    1. The burden for ensuring that goals are reached, for maintaining the pace of the conference, for coping with problems that arise, for deciding when to depart from strategy (for instance, to terminate) if the strategy fails, and so on rests primarily with the supervisor. In the postconference analysis, feedback should be provided to the supervisor with respect to his or her performance.

    2. When the conference has been completed, it is sometimes appro-

priate to invite the teacher to comment on the value of the conference, on points that have been made, and on follow-up that seems
fitting.

V. The Postconference Analysis

   A. Purposes

      1. To reconstruct, as appropriate, the events of the conference.

      2. To assess the conference in terms of:

         a. the supervisor's own intentions.

         b. supervisory criteria.

         c. apparent value of the conference to the teacher.

      3. To consider the implications of this event vis-à-vis the development
within the supervisor of greater professional skills.

      4. To evaluate the supervisor's skill (in each role, and for the group
as a whole) in handling the several phases of the cycle.

   B. Commentary

      1. In a sense, this analysis represents supervision's "superego," its
conscience. It provides a basis for assessing whether supervision is
working productively. Pluses and minuses are examined, and the
supervisor decides to modify supervisory practices accordingly.

      2. Participation in the observation cycle, and especially this part of
it, helps the participants to understand better the intellectual and
the emotional dimensions of the teacher's work.

      3. Among the matters to discuss are: the techniques of the supervisor;
implicit and explicit assumptions that were made; values; emotional
variables; technical and process goals.

INDEX